A Man And His River

Hi Vic

Enjoy this – do you
have a puffy jacket?

Love
Margaret Anne
+ Emily Anne

Xmas 2024

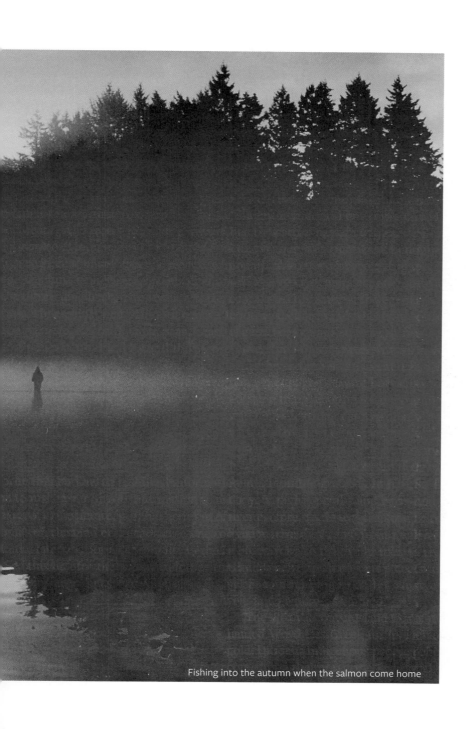

Fishing into the autumn when the salmon come home

“This is a story about life and death on a wild river that has carved a path through a rainforest and through the bedrock of a poet’s heart. DC Reid wrecks cars, flips boats, and communes with bears as he searches for salmon, casting heavy lures ‘that fly because their weight cuts a hole in the air’. Along the way, he dispenses a wealth of fly- and gear-angling knowledge.”

—Mark Hume, author of Trout School and Reading the Water

A MAN AND HIS RIVER

a 25-year love affair with a wild island waterway

DC REID

Cataloguing data available from Library and Archives Canada
978-0-88839-728-7 [paperback]
978-0-88839-734-8 [epub]

Printed in China

PRODUCTION & DESIGN: J. Rade
EDITOR: D. MARTENS

We acknowledge the support of the Government of Canada through the Canada Book Fund and the Canada Council for the Arts, and of the Province of British Columbia through the British Columbia Arts Council and the Book Publishing Tax Credit.

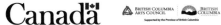

Hancock House gratefully acknowledges the Halkomelem Speaking Peoples whose unceded, shared and asserted traditional territories our offices reside upon.

Published simultaneously in Canada and the United States by

HANCOCK HOUSE PUBLISHERS LTD.
19313 Zero Avenue, Surrey, B.C. Canada V3Z 9R9
#104-4550 Birch Bay-Lynden Rd, Blaine, WA, U.S.A. 98230-9436
(800) 938-1114 Fax (800) 983-2262
www.hancockhouse.com info@hancockhouse.com

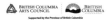

Table of Contents

For the Nitinat River. Thank you for your time, and what you have taught me.

Introduction

I still don't know why I fish or why other men fish, except that we like it and it makes us think and feel. But I do know that if it were not for the strong, quick life of rivers, for their sparkle in the sunshine, for the cold grayness of them under rain and the feel of them about my legs as I set my feet hard down on rocks or sand or gravel, I should fish less often. A river is never quite silent; it can never, of its very nature, be quite still; it is never quite the same from one day to the next. It has its own life and its own beauty, and the creatures it nourishes are alive and beautiful also. Perhaps fishing is, for me, only an excuse to be near rivers. If so, I'm glad I thought of it.

A River Never Sleeps - Roderick L. Haig-Brown

Vancouver Island is the largest island on the west coast of the Americas, stretching 500 kilometres long and 160 wide. I have fished some 50 of its rivers, over several decades. It takes many years of patient and persistent fishing to understand every island river, as each has its own 12-month calendar and up to nine species of salmonids that show up at different times. You may have to cover 25 km over and over, year-round, to know where you will catch a fish and in what month it will be there.

The river I return to most often is the Nitinat (pronounced Nit-Nat), a soft river among the 123 watersheds, from Sooke in the south to Cape Scott in the north. I have told so many people where I go, I need not tell them anymore; they know I will always say the Nitinat. Or I will lie, to keep the river secret. They know that, too.

The Nitinat is an easy river, meaning I can easily get from one side to the other by wading in average water levels. That is its appeal for me, like my own stream in my childhood, Fish Creek, south of Calgary. I should add that, in honesty, there are other rivers of greater virtue. The Stamp, for instance, with its greater flow and its larger steelhead runs, enjoys the character of its great slate ridges, its runs and rocks the size of houses. It has long miles where there is no one but wilderness and going downriver on a rubber kickboat. It's Money's Pool, where so much Van Isle fishing history was born.

Roderick Haig-Brown on the Campbell River. I was Haig-Brown angler a decade before publication of this book. This involved putting on events for people, giving a Haig-Brown lecture, giving casting lessons and talking about fish, and, these days, fish farms, which need to come out of the sea. I also stayed in his house, which was an awe-inspiring experience. I had access to the great man's life, including a hundred images of his family, all the way down to his American Express receipts still left in his desk. I took more than 500 images for my files. And have come to realize that I am the angler/writer who came to do the salmon restoration work he wanted done, particularly all the time I have put into the issues of getting fish farms out of the ocean, and for which I have won two awards for environmental writing, the **Art Downs Memorial Award** and the national level **Roderick Haig-Brown Award.**

Then there is the Campbell, and Haig-Brown, his Nimpkish, largest river on the island, and the Gold. I have fished them all, and many more, but I return far more often to the Nitinat. It is not always on my mind, but I always return. It holds my past—it's where I destroyed my first Subaru station wagon, taking it down tracks and less-than-tracks where even trucks with winches don't go. And where I have destroyed another—a white Subaru station wagon.

I went down my river the first time with guide Bill Patterson long ago, after getting a ticket for speeding and then increasing my speed because the stop made me even later. That day held my first sighting of an island bear and the understanding that my eyesight was failing. Then, heading out on my own the following May long weekend in my little blue 9-foot dinghy, from the boat launch where we had landed. I drifted into the unknown, tipped on the first corner and thought I was going to die.

Then, it meant finding myself alone with bears and coming to terms with them, and coming to understand a salmon river: the smell of killing fields, maggot-filled white carcasses, eyeballs pecked out, red coming away from sockets. And the endless shriek, the endless importance of thousands of gulls so adrenalized by so much food they cannot keep themselves from screaming. Also, carcasses stuck like newspapers in the trees above my head, evidence the river had been higher than me.

Then the day I almost drowned among carcasses in soft water behind a new log. The day I almost went under in the swamp. The day I fell backward from a broken alder into the river a dozen feet below and escaped, thanks to falling on my pack, which landed first on the rock beneath the surface. The day I stepped off into winter blue and never hit bottom, into the gasp of cold when water came. The day I followed a rolled-up coho around the outside of the boat launch in a river I know better than any other and, in that assurance, nearly lost my life in my mid-fifties. The river was faster than I thought and deeper than I guessed. As I went under, I luckily grabbed a root before the rest of me swept under sweepers. I hung in the wind of water, unable to get neoprene feet beneath me, until I slid into a back eddy, fish gone but life retained.

There was the day I sweated in 10-foot-deep blackberry and huckleberry and climbed an old stump, not seeing anything but clear-cut, until I finally spilled onto gravel, soaked by my own liquids. Idly eating berries, head down, I followed my tire tracks deeper in, and on the way out, jammed on the brakes on sighting a broken sign in the road. Backing up to read it, I learned the whole area had been hit with herbicide to kill the vegetation. I sat wondering about bears eating berries, wondering about myself, my fingertips of blue.

These days and so many others. On my own, when predator eyes were on me, I once had to keep myself from running back to the car. You may have felt those eyes on you and come to understand them. Many days and many years later, I look up, aware I am being watched by cougar, wolf, bear, or elk, and move into a clearing, make a few "Hey-ahs," and carry on. There is now no fear.

I have come to know my river. It is an excellent salmon river with a hatchery and hundreds of thousands of chum lining the bottom like brown arrows, then like Tutankamen, hooks ripping flesh, they're so rotten. In a good year, 20,000 Chinook; 30,000 coho. But only 100 winter steelhead and perhaps 150 summers, and the good fortune one year of catching almost as many as my fingers, the equivalent of more than 2,000 springs. I have come to realize I know this river better than any other, and that familiarity is a kind of love, too.

Send me down with spinners in coho season or a Spey or switch rod across river from a run where I know steelhead stop behind one rock on their way up. The fly must be cast upstream under branches that touch water and held to connection for the trip through one-rock holding water. Then, watching the rock it catches on move away, I understand I have connected with the true part of me.

The Nitinat is not without history. It was clear-cut in the early 1900s. In a jungle of regrown forest, railway grades that moved great logs remain. So do booming grounds in Nitinat Lake, the odd fresh- and salt-water body. Twitching crabs and barnacles may be found on shores beside the river estuary. There was the swindle of Clo-oose, where the crazy minister lived, where they came from England to land they bought for erection of a boardwalk, so they were told, to rival Brighton, Blackpool and Atlantic City. To start up an antique store, wares dumped on a beach with 10-foot swells and nothing to do but survive until they could be picked up next year and go home, swindled.

The 1864 Vancouver Island Exploration trip under Robert Brown probably named Worthless Creek for its lack of "colours," as they called flakes of gold. Ditidaht Indigenous people beheaded four Huu-ay-aht men who had come upon their territory. They stuck them on poles by Hobiton Lake and its early run of sockeye that enter in April, long before summer. These legends we humans make, by doing them and telling them until they stick.

This is my river: smaller and without houses, unlike the historic Cowichan, closer to my home, the one I should have taken to. The question can be asked about coming back. What can be the answer, other than reasons that don't quite answer the question because it is without thought; like what a child and a parent have between them; a man and a woman or man; or woman and another of her kind.

I enter still from Youbou (pronounced You-bow), down the rutty, potholed road where I have destroyed two cars, and work on a third. Where I now speed, 60 feet above the lake, there is a slide slowly eating the road. Someday, passing a logging truck or simply not noticing, someone is going to go over. That sport of chance, of probability you react to without thinking anything about it. That is my river, and everyone else's.

Here is what I think about knowing a river well: it is the coming back, the familiarity, the knowing. My river is all rivers, of course. In looking, we apprehend water that flows and in that flowing, passes each second more water, but not the water that just flowed by and thus a presence that is and is not the same in one. We call this time, and it is what we breathe and flow through during our shortness. Make haste to your river. Let me tell you about mine. And at the end of my stories, technical information that will make your fishing better.

Gear Note

I have put most gear in this book with technical information and brand names. The purpose is to give you specific information to make your own gear decisions. Also, if the specific piece of gear has gone out of manufacture, they give you information for buying new gear as it comes on the market. An example is Skagit Lines and Skagit rods from Rio in the late '90s, for a shortish Spey Rod and roughly 25 foot, heavy heads. See this link for the evolution of Skagit gear over the years: https://flyfishusa.com/skagit-lines.aspx. The same is true of all gear: it evolves.

Chapter 1

FIRST BLOOD

... he that hopes to be a good angler, must not only bring an enquiring, searching, observing wit, but he must bring a large measure of hope and patience, and a love and propensity to the art itself; but having once got and practised it, then doubt not but angling will prove to be so pleasant that it will prove to be, like virtue, a reward to itself.

The Compleat Angler – Izaak Walton

Green glows from the dashboard. The speedometer reads 110 km/h. My tea is on the dash, steam on the windshield. Headlights open a tunnel in the night. Curving down the long dark hill, I watch numberless raindrops explode on the glass in front of me.

As I relive these images, my first trip to the Nitinat seems long ago. Many decades, in fact, and so many images have piled up behind my eyes, including the next one: red and blue lights streak toward me on the corner where the road bears left into the little town with billboards and a boarded-up Reserve. Red and blue tracers snap past so close I could have held out a cigarette to have it lit. The dome of lights makes a U-turn and comes rocketing from behind. It's not going past me, but after me, and I say, "Damn," in green phosphorescent light.

I pull over where there is no place to pull over, and the bullhorn says, "Stay in the car." The policeman does the saunter up and shines his flashlight so all I can see are the veins in my eyeballs. He hands me a ticket: 107-kms/hr in an 80-km zone. One hundred sixty-seven bucks, before sun comes to the day. I cross the Koksilah River into streetlamps. Then the dusty cement-hopper chute, car lots, Duncan Donuts, the southern fringe of the only town in BC with a policeman at 5 a.m. No highway divider to let me pass into the safety of houses, where dead cars sit like great insects on their backs in front yards.

Having lost 15 minutes, I turn left on Highway 18 and redouble my speed, my low-horsepower Subaru pretty much floored. Then I hit Youbou, a sprinkle of hillside houses and potholes the size of my car. Up past the mill with its arms and spouts and broken limbs, churning smoke into the moon. Past the little creek on the little bridge with a sign that says, oddly, "Traffic Alternate." I'm looking under trees to a creek as beautiful and magical as any in Disneyland. Around each rock, water trembles and tumbles perfectly.

Then I whiz past Pine Point Recreation Site. Past Robert street—the only street my eye will catch every time I leave. Past Maple Grove Recreation Site and a few new clear-cuts brought to a tree "Farm" near you. Then chunking under my tires from strippers that lift logs and zip off branches without straining. Past Little Shaw Creek and slithering to the signs at lake's end: one for Kissinger and one for Nitinat.

Then the big pond in alders where beavers busily make a den. And across the three bridges, Vernon, Granite, and Jasper Creek, bearing right on the one-way section. When I screech to a stop at the T-junction short of the Nitinat bridge, I see a truck waiting. Its hung-over young guy turns out to be someone I have come to know over the years: Bill Patterson, cheesed that I am half an hour late. At this point in my West Coast fishing education, I don't know there is such a thing as "first water": the fish can be stirred up and biters bitten for someone else before you arrive.

This is the first time I've been on a river in over two decades, having had a wife whose version of roughing it was going to a hotel without a swimming pool. Over those years, my pack, Primus stove, two-person tent, and knives with 20 implements slowly vanished from my life. Now, having removed myself from her, I find myself adrift, without camping gear. I will soon find out I am afraid to just push off down a river I don't know. To resume being myself.

"Ohhhhhh," I say to Bill as we rattle along in his red truck, crack snaking across the windshield. Down among second-growth fir, alders slap windows and scrape sides. We come to a smaller flow, which I am told is also the Nitinat, at its upper fishing boundary of Parker Creek.

Bill busies himself with his drift boat, one of the quaint—or so I think at the time—double-enders designed to keep water out in rapids. I am looking at stones here and there, at the water and finally up. Across from me, a bear stands, smelling my steak insides. I back up slowly, keeping my eyes from the bear's so as not to stir it into attack, until I am on the other side of the boat Bill is preparing to shove off the trailer. I get in the truck and yell back through the window, "A bear."

Bill shrugs his shoulders, "Only a three-year-old." He pushes the boat from shore and motions for me to get in. And then we are off. The first time I have been on a river for decades. Having grown up on Fish Creek in Calgary, I came to regard that water as my own private game reserve. Because I knew it so well, I was the one who caught the most fish. I carried home years of trout on willow branches with a side branch cut to form a Y. I strung it through the gills and walked the corpse, its colour draining, through noonday sun.

Over the edge into Parker Run, we are among rapids with stones like knees and bones of ancient animals. We bump through them to the pool below. During this slower drift, we are among trees drenched with moss. Without leaves, like anonymous sad animals, arms lifted, as though asking for some sort of help.

"Whoa, there's a tree come down."

I look forward where Bill is pointing but can't see anything but green. Then it dawns on me the fir probably weighs more than his truck. It has been under-cut and, in falling, moved through air across the river and ripped into forest on the other side. We are fortunate. Someone has chopped its branches to get a boat underneath.

"That's a good trick, because it's hard to get close enough to cut branches without being dragged under sweepers and drowned."

"Drowned?"

"I just fished this a few days ago. Good thing it didn't come down while we were passing through."

We lie back and watch the six-foot trunk and shortened limbs move by, a few inches from our faces. We float into a different world from the one I know. Silver willows, half-mile-long lines of gravel, cedars so huge they don't seem real. And we pass in silence, oars lifted, a sprinkling of drops on the water.

The anchor line is lifted from its crimper and the pyramid-shaped weight is lowered. The pool is deep and long. "Most of the fish are on the other side, a foot from the bank."

For me it is almost mystical: the mouth touching air, bronze shoulder, dorsal fin, anal peduncle and finally tail. "The square tails are coho."

Bill casts a long, lifting curve up and over the river and then down to the water a foot behind a branch, two feet from the bank. When I try, I can't even get close. And, of course, my line becomes a nest for magpies. I hand it to Bill and he sighs and hands me his rod. As I learn later, it has a dink float, some sequential, large split-shot to take the offering, on about two feet of leader, to fish eye level.

"Mend your line," Bill says.

"What?"

"You missed a fish."

"What?" I can't see a thing and wind the gear in and cast again, resulting in another bird's nest in the reel. Bill hands me the other rod. "You have to have your thumb on the line in the reel." And, sort of sideways derision, "I mean, you write about fishing ..." but he doesn't add the rest, something like, "but you don't even know how to cast."

Bill looks at me, hungover and green, sorting out the reel. I'm watching my float float merrily along, when he shouts, "Fish. Fish, Dennis."

"What?"

"You've got to mend your line."

Not wanting to look like an idiot, I have no choice but to prove I am by opening my mouth. "What do you mean exactly when you say mend your line?" I'm not going to tell him this is the first time I have ever fished for salmon in freshwater. It's too embarrassing.

And then there's a bear, on the other side, looking smaller than the other one. A semi-load of logs thunders dustily along the road high above. As if sensing my thoughts, Bill says, "They won't bother you, if you're in the water."

And suddenly I feel safe—only years later did I realize he was bullshitting me—and, strangely, I believe it even to this day: if I get into the water, a bear will not attack. "Mend your line, Dennis." The line from the rod tip should be connected, completely in the air to the top of the float."

I look between rod tip and float and realize I can't see the mainline at all. My eyes—my glasses—are too weak. When I reel to get the extra line in—the line I can't see—Bill says, "No, you're pulling the float and gear out of the fish." Not only can I not see the line, I cannot see the bite, either.

Bill explains: "Chinook, more so than coho, will touch a yarn fly—as simple as it comes, chunk of yarn slipped through a sliding knot, then pulled snug on the hook—as it goes by them at eye level. When it bumps them on the nose, they hold it for a few seconds and then they let it go."

"Don't they chase after it?"

"Dennis, remember, salmon are not eating in freshwater. But they line up one after the other and you use this group to improve your chances." The yarn fly passes through the pack of them and a fish "passively" bites the yarn and lets it go. It does not move, unlike a fish that comes after a lure and then snakes off, hooking itself.

"Passive, you say," and hand him another bird-nest rod. I am looking dubious I guess, and he hands me a rod that has a fish surely hooked on its other end. A fish as thick as my chest and long as my leg races by the boat and we are looking down at it. "Jesus, that's huge."

"That's your fish," Bill says, and I come face to face with the reason for fishing salmon in freshwater. The black mouth, the slide of water in and out, operculum gasping, rows of gill strainers, and short black bits everywhere. "Leeches," Bill says. Finally, leaning over the side, taking the hook from its big black jaw with pliers. It drifts down and away, like an airplane from a pack of fighters.

My next cast results in another bird's nest, and under his breath, Bill says, "The backlash kid." And here I am, the guy who's supposed to be this master fisherman. I can't even cast the lure. The rest of the afternoon goes like this: snap of line and Bill hands me a rod with a 30-pound Chinook on the other end, or a coho as much as 17. I've never seen fish this large, nor one after the other. My largest trolled up salmon to this point in my fishing career is 27 pounds.

Bill casts, watches the float, snaps the line against the air and hands me the rod. He takes from me the one with the bird's nest. As the sun progresses through the trees, Bill hands me 20 rods in a row in my introduction to freshwater salmon technique at Worthless Pool, named a century ago for its lack of "colours," meaning flakes of gold, by Robert Brown on the Vancouver Island Exploration Expedition, 1864.

"Yeah, in a passive bite, the fish won't hit and hook itself."

"Passive?" and thus begins my education. It takes years for me to understand Chinook do not move; they fin in place, bellies to bottom, and any flotsam that floats into their face, they hold in their mouths and then let go. You don't feel the fish snap and run against the line, because they don't—just touch and release, touch and release, bodies not moving an inch. Then I realize: if they don't whack the lure, you can't strike the lure, if your line isn't mended. Ahh.

Afterwards, snapped-off cigarette smoldering in my tired fingers, the boat runs into a rock and I am whanged into the thwart so hard I have a dent in my leg to this day. Of course, blood comes gushing out of the crease. First blood on the Nitinat. Not the last I will shed. Not by many gallons.

"Coho like shade, even as little as a foot wide will be where they sit."

"Hmm," I say and look into the skinny water where, true to his word, a fin or two is moving up.

Around the corner from the boat launch, we pass through tens of thousands of chum; so many, in fact, when we are among them, the water shatters and we are soaked to the skin. We laugh through our soaked mouths, water running down our faces, chests and legs. We pull the boat onto the gravel bar above the bridge and bump off in my car to retrieve his truck at the top of the river.

Just as he's firing it up, he says he has a party to go to in "The Port," localese for Port Alberni.

"Don't drink too many beers," I say.

And the answer: "It's not the beers I have to worry about. It's the rum."

Driving out in the dark, on my first day on a river that will become mine, I miss the centre of Jasper Creek bridge. The car bottoms out in a pothole, twanging off, I discover the next day, a hubcap. It is the first of nine I am going to lose from this maroon Subaru en route to the end of its life.

Chapter 2

DENNIS ALMOST DYING

The better part of a year later, after the warm fall afternoon Bill and I passed among the shades of Worthless Pool, I make a decision. I will take myself down to the Nitinat and try fishing on the long weekend of May.

I put my blue dinghy, all nine feet of it, on a long green foamy I used to use for camping. I put it on the roof of my car and pass the rope over and down, through the car windows to the other side and up, over the boat and so on. Along with me comes my $12 Kmart special rod, with three flies: a huge Royal Coachman, some Atlantic salmon fly, and one made of orange and brown. I do not know how ugly these flies are and how useless. That's because I know nothing about freshwater fishing on the coast. And I am nervous, having stopped being a river person for almost 30 years. Much of that time, I was married with kids and had a wife whose version of the outdoors meant walking to Dairy Queen.

So, to the water I have so frequently thought of as my real home, in earlier years of my life, I return, apprehensive, pushing doubts away. I do not know what lies below where I will launch—waterfalls, deadfalls, whatever. I do not know about the Nitinat wind, but I will soon learn.

I tie a dumbbell to a rope and tie the line to the bow. I put oars in the oar locks, fire in my spinning rod, the one that sometimes its bale does not flip back over. Twenty-five-pound test line as well. Lunch. Water bottle, camera gear, tackle box, pack sack, knife. But not a coat, no lifejacket. I swirl away from the launch, oars in the air, turning in a circle beneath the bridge, into my own deliverance, without knowledge of what is in front of me.

When I have drifted down the half mile to what I now know as the Stump Pool, I decide to tie up and fish from the boat just below the fast water that turns to the left and drops into a deep pool. I will be casting Buzz Bombs, some ancient Mepps Aglia, used for hunting cutthroat in the Altrude lakes in Alberta decades before. And a Dar Dev'l, Len Thompson, red and white spoon.

I dump the barbell over the blue dinghy's downstream side and the line goes taut. The boat rolls over and I am flung to the bottom of the river. I know in this instant I will die, not thinking that I am a father, former husband, only the knowledge, in terror: *I am going to die.*

Then my feet touch the bottom and I look up several feet. All around me, in the water column, is my gear: fly rod going down, oar, packsack. Then I am angry and push so hard I come up under the upside-down boat. I push it to shore, which sends me back down to the bottom, only 8 feet this time, where I push again and, by a slow, inchworm process, come up neck deep and struggle up the sliding, watery gravel.

Expletives I yell, and drag my upside-down boat up the bank, realizing I still have my spinning rod in my hand. Fancy that—drowning, but with priorities: I will not lose the rod until I am dead. I throw it down and fetch my sodden packsack, my sinking tackle box. I have lost: one oar, one fishing rod, my water, my vest.

I'm shouting obscenities as my oar floats calmly downstream on the opposite side of the very deep pool. I grab my spinning rod and cast my Buzz Bomb, trying to snag the oar. If it is lost, so am I. I run down my side of the bank until I have to wade through some very sinky mud that closes on my thighs, casting and retrieving as my oar trundles along to the horizon. While I am shouting: %!@#%$!@#@$!@#$—which means *spirited lament*—I go in up to my chest and can go no farther.

Then a strange thing happens. The oar turns to shore and starts coming back up of its own accord. Ah, I see: it's in a back eddy and the water carries it up the opposite shore. I struggle through mud, lifting each leg and placing its foot down, pulling the other, causing the first to sink in silt from a thousand trees felled the previous century. I am too angry to notice that each step sinks farther than the last. I cast like a fiend, Buzz Bombs strafing the air, breaking trees off their roots, white-coloured lead breaking the sound barrier. More expletives. A million bombs sent flying, but not one snags the oar, its black plastic oarlock.

I run up my side of the river a good hundred yards, to my sodden stuff, but the hook will not catch. Line passes over the oar, but the hook slides off. Then the oar comes to rest, drifted to the head of the back eddy and swung so the blade touches the big rock at its head. And there it stays. This is my chance—my only chance—to retrieve it. I turn the water from my boat, and rub-a-dub-dub, like three wet guys in a tub, kneel in the bow. With my remaining oar, I put one vertical stroke down one side, then a vertical stroke down the other. The river works on me, running me out of reach as I reach out my longest finger for the second oar. The river carries me away, one stroke on one side, one stroke on the other.

Just before sinking over the horizon, I am spared. With the luck of the forest, maple trees with their green hands, elk with velvet knobs of antlers, I am gathered in the back eddy and carried upstream to my oar. When I come even with it, I simply reach down and pick it up, as though nothing has happened.

When I regain the other bank, I open my pack and water flows out. I take my camera and water runs out; it and my flash and all the film have been ruined—requiring purchase of others—in the first millisecond after my open-mouthed face hit water. There is another long list of curses. My tackle box I empty and later, water leaves a red crust over everything. My lunch is something left to bloat in the sea for weeks. Banana squashed. Coca-Cola disappeared.

I shiver in weak sun that to this day, more than two decades on, is cold on this north-facing corner. Haunted trees weirdly cry with their load of moss, tons of baggy, green fat. It crosses my literate mind that perhaps I can retrieve my no-name Kmart special, one with line guides fixed with electrician's tape, a reel that grinds out line at the best of times. It does not need a drag. Rust does that well enough, since I was 13 and laid my handful of change on the counter.

I row out into the river, look down through the shifting lens of water. Way down there is my rod. Out goes the dumbbell—over the front end this time—and it tethers me back and forth in the current. The spinning rod tip with its Buzz Bomb goes down, down, down, and I try and try to latch the fly line, or rod, or any damn thing. To the eagle and mink, to otters and elk, to cougars, there is a screaming human on the water, like Jack Nicholson in *The*

Shining, making fists and groaning when the hook misses the line. Twenty minutes and more, until—can I be so lucky?—the fiddly line is snagged.

When I pull, more and more comes up. When I get the fly line in the boat, I have to pull, hand over hand, the backing from the reel, until every yard is sitting in a pile beside me. Then the reel end of the rod lifts from the gravel and comes to my hand.

And, now I hear it, a presence in wilderness of rock, water and stump. I can hear it coming up the valley and turn my head to understand. Trees complain as their limbs brush their neighbours. On this day, I have little knowledge of the river that will become my own, and it will be years later that I realize wind comes every day there is sun. By noon, wind breathes up the 20-mile lake and then the 20-mile river. Thirty miles an hour, until sun sets and it forgets about blowing for the day.

Sitting on shore in my yellow canvas shirt, I do not know what is in store. But I cannot go upstream, only down. I swing out, feet in water in the bottom of the boat, and the first wind brushes my face. Here I am, drifting down, oars in the air, watching trees do their version of tossing like broccoli, bending into and out of faces. My oars hit the water and I cannot understand why water should be pushing the blades downstream. Until I realize the wind blows so hard it is blowing me *up* the river.

In my cotton shirt and bare legs and wet crotch, I begin to row, sitting backwards, passing feet-first downstream. My afternoon becomes this: row and row and row and check the trees to make sure they are not going downstream; the big firs with their coats of Spanish moss; the big maples with leaves as large as platters; the ferns exotic as peacocks; and, my fear, as I get colder and colder and my shirt will not dry.

The bones in my limbs lose their purpose and muscles become numb. Hairs on my arms blow from red centres of puckered flesh. I pull over to rub myself, run up and down the bank, arms around myself. I stare into implacable, not-there eyes of forest, thinking of Kurtz in *Heart of Darkness*. His civility was stripped in jungle that didn't care, as it threw more beauty at his feet than he, and now I, can imagine.

My feet are onions in wet runners, my legs white, their fur of black hairs rising. I am not able to stop shaking as I row downriver, to what end I have no knowledge, but down into wilderness, farther away from where I know not that I am, not having thought to bring a map, or look at one in advance, knowing only that there is a pull-out somewhere down in the wilderness. Tree leaves come free and fall around me like rain. Fir needles are a red tide around the boat, migrating upstream as I row and row down, hunched in my wet yellow shirt.

Where the river makes white noise, I raise my oars and look at a log in knee-deep water beside me. When I see a fish dart from the log, I rise up in my seat to see better. And then, when I am just passing the log, so close I could touch it with my oar, the log transforms itself and moves away steadily, toward the opposite bank. I realize it is a fish, the biggest fish I have ever seen in fresh water, and the river moves on, carrying me with it, teeth rattling against one another. I do not know that this is the first Pacific steelhead I have ever seen. A log. Mistake a fish for a log. From here, it seems long ago.

My day ends with my boat pulled over to the gravel bank, where a car shakes itself along a wash-board road above and dust rises like a kind of intelligence. My eyes perceive that this is the road beside the river. Had the car not gone by, I would not have seen there is a road so hidden, just above river level, within the second-growth jungle that is the rainforest. I would have missed the last place to get out of the river.

And if I had kept going, I would have never come back, because the river would have taken me all the way to the lake in the distant white that is the stars, me looking up from my cold, wet, yellow, canvas shirt. I turn left and walk the rutty miles back to my car, it having to be upstream after all, and thus there is no point turning right and down the road. So long ago, it seems, dust on my runners, dust on my knees, eyes on the gravel in front of them. One step at a time.

Tadpoles – A common summer sight is huge numbers of enormous tadpoles, that become huge numbers of teeny tiny toads. They are found at many places along the Nitinat River. These were at Dennis' Pool. Glass Run is another hotspot for tadpoles and toads, as is just above the Hatchery Pool, and beside Worthless Run.

Chapter 3

DENNIS' POOL

Cool water surrounds my thighs as I cross the Nitinat River after fish I think of as my own. I walk a corridor of conifers that talk with the sky, of willows that crowd the banks when wind turns them silver, then green. They take over, only minutes it seems, after winter flood strips the land of earth.

But this is a summer day, and I slosh the calf-deep channel east of what I call Bear Island. The bear that owns this stretch of forest crosses the lesser channel and leaves wet prints among rain-softened holes of bull elk and the maidens they harbour this time of year. On this day, though, the bear is not at his island, nor on the west channel, where willows make quiet noise in soft morning air.

I cast into moving hands of water above Cutt Corner, where a log stretches down the opposite shore. In the shade of trees wide as a hand-joined couple are Chinook salmon. They touch the surface, moving up, crossing over, then down, crossing over and then again back up, all day long, in a circle. Thousands of fish, each one as long as my leg. While I am early in my understanding of salmon, I already see that yellow leaves and white bubbles moving up means something very large is beneath.

A piece of silver and gold monofilament crosses the sun. A lure lands short of the other side, where fish are always found. They are never on your side of the river.

I wade cool hands of water that slip round my thighs, then deeper than a man likes to go. Water rises to my ribs and I cast into shade on the east side of morning, where long spears of shadow cut across the river. I can't see a single fish, though I know there are many, keeping out of sight of whatever predators may come.

I send a high weight-to-volume spoon as far as I am able. The Illusion, Kit-A-Mat, Ironhead, heavy lures that fly because their weight cuts a hole in the air. My lure travels the morning sun, into the shade of millennium-old trees, big arms spread out. Some are broken from battle when winter is in their hands.

And the small bereft call of an eagle, in its tree above the blue river. Its perch the winter river will take from it. But not today. I make the bird the small king of my day. The sun is in my chest and on my arms.

Then the sound of my line—sffft—into the strike. A large fish easily clears the water, tail passing up and over its head, then craters the river. I am pulled so hard I rise on my toes to keep from falling face-first into the tow of the fish. It simply moves upstream, and as though an invisible string is stuck to my sternum, I follow, dragging bottom. River bulges against my chest.

There is no word for a salmon this big, other than it is a great beast of an animal. No mere fish, no hold in the hand, blue brook trout. This is a fish so large that when its head comes clear of water, it is as big as my own. I am in its element among its holes the size of cars.

It seems to take all morning, landing the largest fish of my life. It boils dust on the bottom of the glide. Its game of tic-tac-toe, its spider-web flight, turns me in a circle, tip of rod pressing downstream, water moving me deeper than I was before. Then up, between me and my shore. The line cuts like a submarine conning tower. Its *zzzt* is the only sound in front of the eagle, far above, sun falling in pieces around its shoulders.

A long time later, the great fish comes to me. I lift my rod high, right hand reaching, it seems, into the eye of Chinook. There is no other way to put it than, the fish looks at me and into me. I feel its incomprehension, its fear. It shushes against my beating chest, so large it is as thick as I am, with a mouth into which I could stuff both fists.

I wrap 20-pound test mono around my right arm, drop my long rod and golden reel into the river. From my mouth, where I've pushed them during the fight, I pull needle-nose pliers, and the beast eddies close, eyes on my eyes. My fist is small in its mouth as the pliers retrieve the hook of subterfuge. And this hand, as so often happens, releases ribbons of red that are my blood. The teeth are a line of pins in black jaws, meant for holding and shredding prey.

When I place my hand beneath its belly, its alien, three-chambered heart beats in my palm. I point its head into the current. My other hand can't grasp the wrist of its tail, so I stuff cold silver to my chest. Bending low, chin on water, I ship mighty cool water into my armpit on a golden day.

When it is ready, it lets me know. It moves its head side to side, which is the first movement of flight: how a fish understands freedom, making its body serpentine like a scarf in wind. The curve pushes down a black and silver body and the thrust of tail sends me clear off my feet. And then it is gone, back to its shade, back to the others in the invisible country of cold blood.

There is nothing more to do. Nothing to say, other than words of appreciation. "Thank you," I say to the forest. "Thank you," I say to the fish. Words that make me part of the water and part of the land.

All day long, I cast into the invisible, and pull out the beautiful: fish I can only see, sipping air where no one else can see them. Small bubbles rise from mouths that angle down to stony bottom. Shade is a dark medium that cannot be deciphered, unless your eyes are open.

All day in a cool river as deep as I dare, letting fish pull me where they will. I catch more than I thought possible: an even dozen to 50 pounds. I cast until my arms cannot withstand the hundred-yard runs, and I must quit—something I have never done before. Arms at my side, I offer up thanks, once more, to the fish still mouthing air in their shade.

My last deed is to name this nondescript run: Dennis's Pool. It is hardly more than a glide, and in the river I will come to know, never more than simple. In a future summer, wader-less, I will walk across up to my neck to understand the water where salmon lie. Where they wait, for the river to rise, for rain to tell them it is time.

Rod over my shoulder, I walk back into the person I have become over the decades. This private person, whose private meaning is being alone with fish. In my future, the small glide will reward me with more coho and Chinook than almost any other place in the Nitinat. A place most fishermen pass by, thinking it is shade, and the gloom and coolness forbids them entrance.

I return with striding sun. Upriver through shallow water, now on the east side. From the forest ten feet above, broken turf has been made into a sandy trail. This is where elk make their crossing. If a man is found walking in sun that sweats down his back, they withhold their presence. I give in to the forest without fear of being watched—the seventh sense we have of feeling eyeballs looking at us, a strange feeling. Bear Island is left behind, and when I turn back, a line of elk—males with crowns of bone, females the size of horses with delicacy of muscle—are moving down the bank.

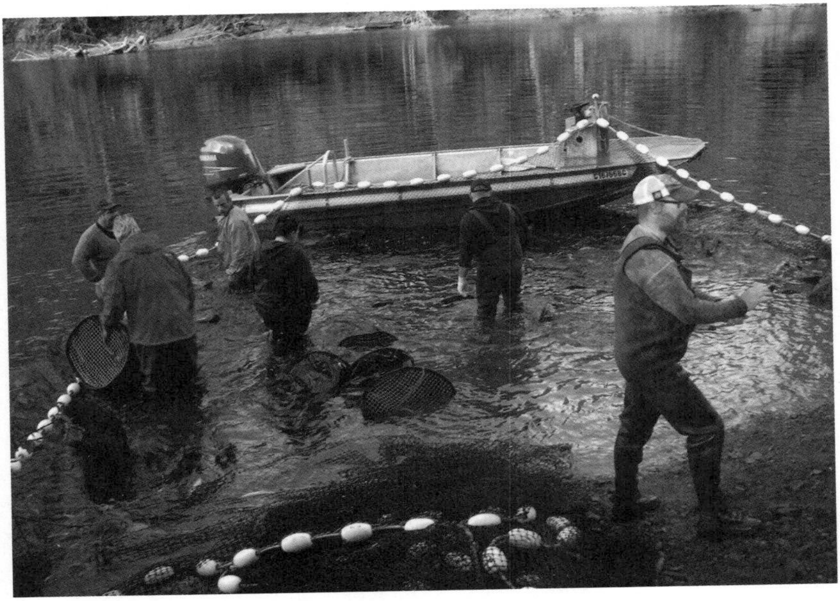

Just up from Dennis's Pool, the Nitinat hatchery takes Chinook broodstock at Red Rock Pool. The boat pulls the net around the pool in a circle ending close to the start, so both lines may be pulled in. When the fish are in the smallest space, they are lifted in mesh containers and loaded on a truck.

Sun drips down my glasses. I trudge into my shadow like Huckleberry Finn, rod balanced on my shoulder—the gift of fishing often. My hands are in my pockets. There is no one to whom I can tell the tale, who can live it my own private way. I thank Mark Twain, too. Thanking nature is my only fishing ritual. Its gift of pleasure recognized, on a half-mile of squelching, ankle deep in a place of caddis and brown algae. I look up to endless tons of gravel and seagulls, important in their whiteness. Nature and me, two fingers crossed.

Where I cross, the river is at my waist. I brace with spread legs, quarter down, river pushing me into itself. But not all the way. Not this time.

Minutes later, I am breaking down my rod at Red Rock Pool. A guide I will someday come to know has dropped his drift boat, and clients, while he runs back up for his truck. The husband is a large Scottish man with a beard. "I fought it for half an hour and never even got a chance to see it."

This is their version of the best fishing of their lives. "It was glorious," his wife says and gazes into the wilderness that is Canada. To hook a Chinook and never get a look is a memory the length of a life.

"How did you do?" the man questions.

I simply shrug, for I have lost the ability to speak. In silence, I offer final thanks to the day. The beauty of the open eye.

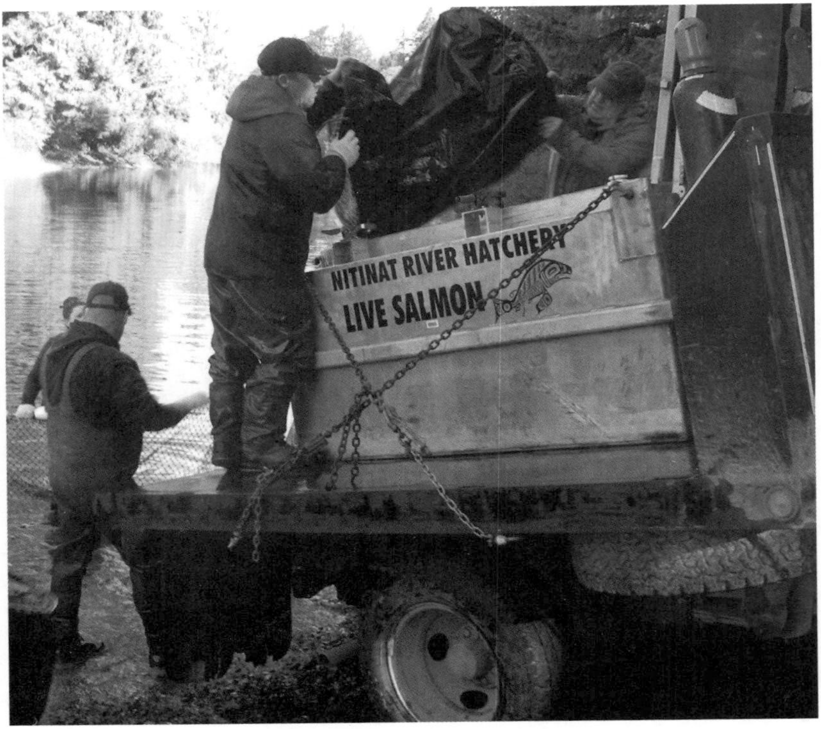

The mesh bags are lifted to the tank on the back of the truck, dumped into the live-well (it has oxygen) and then the truck beetles to the hatchery, about 5 minutes down the road, where the fish are emptied to ripen in the raceways until milt and eggs are taken and mixed.

Chapter 4

DENNIS ALMOST DYING, REVISITED

This day is in mid-September, before the rains begin. As so often happens when sun hangs over southern trees, morning calm retreats, a breath taken in by the sea. Later, the breath will be let out. Nititnat wind will blow from the ocean, up the long lake and into the treetops, 30 miles per hour. All around me are broken wooden heads from years of wind.

But it is early now. Dew is wet in the shade of Douglas fir. Maple leaves as large as my chest pull from their trees and fall in yellow piles. I cross the rocks of an empty seasonal stream. On either side is a line of golden pine needles, evidence of fallen water. Down where the winter stream will push gravel from its throat are white stains of seagulls. When I burst from willows, ten thousand wings sound the applause of invisible hands hitting air.

Beyond the white seagull beach, the river is shallow and soft-spoken. I walk past almost human paw prints, past drying hulks of Chinook. A spiky hand has ripped off their heads, and the rest are left to rot and thus taste better next time.

I begin to re-understand knowledge I knew as a sunburnt kid: in crossing a river, turn 45 degrees down-current and half run, half fly, letting the weight of water carry me to willows on the other side, to their green-skinned knuckles.

I am deposited on a beach of gravel and silt that stretches down half a mile, beyond the island and its bear, all the way to Cutt Corner. In front of my feet are tens upon thousands of tons of clear-cut logging gravel from a century ago. It comes to me that the slow disgorging of gravel by winter flood is the river cleansing itself, over the decades, of what men have done.

Sun is in the crowns of eastern trees and the bear of the island inhabits the right channel. He—it is probably a he, for he is not with cubs—is not full grown. But he is big enough to kill a man and so I step down, kicking stones, looking at the bottom—shambling ... like a bear. Tan algae and caddis larvae lift; they are carried with current that can have as its metaphor only time.

I clear my throat and let out a long "Hey-ah" to alert the bear that I am coming. He is snout-deep, pounced on four feet, trying to sink a claw into shredding skin. Large canine teeth and bear head pass completely underwater. I am surprised how clumsy he seems. I have seen the ads of a bear standing on a rock in a river and the hapless salmon leaps up into its mouth. We have all seen this.

And then to find the advertisement is intended to make me send money to an envirocorp; that the immutable image I and all of us have seen for decades is untrue. The bear in front of me jumps here and there, having little luck trapping fish in forearm-deep water. Still, it could kill *me,* and I stand, fishing rod over my shoulder, blowing my whistle, as though its toots will save me. After an impatient tooting minute, I say, "Time to go, bear. I want to go by." The bear yawns at me and closes its eyes. *Whatever,* it seems to imply and then rises indignantly to walk away, elbows—if they have such things—pointed outward. Claws pull it up and into the forest.

This is when I name the island Bear Island. I am very alert, walking the left-side channel in knee-deep water. Down the dozen-foot bank the bear has climbed, footprints have shredded the greenery, as many as a team of particularly beefy football linesmen. Some look like horse hooves, and I relax, knowing they are elk.

Below is a stump, apparently grown from the river bottom. It would have been pushed on a flooding winter day and deposited here. It must have taken years for a restless river to scour a hole big enough for its root ball—some are 20 feet across. One day when the water was perfect, it dropped the ball into the hole and lifted the log, with its diameter wide as I am tall. Amazing strength. None of the ball is visible and a good 70 feet of log rises at an angle. In salmon season, chum sway in its calm, waist-deep lee. I call it Lonesome Pole. Decades later, it is still there.

I cross the river in the Pole's shadow, water to my stringy shin muscles. It won't be this easy every year. Over time, a river changes. One year, a new channel gouges gravel just below The Seam. A full 12 feet deep. Again, thousands of tons of rock, moved like it was sand. All from clear-cut logging.

I will stick my head with its glasses into the water. I will see big rocks, from before the river was choked. Another year, the opposite, when the seasonal stream falls white from rock to rock. The entire pool will be filled with gravel and less than knee-deep. On the bottom lies a hundred-yard tail of boulders, each heavier than I am. Two hundred pounds each, picked up and carried by the dumb weight of water.

I am thinking about what made my eyes open in the dark, what pulled my body from bed to drive several black hours north and west: I have come to walk the banks of Dennis's Hole. I stop and eat a sandwich in sunny September, river gravel white with bird droppings. Now I understand why the name "shithawk" is appropriate for seagulls. When I move my arm, a thousand lift in a mass, comprising a single animal.

In shade near the eastern bank, salmon touch the surface with open mouths. They lift easily, gently, one and then another. When they touch the sky, they look like rain. This is the first time I have witnessed such behavior, which I will come to understand as calm, alert fish, the kind that will bite a well-presented lure. What I see is easeful fish, neither turned on nor stale after a string of sunny days. Waiting for me, in another year, in *my* spot.

My left arm snaps out monofilament, slipping softly through line guides, and my spoon, a spot of gold, arcs across the distance. I land the lure above, so as not to spook the fish. I noticed once, on the San Juan River, when I stood in sun, high on a bank, above a bottom speckled with coho, that when my spinner hit the water, every salmon ricocheted like a pinball machine. I spooked them so soundly on my first cast that on my second, the fish spooked simply with my arm moving through the air. They were looking *up* at me. That was the last time I stood above fish I wanted to catch.

And then the lure stops. I am tugging on the lure stuck to a lousy rock when the rock moves upstream and I am hard into a large coho. As in previous years at Dennis's Hole, I am pulled onto my toes as the fish bolts a hundred yards upriver. Then the line goes slack, meaning the coho has turned and is running toward me. I stump backward, reeling as fast as I can to catch up.

The fish streaks through long, pyramidal shades cast by Douglas fir across morning water. A thousand coho scatter into the sun. I had not seen any of them. I recall Bill Patterson, on my first trip a few years ago, telling me coho travel and rest in shade, even strips as narrow as a foot, and are completely unaware of my presence.

When the fish comes closer, it bears the four-angled mouth of a mature, handsome buck. You see these angles in Indigenous carvings and paintings. I reach, and the buck does the "coho roll," meaning it rolls round and round like an alligator with prey. It is instinctual, meaning genetic: coho are the only species of five that will roll this way. Once, fishing for halibut, bottom-bouncing a lure 250 feet down, my line went limp. I reeled in a jerking coho that had rolled so completely it had shackled itself into the braided line, with 100 feet down to the lure. In other words, swimming happily about 150 feet down, it had the misfortune to bump into the only fishing line for miles. When rolling to get free, it become more and more entangled.

I bend over a fish that gives me the old face wash. I can't say how many times I have reached for a fish only to have it soak me, my hat, my glasses, dripping off my nose, my chin. As though they have a sense of humour. Pliers are taken from my mouth, where I put them during the fight. I slip the hook round and it comes neatly from the jaw. Kirbed hooks, in the days of barbless hooks, are far better than Siwash-style for hooking a jaw. If a lure comes with a single straight Siwash, place pliers across, gap to shank, and bend 15 degrees.

The rest of my day is as memorable as the one when I landed so many Chinook I could not cast anymore. I stand in shade, managing air-sipping chum and coho, working them, fish that, having porpoised, slip down, leaving lines of bubble.

When I turn upriver there are more seagulls than I have ever seen, rising and falling, as though the ground has freed its boundaries and is testing new powers. At Bear Island, ten thousand are so excited over so much food they can't help but scream. I return through undertaker shrieks, webby feet standing on the corpses, pulling out eyeballs. And bloody cheeks of blind, dead fish.

Afternoon sun melts my back as I move up, one leg lifted and set down, then the other. Slow, measured, not falling over. I skirt willows where I crossed earlier, one hand holding a branch, one foot moving. Sun throws watery shadows from the western shore. My route is in shade and the bottom clear no more. I spread my legs, move the upstream leg first, wade to my thighs, my waist. The river begins moving me down. Then to my stomach, my ribs. I am fully committed and there is only going forward.

And then my toe does not touch, and I am gasping. I turn back, beat water with my hands, look from a green tunnel, 20-pound pack taking me down ... and then my mind comes back to me, from the shock of frigid water invading my waders. I have to get to the road side.

I turn myself around. One hand reaches out, then my other reaches over. I turn them over and over until my toe finally touches down and I drag my carcass, to crash in the gravel. I am surprised to find my rod in my hand—proof, once again, I won't let go, until I truly do drown. There is no human being for miles. Only me on my back in bird shit. I call this The Seam, among the best coho places until late October. I have been lucky: pulled out just above a 12-foot pool, where my pack would have taken me down.

And then I see them: coho lips touching sky. There is no more dying and no reason to leave. Gallons of water on each side, my legs widen like Alley Oop. I move waist-deep to keep from breaking my waders, ripping suspenders from Velcro.

Afternoon flow is in the treetops, shaking beards of moss. Wind skins the water and a coho reaches out to smack my lure with the particular "rubbery" bite only coho possess. Sun marks its progress down the treeless clear-cut to the west. I am fortunate. Wind makes the fish confident, and I take one and more, wind in the hair on my head, my ears, wind in my eyeballs, so they stream with tears.

Later, I lie on my back in white gravel, poke my feet in the air. Gallons of water drain across my chest, gurgle into stones below. At the car, I take off all my clothes, save underwear, pull on a scruffy t-shirt scrounged from the back. I lean into the heater, steam making my windshield invisible. My maroon Subaru insinuates into Nitinat turns, as I hope not to be stopped by police. How to explain sitting in wet underpants, a ripped t-shirt? Next day, it hits me: go buy a wading belt. And I actually do.

Chapter 5

THE INDIGNITY OF WILDERNESS

Once upon a time, philosophers more intelligent than I opined there was no God. They saw no single, conventional Christian God, no he/she/it of a God, nor committee of willing supernatural types. Nice, symmetrical logic pointed out that if God was perfect, it was impossible for he/she/whatever to create something not, well, perfect. They rested their case, as lawyers pointing out the mens rea of it all, thumbs in imaginary suspenders. The individual, pudgy lout each human being struggles to be demonstrates that there is nary a single, perfect specimen among us. Hmm.

Once overcoming alarm, I was impressed with their erudition. We are not perfect. And, neither our pudginess nor loutishness is the less-than-perfect attribute. At two score and thirteen years, it came to me: as we humans have to take a number two, we are not perfect; not even close. Having to do a loo is far less than perfect would do. Thus, there is no God.

Many, like me, must feel the need for privacy when God does or does not have me stop for the unmentionable plop. I enter my private room, when no others are there, ensure no door may be opened by another of the less-than-perfect crew; that no mirror is placed just so I must watch my fact of doing the less than perfect act. On porcelain squatting, only one thing men will do is s_itting on the loo.

When not alone in my own little home, I have learned to wait until I return. Privacy and quiet I seek to do my, er, pooh. Doing the deed in unfamiliar locales leads to conclusions not in tune with my quest for number two. Most of the time a place do I find, with a lock that won't bind, and cannot be used, for wouldn't I die if someone came by?

There are other negativities, too. What if you do the unmentionable two only to find, at the end of your time, there is no paper on your roll? And what of the chemical toilet, where one might need to jump to avoid splashback on your rump and still not been entirely successful, and had the icky chemicals commune with your most private parts which most other, perhaps more perfect, animals can see and lick clean?

Every morning I head north in search of fish, my car cruises into the wet or dusty Payless Gas, because its gas is cheaper than that in my home town. They know me here and know, even if I do not ask, the products I want. They move through their store and return with things I'll find useful in my day: two cans of Coke, two Captain Black cigars, two tuna sandwiches, two chocolate chip cookies and one very large tea with two teabags, to open my eyes. They do this because I have asked them so many times. They ask for my Air Miles card, the one with numbers worn off so they enter the digits by hand. Then they give it back. Problem is, I've already closed my wallet and put it in my pants and have to haul it back out. I put it away again, and seconds later they give me the receipt I have asked them to give me, for the meals and entertainment stack of my income tax. So, I have to get my wallet out again because I have gotten up at 4:30 to go fishing and no brain cells yet exist and there is no indication any are about to show up soon.

I have managed to train myself to do the sit-down thing in their little orange loo. I do this because I have got to know them and to trust them, a little, though many "clients" might have sat in the night with evil intent before my station wagon varrooms to a stop. I walk with their key: a two-foot orange handle sans squeegee on one end, for my do in the loo. This unstealable key has the highest coliform content in Canada. So, I look at it and look at the door and the sign for a man has only one leg and makes clear the washroom was cleaned last year.

I know I will come to grief if I come to rest and ponder on the roundy seat that one's male appendage always seems to contact. So, after washing the key in the sink and flushing the toilet with my toe inside my shoe, my elbow pushing the paper holder so the paper starts coming and I can use it to cover my fingers and push more paper out, so I can hold the orange handle, paper between my fingers and dry it off, because it would be embarrassing returning with a long, wet, orange windshield-washer key.

One dark day I race away on the long, straight highway through sleeping towns on sides of hills to the car-challenging gravel that leads to fish. Along the way I remember I've forgotten to remember I am really in need of the washroom I forsook. I had a load of chili the night before, a Caesar salad I love, but can't quite digest the raw egg in the mess. French bread with butter my lactose-intolerant intestine won't tolerate, and garlic. I have eaten two bran muffins while my Subaru has eaten the Malahat, its cat eyes going de, de, de. And now with my tea and oatmeal chocolate chip cookie, I am, frankly, in agony.

I'm standing in my waders, literally holding my rectum from opening—sorry for being indiscreet—when I know I'll have to go; no choice but to be doing my twoing that proves there is no greater being looking over me. The indignity of it all. So, I grab my packsack, fishing rod and my hat, sunglasses and boots, vest with my scissors swinging blindly, blades well open and ready to cut. I've never done such an evil deed before, nothing of so little dignity. So, I don't have a clue as my face turns blue how to make the thing come cleanly from, well, where it comes from.

If, for instance, I push my pants low, do a knee bend and let flow, I'll probably go in my pulled-down waders or fall back in what I have just relieved my body of having to hold in. So, I race along, hands on my bum, fishing implements leaking from my pockets, until it comes to me how I can go in the woods: by sitting on a log with my bum as far out the other side as I can manage. But *this* log is three feet wide and there's no way my rear end will slide to the other side, and so I keep running.

At three feet tall, I look left and right until I spy a log a foot high. This one will have to do, as I'm shedding my waders and trying not to fall over into it, all that arrives with the force of the Challenger, the end result of the nonexistence of God. When I come back to reality from holding the log as an excuse for a bog, my eyes in their opening come straight on a plopping that looks just like—you'll remember from a previous book—strawberry jam just ladled on the wilderness, but is actually from inside the prehensile-lipped bear who can grab every berry off a bush and not take a single leaf, twig or thorn.

Of course, I am here among all the bears just looking for easy human flesh. And then I discover I don't have any toilet paper either, and I'm a

Seinfeld skit by Kramer with the smoky hair. Brain coming back to me, I remember I have one of my reels in a handkerchief, and while sitting on the log I'm picking the pieces and setting them down on the gravel and wasting a perfectly good cloth cleaning a lump off my ... er, rump. And that is the end of the parable of the first indignity.

Since this time, I have taken along toilet paper in a Ziploc bag. How clever. It never gets wet, it comes out clean and, bon chance, is biodegradable, as are the substances that pass through me on their way back to nature all over the wilderness of my river valley.

I've even managed, over time and with practice, to improve my skills on the number two manoeuvre. First, if you have no choice but to go, remember there is no one watching over you because you have proof of the nonexistence of one or an executive pack of greater kinds. Second, find a tree with a clear plop zone below. Lower your waders and then, as though sitting in a chair, legs at right angles at the knees, your back comes to rest against the tree and thus you have a good way of staying out of the drop zone, as do your waders that you don't want poop in either, and let fly! Then take out the Ziploc bag in which the important white material has been waiting for its five seconds of fame.

After perfecting my method, I have come to realize there is an even better refinement of the act. And, in the rain—it seems to rain every day you go fishing—you know you want to be out of the rain so you don't get your clothing wet. Here's the deal. You go to the teeny weeny little-more-than-a-culvert crossing of the seasonal stream that comes down into the river where The Seam is and take yourself underneath. You will be out of the rain, with the stream whistling down ten feet from you, a kind of natural emetic to help in the letting go of fluids and solids that should be returned to nature anyway.

In the instant you realize there is no God, you can still witness miracles in this natural world where a mountain is a mountain, then it is no mountain, then it is. Lean back against the telephone pole–sized pilings under the bridge, cars and trucks going thunk thunk above, and plop to your heart's content. No one will see you, no one will suspect you, no one will ever know.

It's truly a miracle. You can stand afterwards, clean and raring to go and saying to the underside of the bridge, "Thank you," holding your hand out like Queen E and doing the thing she does to sprinkle royal largesse among the hurly burly under-toads.

And you can experience the miracle of nature: I have gone back to the little "chair" to check nature's progress processing my little leavings into useful things like nitrogen, carbon and hydrogen. I have deliberately gone when I didn't need to go, and every time, the spot is completely, utterly, absolutely clean. No droppings, no ploppings, nothing. All of nature has gotten together to do the right thing for the universe.

To this day, I have never found my insides come and awaiting decay, nor one white sheet. And I use three per time so I can fold them over so the fingers of my left hand are completely obscured, so I can dig into my ____ to get the last little bit that were it not retrieved, I would get that tickling, prickling feeling and have to find a little bridge again. Nor finding one white puff of soft, charming, Seventh Generation recycled paper (doing my bit for the ecology) nor a plopping—and I've left as little as seven days and made a detour to look and see if I can spot someone, like, say, the tooth fairy, or poop fairy, or wolves or bears that have found it's just great to eat.

I experience epiphany after epiphany under the little Seam culvert. Perhaps the intelligentsia might be right; there is no immanence, for number two is true. But maybe there's a kind of honey-pot god and he has his eyes and hands on the aftermath of eating, keeping his universe clean. If this were true, though: where is his stash of them and what is he doing with them? Hmm.

Dennis and Dented Car – This is the first car I destroyed on the Nitinat, and other, back roads. Like all my other cars, this maroon Subaru was always covered with mud. Note to the right of me the dent in the bottom of the car. This ran from one side of the car to the other. The story is on the next page in paragraph 2. I am a lucky man.

Chapter 6

THE SEAM AND ME

Loud music, and my hand hits the alarm clock. 4:30 a.m. Then rain streams down my windshield in phosphorescent dark and the Malahat Drive takes me up, over the rock to the rest of Vancouver Island. My hands are on the wheel when the car begins skidding sideways. My eyes look out where I have just been coming from. Then at the dark, mountain side, not sky. Then my tires bite cold, wet asphalt, and once again, the car points down the long, black road north, to my river.

Strangely, this has happened before. On another highway, going to another place in the dark: a stream, flowing across the highway, carried me into the opposite ditch. The boulders threw the car in the air so the bottom hit the mountain—or I would have been killed—and the impact threw me back onto the highway, brakes skidding to a stop, one tire blown. Later, the car limped back to town, only one lug nut on the rim, a two-inch dent across the car bottom.

In both cases, once I moved clear of danger, the incident slipped into the land where memories pass unhindered into forgetfulness. And then I wake again, the Subaru screeching down rocks. Not rocks beside the highway but off the highway, where it ends. A day of fishing never seems complete without a jolt of gravel. A long slithery slide into the T-junction on the road to Ditidaht.

My hand on wet trees before morning opens its eyes. Bear tracks on the path. I stroll as though down a street I have never seen, humdrum reality left behind, the prism of work, hurry and kids.

By the first willows, a bear swings its head, sensing a streak of salmon. I cough to be known and turn to the water. Here and there coho take mouthfuls of air, then their shoulders, dorsal fins touch the surface; their porpoising spells turned-on fish. There are thousands, and I will catch fish all day, feeling their wide eyes focused on the purpose of living: to bring another of their kind into existence. Their electricity is contagious, and my body shakes.

I cast my blade across, let it swing to scruffy willows below the circular seam. I cast again and again. I change colour. I have figured out the Nitinat spinner progression: silver, brass, gold, red/orange, pink, chartreuse—colours that advancing coho prefer. Don't use copper; you will catch nothing. But metal is best, or metallic sheen. I move two steps and cast again, two more, and clear my throat to move the bear in his long, wet coat. How can they stand 35 years in wet that freezes me in a matter of hours?

I move up Red Rock Run, looking for the best spot to draw off fish. Then I turn. There, past the bear scat, sand recently released by flooding water, the wash of yellow leaves against fretwork of black branches, stand seven anglers and two guides. @#$@#%!$^%!$^% I think and !%#%$@#. I have gotten out of bed at 4:30 and been aced out of the run I beetled to as fast as I could. There are so many, I cannot move down among them. They cast and cast, dink floats, with pencil lead. Colorado blades glint in thick autumn light. $!$@$$~~$@#!~##@###@$%%#^@^$%^$&^*%$! @#%#%!^%!@#% @#%@~$^%#$!@%!@^$!#$^%&%!#$%$#$!%!$%%^(&*^&*(^%&%$^!$%# $%$&^%*#^%^!%^%&%$^#.

The first rod bends over, and the second. Guides flop here, there with a net, to snare *my* coho, hold it for photographs, flashes of neon, klieg lights in the dim morning. Shouts as from kids on a winter day, sliding down hills.

They are exactly where I would have returned, to plunder the school, thousands of coho bulging The Seam waters. I let my float drift into their territory on a long, long line. I do it again, and again. The closest guy looks up and waves. He's not angry, and I realize he is a tourist, as they all are, and have happened upon the greatest day of fishing in their lives. The guide, with long brown whiskers hanging out, is abundantly happy. His partner leans forward, holds his net as though catching the world. Turkeys.

There is nothing I can do but watch one lazy cast after another fly out, its float plop down, and disappear when another of *my* coho grabs *their* shiny blade. I edge into the crowd, so angry I can hardly spit out politely, "Any chance I could toss a lure in here?"

The guide, who at this point I know little, is Kenzie Cuthbert. Get him to tell you how angry I was, as he did another friend of mine who took him as a guide. Laconically, he motions upriver, where I had been standing. "Aw, they're mov'n up, eh?"

His good buddy jumps here and there, splatting his net, fish streaking away until the line snaps and another round of blade, lead and float is required. It is a cast and a fish, a cast and a fish. Fish leap from the water, racing each other to the blades. But not mine. All I get is rain down my face. After they catch 50, I can't stand it anymore.

I will find another spot better than this, I think. It is early in my Nitinat career and I have not yet discovered these spots. I hump up the trail, stuff my gear in my 100 kms/h mud-encased station wagon, partner of my fishing days.

I drive the water-logged valley toward the Ditidaht village. Under the road flows a creek I will come to know, but do not now. Since the river is larger, the stream must flow into it and offer a way into the back of Dennis's Pool; the glide, in yellow light of early autumn, where I have caught so many Chinook.

I don my gear, force my way through blackberry tangle, down slippery logs until I am knee-deep. Downstream I go, each foot up, across and down. Under two feet of water, the mud is almost as deep. I am in over my waist, feeling toes on crisscross roots and sinking fast.

Would I ever be found—there has been too much of this over the years—should I miss a root and my foot keep sinking? My legs are out of sight, my rod yanked through undergrowth. Right fingers stretch to the thinnest branches, hoping leaves will not tear.

Round a corner, fingers clutching dogwood, is a bridge I know. It goes to private RV sites on the flood plain of the lake; hence, this stream does not flow into the Nitinat. It carries on a mile until it falls into the lake, by the net pens for Chinook.

I pull on stream-side branches, snap off alders, grab a ten-hand of fern and haul my legs from the mud. Then bushwhack through a thicket, branches like stubs of an overgrown moustache or hairs of a well-used toothbrush. I lift my legs over second-growth forest, sweat in my neoprene.

Stuff is thrown in my maroon Subaru. I drive the road I have just come down, past two trucks of clients at *my* Seam; past Red Rock Pool where fish keep turning on the surface, rolling, a fish in the air here, in the air there; a Chinook red and black turns so its tail comes up and over and it falls on its back, eyes crazed with hormones and unable to do other than heed their call. Full of fish, the pool is closed to fishing in the fall.

On the Nitinat bridge, where the river is moving to chocolate, fish boil as far down as can be seen. The hill at bridge end is chunks of logs, rocks, stuff you cannot see to the bottom of, but soon, I am down among sombre trees. Trees like frozen men who never can escape the peaty embrace of moss and fern. Maples with big, thick, meaty limbs.

I step over a log, my foot coming down into pudding that is a 20-pound chum. This fish has not swum into the forest. It has been brought by a bear who will litter the woods with hundreds of fish and the smell of death that is a salmon river in the fall. The pudding flesh of rotting fish becomes more delectable to black snouts that stick teeth inside and rip out brains, shoulder muscle, whose scat is filled with vertebrae and ribs.

A crack sounds from the forest to the right. A branch is broken. I move away, toward the river, snapping off undergrowth locked in moss. The bank, when I teeter on its edge, drops 20 feet to a back channel below the bridge.

A snap in front and above. My head moves sideways. Up the next tree is a cub hardly larger than a cat. And its mother is ... then I'm running through rainforest, ferns the size of ostriches, moss in six-foot beards, baitcaster and fly rods ripping through branches. Then to the mess of logs dumped over the edge by the grader. I fly up rocks, cross mush carcasses, into the car.

Heat pounds from my skull, the only place my body can get rid of it. I float inside my waders. Outside, rain pours so heavily, drops merge on the windshield, leaving it clear as an eye. Rain washes colour from the hood of the car. I am alone with my wasted day and the smell of death. So close it is and so powerful, it comes through the windshield where I sit, hair plastered to my forehead. Above the bridge is an endless shore of ripped-apart carcasses, the white meat of putrefaction. Time to admit defeat and go home, having wasted a glorious beginning.

Before the T-junction, a little track makes a round-about journey to the river, where boats are let down—the place I set off from so many years ago and came to grief. Hmm. I venture in. A huge puddle fills the corner, but below, a spine of sand reaches to freestone beach. Sand is evidence of how high the river will come when rains are so heavy even breathing is difficult. The river rises ten feet above summer's drift of water among stones; it will lift the greatest matriarch tree and carry her, complaining, to the salt-lake below.

Supremely unhappy, I stand wetly on ten-foot-thick gravel, washed from clear-cut forest. I take off my glasses and pull my face dry. Around me, carcasses are held up in trees like bodies at the Somme. Barbed wire, soldiers caught in grey sky, gunned down in the terrible economy of war.

I am lost in the tearing sound of river, looking out at willows, usually dozens of yards up the bank. A chum gently lifts its eye clear of water behind a bush that creates an eddy. In the small slick, a second chum comes up and passes down, then another.

Oh, okay, one last try. Water reaching my elbows—somehow, I'm always this deep—in my bright-yellow down vest. The first bobber goes down so unexpectedly I do not set the hook until the passive bite has ended. But not the next. I connect with a 20-pound fish. And the next obliges with the cheapest thing known to salmon fishing: "wool," pink, purple, chartreuse, orange, whatever bright, gaudy, ugly colour. It doesn't matter. The float goes down, my left arm goes up. Gently turned-on chum take the wool in its passing, and I sink the hook among inch-long, needle teeth.

A rule of chum fishing comes to me: a trick of water hydraulics must be figured out. If an obstruction leaves a patch of soft water, or the bottom shifts down a foot, the chum will be in the slower water where they do not have to swim as hard to stay in the same place. Relaxed, with energy, chum bite more freely; this is the passive bite I have described where mouth closes on detritus, then opens to let it go.

I discover something else: how to process fish. I stand waist-deep, turn the rod away from the chum, and when the line comes within reach, wind it twice around my right arm. Dropping the rod from my left hand, I take the pliers from my mouth where I always put them, draw the fish up with the right, and in one movement, pull the hook free, having not even touched the fish. After 26 chum, I quit. "Yeah, I've caught enough fish today. Thank you." But not a single coho. Doesn't seem to matter on my slip-sliding way home.

A typical baitcaster rod and reel in the autumn. The Penn 965 is a quality reel, and you want to buy quality – it lasts longer and casts further. It is loaded with braided line because it casts further than mono, as well, and an old-style Bolo Spinner, mounted on a Rapala rod. I have since changed the butt and front piece to create a more limber set up that transmits the fish better to your hands, which spells much more fun while playing the fish.

Chapter 7

CUTTING A TRAIL BETWEEN WAYPOINTS

A shovel is fishing gear, as is a lopper and a snipper. Trees slap down the windshield, branches hit the brain like slow, wet bull whips. Those that don't slap down and off, I give the car some gas and push trees aside so they crack, and broken limbs scrape the side of the car. Some could use a chainsaw.

Next, I am poised before the first creek, surveying whether it is passable. It is now, but with the rain there may be later, it could be too full. The gas pedal is hit, because there is no ditch, no mud hole, no swamp that can't be cured with a little speed. Not to mention rocks that hit the bottom, the exhaust and are gone, four wheels spewing gravel onto the gravel wash. I survey the next stream, back up and hit the pedal, so rocks crunch my catalytic converter and my wheels lock to a rocky skid. At the third creek, there is no-go. The other side is too steep, and I'll be stuck midstream, water flowing from the passenger seat to driver's seat and out the closed door.

I get the fishing equipment out, brace my legs crossing the water and jump on the shovel on the other side. I throw the gravel into the water below my feet, the purpose being to chop off the ridge where the creek has undercut the bank, throw it into the stream to form a ramp, not a 90-degree bank. Then hit the gas.

Next, I come to the Y in the road that, to the left, looks like vegetation, though it's not. Years before, I took that trail and ended up at Dennis's Hole 35 minutes later. Straight on, or the right part of the Y, is five minutes to the river on the run named by a guide as The Meadows. There was only grass a few years ago, but willows came and sprung two stories high in only a few years. My name for it is Steelhead Run, as it has several large rocks in a straight line, a blue-green run of current down the middle, four to six feet deep. It cries out: steelhead.

The left is overgrown with alders that, in West Coast forest, spring up far overhead in a couple of years. In Alberta, where I am from, it's lucky if it's six inches a year. Down this Y, I climb over and under branches and get out my GPS. On another day, I took a GPS mark on the other side of the forest where, today, I want to come out midway through Cutt Corner. When I come to a log in a growth of salal and huckleberry, I snip off twigs to mark the spot—no plastic tape for me. Only I will know this trail. I have my white spray bomb, my loppers and snippers and pruning saw. My plan is to cut a path through the forest to the river.

My plan is to cut in a straight line, the shortest distance between two points. I have all the fishing implements and am guided by a GPS. What can go wrong? I paint a circle on the first tree and again on the other side, because one has to come back along the same path. I start chopping the forest in a straight line to the next tree 40 feet away—in a sight line—paint another white circle and so on, until I reach the waypoint on the other side, 800 yards away.

Only there's this problem. The first tree has so much moss the paint has nothing to stick to. I pull off the moss and try again. Only there's one more problem. The tree is white with lichen, so I have to scrape it off. Then I'm snapping 30-foot alders that lean like people left on the margin. They are the most brittle wood in the forest.

Rain makes its slow, inexorable journey down my collar and down my back. I am in neoprene, and though it is March-cold and raining, five millimetres of rubber have me bathed in fluids that came out of my body. I am dehydrating, in need of the very fluids that are now in my clothes.

I yell an expletive on top of the eight-foot-thick log I have crawled up, pulling on branches so rotten they break while I tug on them. I cannot see what is below me; can't even see my feet standing on the log. Vegetative seething has placed more than ten feet of greenery between my eyes and the ground. I can't see whether there are jagged branches pointing up, so I can't jump down. I could end up impaled here, in the rain and wilderness where I never would be found; some weird piece of meat left where no one will eat it. Like a scarecrow. Like washing on an untended line.

I pull my loppers off my back and stand on the log I can't see, flogging the undergrowth with anger. This is supposed to be cutting a route between waypoints, but nature put this eight-foot-thick log in front of me and, of course, it is a hundred feet long, though I can't see that, because of the salal against my nose. I have to climb back down, cut my way to the end, paint a white circle, go around and paint a white circle on the other side. Here I stand, undergrowth above my head so I am looking up through a hole to the treetops far above.

On my next step, I fall through undergrowth, turning a somersault in the green, and am now lying on my back in blackberry thorns, so many sticking into my clothes I am suspended several feet above the ground in growth that has closed over top of me.

A string of expletives! I reach round my body and lop trailing branches, so I can actually stand in the vegetation stretching above me. I cut my way back out, spray-paint another tree and find another route. This time, when I emerge from the many one-inchers that I push down, I spill over a bank and down into a beaver dam.

Why the *heck*, I yell, is there more swamp out here in the forest than forest? I reach up my lopper and hook a branch, so I can pull myself back out of the swamp, paint another tree and strike off in another direction, following the beaver dam to my right, where I know it ultimately comes out below Eagle's Nest Pool, a place I don't want to get to.

I continue cutting, breaking and painting trees. A succession of white circles follows me like strung patio lanterns. I burst into a clearing and fall on my face. There is noise of some great thing and the earth shakes. Bodies larger than my own push my body side to side. A huge male elk, antlers nine feet high, charges so I catch his wind as the bone slices my arm. And then silence, nothing; I am safe, in a hole in the forest where there is no grass, no trees, no vegetation, only what is beaten down and droppings here and there of scat much like large, soaked raisins. I have fallen into the middle of an elk herd. Caught them sleeping and they scattered, thousands of pounds of muscle around my body.

There is the smell of honey, beeswax, the musky smell of elk. I am in an open space of what must be a safe place to sleep so they cannot be attacked. The antlers of the males are fully eight feet across; they are the size of horses and could easily, turning their heads, kill me. But I am safe, sprawled on the brown dark earth. I know this will become one of my most powerful memories of nature. I will never forget its terror and beauty.

I turn to where the beaver dam ends in small, green water weeds. Its giving ground rises around my calves, sinks me past my knees. I turn and pull myself back with branches. Veins in my forehead press out and sweat runs down my face. I beat on trees, branches, beat the forest silly, cut six-inch stumps with my pruning saw, but, caught in other trees, they do not fall. I push and pull and swear as loud as I can, soaked in sweat.

Then I am in a deep, dark spot, where there is nothing on the ground, no greenery, no moss, nothing other than dark dirt pounded flat. Evergreen branches close like hands above me. On my hands and knees, I crawl through the dark hole of a stump hollowed by a century of rot, hairs on my neck standing in fear. Darkness, blackness ringed with delicate vertebrae of chum salmon, broadcast by a careless mouth. I sweat on the dainty ribs like curved needles, and squeeze through dark where a body has lain down, the body of a bear.

And then I am ripping my 20-pound pack through branches. And now, face-first in a muddy stream that flows only at highest water, cutting the land, more than a mile from The Seam to Eagle's Nest Pool. The willow here grows horizontal, evidence of the weight of winter water. From each branch grow dozens of spikes straight up. I force my way through, cutting only those that prevent me from moving forward. Painting white circles on skimpy stumps that I finally realize are useless. I could never follow them.

I am melting so completely, I will melt right out of my waders. I twist my face through branches trying their best to rip off my sunglasses, also covered in the magic fluid I would prefer inside my body.

My body bursts from the forest and I see my efforts have been in vain. I step into rain and ghosts of clouds, wind rising from the south, making thousand-year cedars groan with not giving in. I step onto 100 yards of gravel that wasn't here the last time I came this way and took my waypoint. I look at my GPS and my trail is furry and fuzzy, as though I have taken ten steps this way and ten steps that way and covered many miles in trying to cover one.

I take one more step and my leg goes down to the top of my thigh. I fall backward from the quicksand, so I can pull myself out. I lie back on the gravel, waders loaded with gallons of water come out of me. Rain pushes my face, wind folds back the rim of my hat. My pack is underneath me, my loppers in my right hand, snippers in my left, GPS in its Ziploc bag.

When I stand on the wide gravel verge, no animal or being within leagues, I pull down my neoprene so soaked from the inside out that I am drier with the waders down. Steam escapes my entire body in the pouring rain, in March cold. My GPS blinks out, batteries extinguished.

A shot of my car out in the middle of nowhere covered in mud. You can't get to the fish without taking a route down roads that are old logging roads and poorly constructed for anything but logging trucks and equipment. This spot is the place I parked for the day I almost ended up as cougar food, which is a good tale, and goes to show you that truth can, indeed, be stranger than fiction.

Chapter 8

WALKING THROUGH DEAD CHUM

I shall fear no evil in the valley of the Nitinat

My weariness amazes me, I'm branded on my feet.
Bob Dylan

Chronic Fatigue Syndrome is a disease for which there is no known cure.
DSM III

The mark the chisel carves in marble is
a servant of the greater blow.

Where the Nitinat eats the land, it tosses the tails and
gills, the gentle fungus in green and yellow and grey.

They have come back the shape of rotten umbrellas,
dog salmon, keta-toothed to hold the does in
place and break in the breaking water.

Carcasses in the green tunnel trees, eyes pecked out
and eagles important in their tonsures like minor
deities Ghiberti refused to hit with a hammer.

Spanish moss grows its pasty flesh across the
knubby waders and the Nitinat is a conversation
that falls away from everything it tells me it
is. I am allergic to the blue, blue sky.

Back to my needle. The stainless shank slips among the
layers of my leg. I am the artisan of a tired gargoyle.

Number 29 syringe, cyanocobalamin hangs from my thigh.
First a ladybug climbs down then half a strawberry.

"Things aren't always about who I am," I say to October
branches and suck a thigh until my teeth show.

The Hunger—DC Reid

Pushing my body through bush, I have seen their trees—cedars without branches. Ones they slice low on the trunk. As they have for thousands of years. They then pull the bark out, and a long, yellow diamond climbs the tree. A quick yank and it comes free. The slim wet bark is folded and taken home for pounding and chewing into fibres. For cord, for baskets, for tying reeds and feathers to a head.

In the 1800s, the Ditidaht were the most feared tribe south of Haida Gwaii, capable of putting 400 warriors in the forest. Far more than any other Nhu-chah-nulth from Nootka Sound to Clallam Bay. Those they caught were made into slaves or freed from their heads that found a second death stuck on stakes for wee children to shoot full of spears. The wick-tuk-yu is what children were called, and *the ignorant and worthless persons* is what that meant. They needed to grow themselves up to become useful, and then they were people.

I have found bark-tugging trees when I push through forest at Second Creek. The two maple trees there look like staggering men to me. Maples, unlike most trees, get strangled with moss and ferns, and cry silently for decades. The forest floor is mercifully flat and without undergrowth, so I can walk with my 11-foot rod and not get caught. In spring, fragile bones of wild bleeding hearts rise here. Their frangible limbs cannot withstand even footsteps. They fold back from me and break, revealing my trail through broken stems. I see colourless blood from broken flesh.

Fall is about spatter of sky on brim of hat. The bend of willow in wind. Red Rock Run is between The Seam and Red Rock Pool. Rain calling them home, coho and Chinook move up. Rain becomes the voice of river and then river itself. I see darkness on a bottom that is alive, wave breaking round fin.

A heavy Gibbs spoon arcs across the water. Its fat silverness bumps bottom, and when it hangs up, I set the hook. A fish is on the line. Chinook are the only salmon species that will go to the bottom and pick up something shiny. The trick is bottom bumping where it isn't sticky, meaning the lure won't snag and break off when yanked.

I turn, to ... nothing ... but the thought of a bear. My pack on the gravel seems to have migrated a little closer to me, a little closer to the river. Hmm. I fling spoons and when a 30-pound fish picks one up, I am dragged downriver to my waist and then fight both river and fish. In The Seam's shallow water, I release a fish as wide as my own chest.

Sloshing back upstream, foot in the air, I see my pack has migrated even closer to the water. How does this happen? I hear the sound of distant thunder. It comes from upstream, crunches down to me and passes downstream. Then I understand: it is boulders clunking down, hitting other boulders. There has been that much rain.

Water pulls from my nose, my chin. My bright yellow raincoat becomes a second and subsequent skin, wet as the hat on my head. When I hold up my rod, rain flows down its many feet, spills across my hands and disappears under my wrists, tight and white at their Velcro collars. It pools at my elbows and seeks my armpits. It takes four hours to become wet and cold.

I am touched by something and fall back to find the top finger of a ten-ton tree has reached my leg and given me a scare. On the other side of the river—the tree is that long—its root ball rolls over and over. I am being told the lesson of rain-filled river: "Look upstream when I am rising." Highest water is when trees are lifted from horizontal deaths and transited like cold Medusas downriver and spat out its mouth. Had I been a foot further out, I would have been swept off my feet and ground into the bottom until I drowned.

My pack is a wet green rock ... in the water. I am no longer on an island. Rising water has covered the entire gravel bar and I am miles from shore. I sploosh my pack onto my back and move down to where I will cross. Earlier, it was boot deep. Now it sloshes my waist and pushes me toward the deep on my dog-legging passage.

In the car, my glasses steam and the mirror mists. I am as wet as if I had laid my naked body in the rain. My raincoat, despite salesperson promises of keeping me dry, is not the least bit waterproof, and is soaked from inside out—like my other three raincoats. They are like the waterproof matches someone once gave me, only they have a little problem: they don't work when they're wet. Another inch of rain washes colour from the wilderness. My car thunks the Nitinat bridge.

Comes a wee animal, a brown one with brown tail, little, black jewels for eyes; the bulgy blacks are so beautiful they can bear this cliché. I am standing in the rain, and, 30 feet above the water, it jumps clear out of sight. I lean over, but it is not ruined at the bottom. It doesn't seem to be anywhere and can only have escaped by digging polished claws into vertical timbers and run straight down to the tangle of bush at the water's edge.

On the other side, I turn an acute right and plow through a lake-sized puddle in scrub by the river. In the mud, in six inches of water, I stop the car. I try to find armholes in my raincoat but miss them several times. It is as if the only purpose of wet clothing is to vex you: you can't get your arms through, get the jacket up your back, across your shoulders and sitting rightly on your chest. I discover the law of raincoats: no matter how wet a raincoat gets, you must wear it all day long.

Soon I am alone, casting heavy spoons where river eats the bank across from me. I hear a sound of largeness—something pushing the sky aside—and look around. Way up, a crest of tree falls out of the sky, dividing the air in this valley. It reaches out its great bending arm, lays out linked bones, across the river into the forest on the other side, snapping trees apart. When it hits rock—50 small feet from me—it breaks into chunks and I back away from the waves. Twisted wood-flesh chunks pass, swirl in the back eddy, then pass out of sight.

My eyes lift up to the opposite bank, to layers of white clay and free rocks eons have laid down, then fibrous sand, grey lightness, up and up. Way above are two joined trunks fatter than I am wide. Beneath the black root ball, the bank is cut six feet and perhaps they could go, too. Could be right now, only a ton or two to ruin my day. So different this is from Alberta, where I grew up, with locust heat so dry that when old stumps fall they are still there 50 years later. Not here: forest reaches a paw forward and takes back its own. And anyone in its way.

I have been told of a young man recently, bear hunting in Port Renfrew. A tree fell without him hearing, hood over his head, until it went through the bones of his body. I think how I could have not heard or turned to my own tree just now, how I could have been standing right underneath. There are many dying trees in the forest. Decadent, as loggers call them, beyond use; and when they give up, it takes decades for them to fall. Time for me to move.

I cast my mind to No Fish Pool. There are three firs, thick through as I am tall and, so weary, one leans across the seasonal stream into the heads of the other two. These three stand where river eats the land, eating black and red roots, boulders it rolls for warning. The Leaning Trees, I call them, down Hobiton Main, across the seasonal creek where there is a hole in the road 15 feet down to water. They are going to fall soon.

I leave my car at the Y in the backroad to Cutt Corner. I don't try taking it across the three streams further in. They are high enough to lift my car and swirl me into jungle, never to be seen again. But my body, each foot braced, can get across, trying not to be turned backwards. I mean my upper leg. If that happened, the water would knock me off my feet and I too would go away. Death is often with me when I fish.

Below the streams, I take the path, go over and under alders. They are topsy, leaning, so weak they have no place in the world. This is where I was soaked, with my GPS, cutting between waypoints. That proved pointless and there is no point moving through the second growth forest, because first growth was left where it fell, and it's a jungle. Near the young fir whose branches I clipped, the trail becomes three feet high and thus made by bears. Such paths grow-over, but when bears return, they use the same track, though I cannot find them until they do. And it means getting down on hands and knees to go through.

I move from tugging trees and stand on open gravel on the river's softer side—inside bends are always soft water. Where last high water reached, the whole long gravel flat looks carpet-bombed with miniature bombs. Every inch of every yard of half a mile is cratered, a moonscape of holes and blown earth.

This is not evidence of war, of course, but of massive spawning by chum. They wait for highest water, when no one can come near, and give away their lives. I have seen them on the other side of the forest beside the road, flanks convulsing, asking gravel to let them in. Ankle-deep streams that I cross in summer, and pull a hand of water to my mouth, are now eight feet deep. Now it is fall, and the smell of death goes through me, comes home with me, sometimes makes me ill.

The killing fields are all around me and I shake my head. Millions of tiny pink eyes are the purpose of tens of thousands of chum. All are wasted, because eggs cannot live above water and as far as I can see, all is craters. The waste is as regrettable as it is common. Ninety percent of their children are wasted in every river in which they find themselves, spawning above the low water mark.

I feel very alone in the wet skin of my jacket. Rain on my glasses, water plopping from my nose. Root balls give grudgingly, tons of indifference mowing down everything. A seagull stands on a carcass in Cutt Corner, yellow, webby feet straining against the meat. It pulls its beak with its red load from the body of a fish.

A tree has been stranded here, and I lean back to see how high the black roots reach. Several times higher than my own head. I wade the river side, allowing my float and blade to take the vigorous chum among the spawned-out, with their white fungus eyes, almost gentle in their demise. I toe a dying one into shallow water. It looks at me in weakness, without the brain to take in the small kindness I offer. Its tail of yellow and grey, with rays that stick out like rusted spokes. Its mouth moves in a pantomime of breathing. Open. Close. This is what life becomes.

When I turn back from my orange-tipped float, the fish's mouth no longer moves; its eyes see no more, its yellow body of fronding fungus. I have watched it move from dying to complete death. What we all face, having ourselves turned back into the tininess that can turn again to life. In 70 years, we breathe every molecule of oxygen that has ever existed, that every plant and animal and every human being, Da Vinci for instance, Michelangelo, Mengele, Pol Pot, has breathed in their short time between un-existence and death.

Behind the black-skeleton stump, the gravel bottom has changed. In the lee, the dead have been tossed from the current and drifted together. Their bodies wait for dissolution. The bank stretches down 50 yards, all of it dead fish. Perhaps 10,000, brought together by life-giving water. They are yellow and grey and green—a yellow, buttery heart being returned where it came from.

In crossing to the shore below, at first I am ankle deep in slippery death, my boots coming down among carcasses. Then I am knee deep, trying to find footing beneath the bodies. Then thigh deep in tapioca flesh. Then I am waist deep and as though in fluid, wading to belly button and ribcage. I stand among the dead to the top of my waders, arms held up to the sky. Short days ago they lived and breathed, then came to death, a foot from my face. The only option is to back out, so I do not become one of them. I did not know death could be so deep, so sobering.

The afternoon moves by. I look so deep in the river that when I finally lift my eyes, the forest ripples in vertigo. I break my rod in two and bury the point in cork. My feet crunch the gravel path. The spot of quicksand I slipped into the day I cut my way through the forest has been retrieved. It is now willows that bend from danger of wind and water and so find life.

Below Eagle's Nest, a tree has been deposited from one side of the river to the other. The water was so high, the last storm pushed the log into the forest and mowed down alders and maples, snapping trunks a full foot thick. Nothing can resist the dumb strength of water, and water knows only—if it knows anything—that it prevails.

I climb splintered detritus, then pain snaps up my spine. I look up through the hole I created falling through. Lying on my back, I know something new: in highest water, flotsam is lifted onto the land, against trees and broken wood. When water recedes, the branches, the bark, the beaver-chewed sticks remain.

They settle in the way fingers join and look like solid ground. The first man or animal to place down a foot falls through. Later, I will find the bruise where blood has flown into my otherwise white flesh. It is time to go, to give the forest back to the Aboriginal people who seldom come. I have never met one in the forest, though I see their basket trees, and they swim at Red Rock Pool. A nation they are who think: the land is what we are. My answer is: the water is what I am.

Chapter 9

THE SEAM AND ME REVISITED

Part One—What I have Learned About Coho

What I have learned contains years of rain and watching rivers rise until they spill their banks and run among trees. It is about being ribcage deep in water blown to chocolate: don't fish backward for coho. It may not sound like much but is the major thing to remember about the species in greatest numbers in deepest fall.

What it means is: coho invariably bite while moving upstream. They will not turn back for a fly or lure the way a steelhead will, though the two species are more alike than any other salmonid. First find where coho reside. Most frequently this is a back eddy, which is a circle of current. Analyze the dimensions of water flowing downstream past you, then swirling into the eddy. Notice also the dimensions of the water that continues around the back eddy, that is, flowing "upstream." Now you understand more about the water at your feet than virtually all anglers.

Cast your fly or your lure so, in the retrieve, you are pulling it against current. Try this at the boat launch above the bridge. It is a perfect, circular back eddy. The iron oxide bedrock sticks out 15 feet, providing a perfect water block, and thus a back eddy forms below, as much as 50 feet long, into the bank, and back up, a left bank eddy.

You cover the entire water, first casting out into the river flowing down beside you. Your lure will be carried into the edge of the curling water and then you retrieve. If you catch a coho, continue casting to the same spot, then swing and retrieve, until you have caught all the fish that will bite from that position. Then you let your lure free spool and cover the next ten feet in two-foot slices, and so on, until you reach the tail end of the back eddy, where water spills both downstream and to the left. The left water flows back up to you, completing the circle.

Continue casting until you have caught all the fish that will bite in the deepest part of the soft water. Then walk back up the red bedrock, bend under branches of the big cedar tree with its root I always trip over hunched half my height. You are moving back in rain ... oh, have I mentioned rain? Rain and coho? It is another vital truth: Rain=Coho. The more it rains, the more you will catch. Take yourself into the free-stone boat launch, where, some days, yes, you will be up to your ribs. It's a common refrain: when fall rains its way to winter, it leaves an angler in water as deep as he or she can get. But first, fish the water, before you walk into it and spook the fish.

At the bottom of the boat launch, cast the other way, "up" to the rock you have just been standing on. Work the back eddy water flowing back "upstream" to it. Again, you are pulling your lure against current, meaning into it. When you have caught all the fish that will bite on the particular slice of water you are working, cast to your right a bit and retrieve it back. Don't move out of that next strip of water until you have caught all the fish that will come. Finally, you are flipping up to bushes hanging into the water, up where you were just standing. Now, there is a bear on the rock, looking back at you. Rain drizzles down its chin and it wanders in search of dead chum that dot the forest like lumps of snow, or vanilla pudding, smelling of maggots. As always, willows bend under wind into water; yellow leaves straggle into autumn shouting, "Save me," the cry of everything in its dying. Nature is not kind. Nature kills what cannot resist. And it is cumulative, killing some sooner, claiming the rest a short time later.

The next *profound* thing I come to understand is: coho hold in the deepest part of the soft water—up to two months, before they get "all lined up" in shallow water. Even if you cannot see coho in autumn water heavy and full of detritus, find soft water and cast in the middle—and, as always, draw your lure or fly "upstream." This is how I came to fish Manhattan, having never tried for coho in this pool because Worthless Pool is usually better.

Worthless has two hotspots in its very long slow-water stretch: coho stop below Worthless Creek in the deepest water, as well as up along the roadside under the steep rock bank where you stand in water, yes, to your chest, in monsoon season, while keeping yourself from floating into the fifteen feet of water in front of you.

At Manhattan, aka Toilet Bowl, you will seldom see fish, but estimate the highest percentage spot of the back eddy that curls around the rock at your feet. On my first fish, I could not see a single fish in murky blue-green water but received the rubbery bite peculiar to coho on my first cast and landed a 12-pound fish.

Look for and try all deep, soft water, in whatever river you fish, for example, the Road Pool just up from the hatchery. Coho may not be seen, though thousands may be holding, gently finning, side by side, opening and closing mouths, big black kypes on big red males. They wait for a signal to move, one easy to understand and commonly known, but most anglers refuse to fish: in heavy rain. If it pours two inches and the river pushes you back into trees, you will catch the most coho, some even at your feet.

If you remember nothing else, remember that Coho bite on rainy days because their spawning behaviour differs from other species; they spawn in side-streams that drain into rivers. Small, seasonal creeks can be gravel washes in the corona-sun days of summer and look like nary a drop ever flowed; however, water must have flowed to blow all the trees, roots and leaves away and create the gravel wash.

Greatest rain fills the smallest creeks. They become passable to coho that have waited up to three months. As water taste changes, coho become stimulated, bite with abandon, can't help themselves. You feel the bite in the air. It's electric, instinctual. As mentioned, good fishermen feel the adrenaline jerk; their hands begin to shake.

Station yourself in the first deep, soft water below a seasonal creek. The day I caught, I am embarrassed to say, 52 coho in the Falls Pool on the Stamp, it rained all day. It was raining before I got up and into the car, it rained as I slithered along the highway, it rained as I ran down the path through the big gold leaves of autumn. On this day, I had only one lure, but in the colour we forget is the best—blue. Even Haig-Brown's fly is called the Coho Blue. Late in the season, you think pink or chartreuse, but never blue the colour that will do.

And that day I had only the one, knobby, 50-year-old spoon that had seen its best days decades before because, like a nitwit, I had forgotten my lure "fly box." I scrounged the trunk for anything, and found the one, ancient spoon. If I lost it, I would not be able to fish all day long, so I decided to retie every two fish. And I retied the lure 26 times. If I had not had to retie, I would have had time enough to catch even more.

Coho are so turned on in rain they can't do anything other than bite. I caught two fish four times each. One was a 20-pound male, the end of his kype broken off, nose also broken. I was standing in the middle of Beaver Creek where it enters the Stamp. In the rain, it filled to almost blowing me away. The male bit once and was let go, and then bit once more and was let go, again. After the fourth time, I said to it: "I can see biting once and maybe even twice, but four times? Why would you bite four times?" The fish looked up at me and said, "I don't know, man, but I just gotta have it."

There is one more rule that goes along with: the deepest part of the soft water; and rain. The third is: fish shade. As pointed out so many years before, I have come to understand all coho will be in shade, even shade one foot wide. Stand in shade and look. You will find coho stacked in a line. Instead of moving by shade, think coho and cast your offering in to receive the gold that is fish. Also, because most anglers will not stay in shade, you will find the most untouched coho in shade, too.

I think that's all I know, but, wait, have I mentioned cycling through all the colours in your box, and did I mention moving two steps and throwing the same thing at the same coho from a different angle, and did I mention that all flies and lures should have some metal in them or that the sequence is silver, brass, gold, and for colours, red, orange, glow, chartreuse, pink, purple in the Cowichan; that, failing metal, you have some shiny thing like Flashabou or Krystal flash and did I mention ...

Part Two: The Seam and Me Revisited

You can tell some people everything you know, and they still may not be able to catch the fish right in front of them. The morning I am thinking of starts as always: green light from the dash and jolt of potholes. I pull to the centre, across rocks the grader scrapes aside and that crunch my catalytic converter.

I walk the seasonal stream below the thunka-thunk bridge where, you will recall, I proved the nonexistence of God. I cross in the dark, legs wide, feet fumbling, two-finger-thick cable between my boots. Too dark for seagulls and their screams because they can't help themselves, there are so many carcasses. I stand among white pools like dropped eggs but which are really seagull rear ends. I see a nose here, a nose there. Gentle porpoising says: I am alert, I am moving, I am finding my home.

On my side of the water, I look at mouths that touch sky, dorsal fins, bronze backs. Underneath is a wall of flesh I cannot see but feel in deep soft water where the seasonal creek joins the river and swirls away in The Seam. A back eddy flows beside left-bank willow grown from nothing in three years to double my height. Marks from my snippers reveal white wounds in opening light.

I feel the coho's need so much my hands can hardly make the loop to Palomar spinner to line. Out goes a big Vibrax Blue Fox with gold body and silver blade. Back it comes ... without a coho. I am perplexed because I know cold and rain, when coho cannot control themselves; they take the lure the first time it goes by.

I follow my own advice, moving up and recasting, moving down and recasting, changing colour, adding a Colorado blade, then a brass one, a gold one, this angle, that angle. But no fish will come to me. In the distance, a seal head comes up, five miles from the lake, 20 from the ocean.

I work the school for more than an hour, constantly feeling their adrenaline and hormones. But I cannot touch one. I stand here, idly toeing an eyeless chum, red down its cheeks. Seagulls have ripped the eyeballs from this and thousands of other chum. They litter the banks like leaves, in the smell that is a salmon river in fall. Rain falls off my hat, my nose, and works up my sleeves.

Finally, I stop because there is nothing I can do to catch these fish. I'm glum, watching clouds sift among trees, Spanish moss shrugging like old breath. Out there, my Colorado blade dangles below my dink float and its pencil lead, blade on its leader another three feet down, a bangle nudged by current in their sky. I can't figure it out.

I look around but can't seem to see my float. This doesn't surprise me as my eyes are the bane of my life and missing the orange tip of a white float is common for me. I scan the toppling water where The Seam moves down, and in closer, where the back eddy works back up to me. But, no, it's not here either. Where can it be?

And it comes: This is a fish! It jumps like caffeine to jolt me awake. "Holy smokes," I say and a lot more colourful things. It's a large, large coho, under tension to the snout of my rod. Its head jerks one side, jerks the other side, keeps on jerking as current works on its broad body, moving it downstream. My rod is bent flat to the water, me putting as much strain as 20-pound test can take without snapping. Then the line goes slack and my hands rise high above my head, reel as fast as they can, as I back-step up the bank almost into the trees.

"Thank you, thank you," I say when he comes to me minutes later. His silver side beams up out of the dim like metal made for my eyes only, and to be given back to the river ... unless. I jump on him as he flops here and there, on my hands and knees, neoprene legs slathered with seagull poop.

When my fingernails are firmly in his broad shoulders, I decide to honour him with being the only coho I will take home this year. From my vest comes my short black knife. The blade flips out, so sharp it cuts my own flesh, too. I slit him anal vent to gills and slice behind so blood squirts over the sand, my hands, my face, until his throat pulses no more. His pink entrails and long white purses of milt are thrown back from where he came. I draw a long black garbage bag from my pocket and snap it down, while trying to hold the potent fish that flops around its death. I open the bag in the rain with my teeth and fingers of one hand. Finally, head first, he is slid into the bag and the opening put under a rock.

But he, with his quadrangle jaw, becomes something new: the potentate buck that will not die. Fifteen pounds, gutted, in a plastic bag, flipping around, he yells, muffled, "Hey, lemme outta this bag. I got places to go, important fishes to meet." He carries on, getting on my mind like a murder. I start feeling guilty even though I cannot let a dead fish go just because it asks me to.

I have one foot on the bag as it jumps around and cast into The Seam where two streams of water meet. I let the float float, until, darn, there's another fish. Now I've got adrenaline in my veins, singing the song Klingons sing about passing over to Stovokor. I pull my pliers from my mouth, wrap the line around my other arm, move the pliers down to the blade and turn the hook over. The fish moves from its side, swept by the soft current and, coming vertical again, snaps from sight.

I cast once more, letting the float just float and my heart crunches a beat when it disappears, yet again. Then two very wet guys come down the wash in three inches of rain. "Much going on?" they query.

All diffident like, I try a negative shucksiness, "Not really much, eh?" Damned unfortunate timing, releasing a 17-pound buck in front of them.

They brace across the seasonal creek and take up residence on gravel becoming a strip among willows that say, "I can bend, I can bend," when wind comes to take them in afternoon. Water flows through fingers of vegetation and drops white liquid on their boots.

They are using the simplest method of catching salmon: green wool, dink float, pencil lead. They cast upstream, hold rod tips high, mend line, then, when the float passes them, reel on stream, just like it reads in a book of fishing theory. They do all the right stuff for the West Coast dink float thing, following their floats downriver, reeling in, casting a foot farther, then another, so the wool passes down the bottom in the faces of all those fish spread across the river ... or so they think.

I make a cast, lob it right under their feet, because I have not yet taken a fish from there, and, the white float with an orange tip disappears. I zang the line and yes, another 17-pound buck takes to the air and weeeeeeeeee for meeeeeeee. It dashes here, dashes there, upstream and down, among raindrops falling on my head. When finally subdued, the fish is held in my hands and let go with a feeling that is grand. I'm the Michelin Tire Man in admiration of the golden beauty of nature. I look up with my little good-natured puffy smile, and both are standing there with looks of: You %#*(&)#(%*#%()*% asshole. Negative vibes? Pour moi? And, of course, I start feeling guilty. Really guilty.

The fishing goes like this: they cast and cast and cast and the river rises and the river rises, and they cast and cast and cast. Then I drop my float off the tip of my rod, and darned if it doesn't just disappear quicker than you can say holy s___. And I start feeling reeely, reeeely bad.

These two very wet guys have no raincoats and can only be marginally wetter than me in mine. They stand in their wetness beating brows on my "geez this is fun" innocence. They fish in white-making rain for three hours, not catching a single thing, can't even foul hook one of the thousands of chum resting below the current. They're casting and looking, eyes could kill, at me plopping here and there.

When the disparity gets really silly—I am beyond 10 coho caught in front of them and they have had zero bites, not even a sniff—I feel really bad. "It's just the spot," I say, "why don't you come on over and give it a whirl?"

Leaning to the left, one wades the stream that by now is thundering from the mountains, waist deep. When he successfully makes it to my side, where it is raining so hard many feet of guano have floated up and away, I tell him what is happening. Not what is happening any other day, but right now, this very second: put on a Colorado blade, on a leader below the pencil lead; chuck it ten feet and let it float until it goes down. I tell him and show him what the fish want and how they want the blade presented *right now*.

I wade to his spot and offer encouragement, drop my bobber where he has just stood hooking squat, and, drat, hook a 13-pound coho on my first "cast." I am truly embarrassed. Don't get me wrong, I am glad the disparity comes my way, and after all, they have invaded my spot.

So, the persecution goes: the rain rains, the floggers flog. They cast far, cast close, reel slow, reel fast, mend and unmend, change green wool for red wool, for orange wool, but neither will move to a metal blade or leave the float to float. I, on the other hand, drop the float and the fishy bites. Finally, they give up in disgust, and I, no doubt looking like a very fat turkey across the water as they are packing up, say, "Do you mind me taking back this spot?"

"NO," they say, eyes adding, "you jerk." On my first drop, my float floats in its little foam world and when it disappears both of them say, "#@%!%!@#%' you," real loud, while the hugely entertaining fish pulls my hands here and there and into the stream and into the willows. Bad-tempered oafs.

I refrain from saying something like: "I'm really sorry about this," because they would probably squelch back and pound me. But at least I think about apologizing for my good fortune and decide that's almost as good as actually doing it.

All I have done is figure out on this one wet day, when rain is curtains and their windows falling from trees, and willows shriek in afternoon wind, what the fish want and give it to them, rather than keep on giving what they don't. These guys were not going to listen and they concede defeat as they trudge in wet blue boots up the trail. But not me. Heavens no.

Chapter 10

THE KINGS OF THE RIVER

The king is dead. Long live the king.
- for King Henry III, 1272

Seldom are we are given the privilege of seeing coho larger than 20 pounds. Even more seldom, the chance of catching them. But I have caught the Kings of the rivers. Each year some come to me. Fish so large they fight like Chinook, and the depth of their bellies convinces me the fish in the air 50 yards downstream must be one.

There is a ritual for the Kings: you must let them go. You must recognize them for who they are and release them gently. I cannot kill these important contributors to the river's gene pool, even though it is legal for me to do so.

So many mornings begin with rain coming down my windshield and mud slapping me in the face. Then my feet squish dying red ferns, down the mud gulley and across the broken cedar that has burst its red insides from so many boots to its ribs. Then through the willows that weren't here at The Seam five years ago. Now they are a fretwork of branches, stumps as thick as my arm.

On this "wet coast" October day, the rains have begun in earnest. Water runs down my neck and the back of my down vest. Grey clouds push rags of moss hung from Douglas fir. Downstream, last summer, the river was half a kilometer of knee-deep water, caddis fly larvae on every rock. Now, the gravel is under eight feet of water. At The Seam, I stand waist deep on what was a pile of white gravel several feet above the river. It ran down from a logging clear-cut from a century ago that loosed it from a net of root, moss and salal.

First cast, my rod receives the rubbery jerk that identifies a coho. No charm. No subtlety. Just smash and run so there is no mistaking a fish has struck—it hooks itself, you hold on. And this the first cast into the grey of early day. The fish runs to the other side of the river and turns downstream. The level-wind is cinched so tight it strains 20-pound test and line is grudgingly gained. Then it is lost.

Closer now, the King pushes water aside on his nose-drive into trees that used to be above water. I drop my rod and yank the line. The coho roll thrashes willow, thigh deep in water, and he is tangled before my stringer comes from my raincoat pocket. I have been asked to bring a King home for a soirée to benefit the local hospital.

The stringer needle pushes through the gills and the fish coughs, trying to rid its throat of blockage. I stand holding the line, eyes of the silver fish upon me. I am ashamed for taking this fish, knowing I will kill a King. The next plunge and the needle passes cleanly through gill, mouth, and then the stringer ring. The blue line I tie round a willow, something that is against the law—if you intend to keep a fish, you must kill it when you catch it. It cannot be kept alive.

I am keeping this first fish because it is the right size. It is being kept alive because I want it in good condition at the end of the day. I look into scared eyes that are looking at me. The silver mouth gasps, the silver lies on my arm. Sky keeps raining and river keeps rising. Electricity is in the air. Such an odd thing to feel: the mood of animals in abandon.

I cast and manage the school. I developed this idea when I realized I could increase the number of fish caught—and carefully released—by forming a 3D image of the school within the 3D image of the bottom. It works better for coho on a rainy day. It works best in coloured water.

Once I have caught a fish, I fish that vein until it goes dry. Then I cast inside the school for ones that did not see the other fish bite. Then I cast behind, then to the outside and then in front. I change my position because these are coho; moving two steps down or two steps up is enough to bring my blade at an angle different enough that it will trigger a bite.

"Managing a school" works most frequently with chum. The purpose is to keep the school in a place that is easiest to trigger a strike. By casting around the school, you can make them close in on one another and, as a group, move up or down the river, closer to shore or farther away. The other purpose is to keep some fish unbothered for a while, so they forget their buddies are being slipped from the group. Keep in mind water not cast to for ten minutes and then come back to it. You can catch triple the fish than if you move through the school on a beat downriver. There is no point leaving fish to find fish, nor leave fish that are on the bite.

Morning opens more of its grey, and willows behind me shake so visibly, a conservation officer would know there was a live fish within a rod's length from me. I am worried about being caught, but not as much as I am ashamed.

And then looking up, and thinking, *what, what is happening? Oh, yes, the bite has ended.* I can feel it end. The river has risen so I wade the sweepered seasonal stream, holding branches, my legs like scarecrows in wind. Feeling just as animals do, their excitement, their lassitude, is one of the greatest things I ever feel. I stop and say thank you, to the forest, the river, the fish. To make it important.

I take my leave, walking the forest, around trunks so large I can only hold onto bark to pull myself up the muddy trail. Then the car beats up over the rain and steam is on the window. I bump past Red Rock Pool, past Road Pool, pull into the boat launch above the bridge. My tires crunch on gravel ten feet above summer level, evidence of days the river hugely spills its banks.

I wade into the cut for launching boats and stumble over rocks gathered, on a dryer day, to form a fire circle. The wash is chest deep, and I can get no farther than the entrance willows. Above is a very wet guy on the rock above the back eddy, casting his dink float and orange wool, out into the speeding water, swinging it into the back eddy.

Again and again his cast reaches out, then plop of pencil lead and swirl of dink float like a small orange head being swept away. He has been casting this way, as I will find out, all morning. As I have mentioned earlier, the boat launch eddy is so pronounced you can stand *downstream* and cast *upstream* into branches of shoreline willows, their leaves turning silver then green, in the wind.

On my first ten-foot cast, the pentangle kype of a splendid coho whacks the shiny lure. On my next, a fifteen-foot cast, another coho whacks the thumping lure. Then another five feet, and closer to shore, then into far branches and finally at the feet of the angler. Here, a minty, ten-pound, silver coho leaps in front of his face. His eyes penetrate mine, wetly, in his wool toque, water down his face.

I haul myself among branches up and over, around and under a cedar tree. My feet descend roots polished by boots. He tells me he has caught two fish all day. I can see why: he has been performing the same cast for five hours—exactly the wrong thing—even though coho porpoise everywhere. In my first minutes, I have taken more than he has caught. He hoists his tether over his shoulder and squelches up to his car, not realizing he could have taken a dozen more if he had understood a bit more coho behaviour. I stand on the rock with the river sweeping around the corner and down over my boots.

In my time, water keeps rising. It comes with wind from trees, a boiling sound without heat. Water billows from bottom rocks and spills open on the surface like breath of some magnificent, invisible animal. Behind me water spills over rock and I am left on an iron-oxide chunk. The river continues rising until I need to brace my feet to keep from being carried away. The river has risen another two feet in three hours and almost reached the wheels of my car on the gravel above the launch.

It is late, and I have a date to keep. I race back to the little bridge above The Seam and pull myself through the branches, down the muddy gulley, over the burst-open red log. The river has risen here, too, and light is retreating. I cross the seasonal stream, holding branches so it does not push me away. I stand right in front of the last willow, up to my belly, backed into it as far as I can.

As I have said, coho increase biting in greatest rain. They do so in preparation for moving up seasonal creeks to sex and death. So, instead of casting out into The Seam being pushed over by the river, I slowly push my rod tip down beside me. Less than 3 feet from my leg, coho begin their move up the creek, though I cannot see them nor my feet. The lure is three feet from my boots when, yank, it is pulled away and out into the greater current by a red regalia coho that swings, tail over head. Subsequently it is released with my red-handled pliers.

When I let the fish go, I rest my rod on the surface, river moving up my left sleeve to my elbow. The spinner twinkles, inches from the rod tip, when there is a splash and the line tugs out into the river once more. When this fish is released I leave the lure spinning on the surface at the rod tip. Behind it a seal pops up—many miles from the sea—giving me a heart attack. It is now I think of my gonads, underwater, unprotected, the seal less than a body's length from them.

Spooked, I turn in wind of water, reach across to willows as my feet leave the bottom. I hang, drifting among stumps. There are dozens, and I can't see where I left the blue tether. The river has, over the hours, pushed in branches and woven them in a tight glumph. I lift my neoprene leg over and start at the beginning. My arms reach down the first stump.

I move among branches to the next stump. My hands reach down until my face comes level with the water. The rising river has left my blue stringer several feet down, farther than the length of my arm. I crawl under and over branches, logs and flotsam in dying light. When I contact the tether, I can feel it but not see it. My body floats on branches, my head underneath a yellow pole pushed against a wooden fencepost.

4:30 light leaves only grey. One hand down over the other, I pass beneath the surface. My waders ship the cold that gasps my body. I feel the first knot and untangle the needle, then the next. And then I must surface for a breath. The fish pushes my knee, but I can't see anything. It comes to me I could end here, branches pushed so hard I won't be able to move.

My gutting knife pulls from the pack on my back, and I pass down, holding my breath. The fish I seize from gill to mouth. In my left hand the knife saws blue line I cannot see, and I break the surface, waders filled with water, tugging the fish with both fists.

We could have died among the willows, but we move away from danger, again. Waders the size of Alley Oop, I hold the gagging fish and fall into the forest full of rain. This is how a King is retrieved. This is when he dies. My body is electric with the danger I have faced; one that, in time, can only be described, once again, as one of the most important experiences of my life.

Jittery success follows me all the way home. Turning in on the wet forest road called Linnet Lane, I come from the dark two hours to offer my portion of charity. A 20-pound coho from its long green garbage bag into the sink. Then the leaves are washed away, the head removed, the tail, so the King is simply a chunk of flesh another animal will eat. The only animal that can raise the death of another, because we can think it, and speak upon its death: Long live the King.

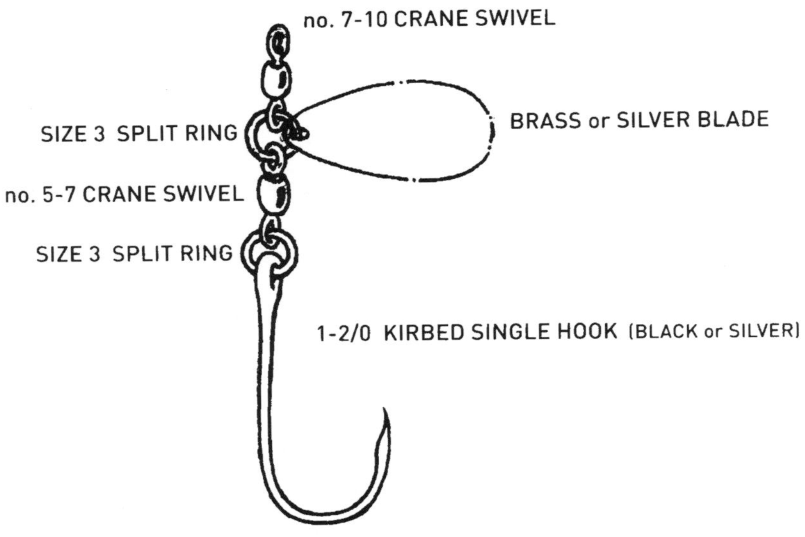

A simple, cheap, self-made Colorado Blade is an alternative to the more expensive Blue Fox spinner. Put a weight above the blade to make it cast farther and sink faster.

Chapter 11

AUTUMN BEAUTY

All the people have gone home, and all the trees have lost their leaves. High water has run through the forest and stolen the gold that littered the earth. It has left clean grey sand among white alder stumps growing thick along the northern shore. Alone with myself, I look up and am stopped in tying spinner to line, to see autumn beauty; this run every other day is nondescript, up and around the corner from Worthless Pool, down and below Toilet Bowl, so called for the whirlpool in its middle.

White stumps poke from newly laid sand the river lifted from clear-cut forest and dropped in brooding, rainy days of November when summer was replaced with winter. The light now visible among black-handed trees reminds me of horses and their flight across winter snow, gold poplar leaves. Downstream, cedars green, almost ghostly in rain that has drained the air of colour and replaced it with luminous light that is West Coast winter. Over shores, where they crowd, are tough seedy willow with red vein rootlets the river tries to take.

I am alone without truck sound from the road high above, without shrieking gulls who cannot contain their glee for the tens of thousands of eyeballs left to plunder. Just me and cinnamon red coho, chest-sized maple leaves pasted here and there like Salvador Dali's pocket watch.

I stand behind the little island below the log jam that closed the channel by the hill. I have waded across, legs placed wide against the sucking current and stand in soft water that holds and sways me.

Down a ways are bright red bodies offered up to sex and death. The river is risen into tree roots and coho are lined up like red arrows a foot or two from shore. In the middle there are none, but on the far margin, as on this side, red arrows point upstream and waver as though uncertain of their existence.

The coho are not in mating ritual among the roots. They are waiting. They do not spawn for almost three months after coming into fresh water. It is almost December and there they are on both sides "all lined up."

Close by fish can see me, as they fidget here and there. They have changed from earlier in salmon season, when you cast from shore into deep, dark, soft water, and they loom from the blue to tag a silver spinner that looks nothing like food. They ate their last meal months ago in the ocean and respond now because metal stimulates them to bite. I wade the middle of the river, cast into shore, among red veiny roots, in foot-deep water. When the lure passes in front of their faces, the closest fish let the current move them down and out of my eyes' reach.

So, I cast further down. As the spinner lights up, it moves across a dark shape that, with a wave of dorsal fin, follows up and into view. And then comes the behaviour that separates these late, resting fish from all others: its head moves to one side, so that eye can see the spinner, then the snout moves to the other side so that eye can see the spinner. The vibration back and forth increases until the fish, eyes locked on, closes its mouth on the silver and chartreuse spinner.

I set the hooks hard and the spinner flies up out of the water, just misses my face and gets stuck in trees behind me. My hands are senseless with excitement and I remind myself: don't set the hooks when you see the mouth close, set the hooks only when you feel the bite telegraph up the line to your hands on the rod.

I wade through water to my pelvis and untangle my line and spinner from willows. The fish I have seen and lured will not come again. They are spooked and leave a hole in the water where the spinner flits its way brightly across the current to my rod tip. There is only one option: commit to the river and let it take me down, hoping it does not get deeper than my waist.

My car out in the middle of nowhere covered with mud, as it usually is. Be prepared to wreck a car or buy one that can take the punishment. This car, as well as my new Jeep Grand Cherokee, has a button that you press and it lifts the car higher off the road, up to 2.5 inches, so you don't hit as many rocks and stumps.

I cast to fish that cannot quite see me. I swing the lure within 18 inches of their snouts and when they follow, again the snout twitches to let its eyes lock on. When the twitching occurs, the fish will bite every single time. The first rubbery bite transmits shakes of a head I can just see: the 15-pound coho shakes because it does not have hands to reach in and take out the hook.

When the fish is on its side beside me, black mouth opening, when the eye is looking up at me, I wrap the line around my arm, take pliers to its mouth and allow it to drift back to anonymity, having only come in contact with me and no other. I don't kill them. I let them go.

I cast to the left to pull a coho from the roots, cast to the right to pull a coho from the roots. Cast and step. Current cuts sand and gravel from beneath my feet and water exerts its emotionless strength. I slowly give ground, heels dug in, going where the river wants me to.

I look up to anonymous forest, its language of slow beings passed on wind and fog. Moss drapes limbs that move like scarecrows. Autumn Beauty, a run so gorgeous it is worth waiting for all year. I cast, and uncertain darts leave the cinnamon shapes, mostly bucks with big bent jaws, kypes like beaks of freakish birds.

My afternoon is being ground downstream until I must push to shore, for water farther out is deeper than I. There is the soft flood of understanding something for the first time, something wild and worth saving. I have fished a lifetime and feel honoured to understand fish, how to change technique for locked-on coho. I give thanks to wilderness and what it teaches me. For the first time, I say: coho season ends, long before the spawn, with coho "all lined up."

My feet are numb and I can't feel my shins. I drop my rod and run up and down the small beach in the middle of luminous nowhere. I could shout as loud as I please. No one would hear me. Even ears under water, so close. I can't return the way I have come. Water's strength is against me.

So, I lift my leg onto the mesh of root and leafless branch. I move among white trunks rising from sand so fresh it looks as though some minor god has mixed the two together: lichen spots on branches; sense of winter and death; sense of being alone; of being at peace. But soon, pulling through clinging branches, white stumps, I see tracks so new, sand has not fallen from the ridges into the print.

The prints look like those of a chubby, pigeon-toed child—one set large, one small. I am following a mother bear and her young cub, though I cannot see them. And I must follow them, for the log jam that closes the side channel is much too rough to climb across. I have no choice and my chest feels no fear. I walk behind the mother and child.

The tracks are less than 30 feet from where I passed downriver, flinging my spinner left and right, drawing fish and feeling fortunate to understand something very few people do. I am the last human being to come before winter closes completely and the fish attain their purpose. Once spawned, the red bodies settle back and come apart in the luminous winter, dead flesh drifting within its home.

I think about dying. The world going on without me. The definite me. The body that holds these molecules of carbon and nitrogen and oxygen for its time and then releases them. I think of the times I have been foolish with my few short years.

Earlier, in the Little Nitinat, I cast my fly across winter-swollen river. It lodged in a bush, and to avoid losing another fly, I waded deeper, hand held out until I edged into the bush on the other side, water so high my head looked like a small ball. On my back was a steelhead bag the hatchery had given to me. It had an opening at one end and was closed at the other. If I caught a steelhead, I was to put it in the opening and draw it shut.

But I had not caught a steelhead and at that time not one coho. When my fingers touched the twig, I felt the bag fill and pull me away, twig breaking in my hand—not the part with my fly.

Downstream, I ran, backwards, stumbling over rocks way down at my feet. In pure luck, water pushed me and my hundred-pound sack into the shallows. I was so angry I threw the bag and rod on shore, moved back upstream and came down on a diagonal, running like Chariots of Fire in water, not on sand. I reached for the branch as water moved me by; it broke and gave me back my fly. Thirty-five cents. That is what I saved, on a day when being off three inches could mean the difference between life and death. Foolish. On the other hand, that led me to Autumn Beauty, and that led me to understanding.

Now I am standing in the forest under big cedars with roots exposed like legs of naked old men. When I take off my cap, my body gives off steam, up from my chest, out the top of my head. Above Toilet Bowl, around the corner, is a major run for coho to wait until sky fills their side-stream. Coho Alley, I have named it. It is good for nothing else; too shallow the other 11 months to hold a fish. But in the window between all the people going home and bears deciding to sleep, coho let themselves go and lay pink eyes beneath Big Bend gravel.

I will come back another day, on the other side, on a back road I will not tell you about. I want you to look for and find it, so you come with respect for fish that line the shore with red for half a mile. I will return to cinnamon fish, for this is my favourite fishery. There is only me and the coho and that is the way it is supposed to be. All lined up. The fish. The me. The end.

Chapter 12

DECEMBER COHO

I could simply give in

It is morning and I am kneeling
in the river that trembles my hand.

There is flesh in this morning,
the fragile of sockeye, living on

in winter where they should not live.
There is the beat of a hidden heart,

and the river gives and takes a life.
My hands grow ghostly

at the ends of my arms.
The flesh in them will not end today.

The blue-green knowledge
of water is: Sitka, cedar and sedge.

As though a coastline makes a difference.
A ragged place of feet in boots and laces

come free. Only the legs keep moving,
scattering salmon that should not be.

Their purpose is as ours: to make
an acquaintance and break

in water the colour of thought.
I could simply give in to making life.

My feet, trembled into nothing,
run red rocks from the basement

of time. They know no other
purpose than striding the Taylor,

the Elk, the San Juan,
any source of knowledge

that is passed to the tree
after it is passed through me.

These Elegies—DC Reid

I have passed in and out of the valley of my river so many years I know the pot holes by name. I have learned to love late-season coho after the brown river rubs algae off bottom and leaves the rocks luminous, as though polished by a tiny workforce for late red fish that seek their end.

In years of passing down Coho Alley, mid-river, I enjoy as much the push of winter green on my legs as fishing for late fish there only for my enjoyment. I fish this special time alone, for years, before wondering if there are a few fish for me in the last month of the year.

So, I return for salmon in December. I look for ones new to freshwater, not ones waited three months, worn by water and wearing patches of white down their backs. They serpentine tree roots, waiting their time to die. There is so much of that on a salmon river, so much it inhabits me, and I can't turn away. The rotting flesh smell gets in my clothes, the air, my car. Flesh disintegrates in the river. Soft, pale, pink blobs comprise the greatest part of food for months—for steelhead and fry. Maybe roe is the best thing to fish for steelhead because it is the smell of adrenaline in wind, of life about to be.

I look sadly down the path to Poison Slough. When I step from the sidehill my boots slide until I am up to my waist. I feel for bottom, but there is no way to cross and climb into forest where wind will later shriek and river lick Douglas fir root balls, and six-foot butts, into death. I return through spatter of rain to my car. The wound of wind begins moving through trees like a river.

December 8, and I might have to wait another year. Uncommon for me, I feel I should give in, though I have risen at four and driven 157 dark kilometres to Nitinat T-junction, and 16 extra kilometres to the end of Hobiton Main. I bump back up the road and stop for a last look at the hatchery.

Across the tarmac go my boots, across puddles with skins of wind. Past the aluminum screw for lifting tons of fish from holding tanks, to be stripped of egg and milt. Across what passes for grass, tuft here and there, then ting ting down the iron-grated intake where fish obligingly swim right in to be lifted out.

I stand on the grate and look down to something I have never seen: 2,000 coho, brown and brassy, 20- to 30-pounds, gently finning into death. They don't know this, only swim and swim into water that draws them home.

And never reach the end. No spawning, because a gate prevents them rising. A mass of bodies, and all useless. And the mystery of fish, moving heads to one side and the wave flowing down their flanks. Then the heads to the other side, so they fly in the fluid of life on this small blue-green planet in its unimportant corner of the sky.

No December coho for me. It's not legal to drop a spinner in a hatchery. And though the square of wet is cheek by jowl, there are none below, where my boots squish to the brown river, where water is rising, against the very fish it nurtured. Ones fallen from the grate are sent backwards, because they can no longer resist the current. Back to the lake from where they will not return to spawn, the only business of life.

I reel in extra line, break down my rod, wrap a purple elastic around ferrule and butt. I sit in my wet yellow raincoat, steam rising on my windows, and admit defeat. It is hard to do because the drive to capture fish and let them go is strong in me, like little Useful Creek I will soon speak of, its perfection. We strive: to catch and release, catch and release. And never get to the end of it.

One last look from the bridge near the junction where I will turn from wilderness. The brown serpent carries a tree, root ball turning as it goes. It touches the bridge below my feet and I feel the bridge roll and spring back from many tons. I turn and watch the great log grind the tailout. Down there in a shaft of afternoon light is the head of a steaming elk, antlers farther across than I am high, and the snort of vapour from its nose. I can do no other than hold my breath as it runs for me and, instead of up the bank and right through me, it passes beneath my feet, under the bridge—which I did not know was open air—in wetland filled with plastered green ferns.

The brown buck passes through bush to the narrow gravel verge and without hesitation moves into the river and swims right through the brown, then out into the forest and is gone. I am left standing in late, dappled light in fall silence, as though this huge voluptuous male animal had never existed. And that, I think, will be my last image, in the season that late fish are dying.

Silence is replaced with distant canine voices. As they come, I see the pack of wolves snuffling as they run the forest down. Surprisingly, they look like dogs, huskies, the Littlest Hobo, but dogs, hardly killers. But my breath is held, and I wonder: will they come after me if they can smell me as surely they do the elk?

They smell so well they follow at full speed, running through trees, running below my feet. At the river, the large ones leap and swim across, while the young end up swimming and being carried down to the tailout at pool's end. Then the thrust of legs against gravel and up into green where others have gone. One magical image replaced by another, and I knowing there is only one end for the elk.

The forest is full of water between gothic trees. The brown serpent gathers at the bridge, logs giving ground grudgingly where the best coho water is off limits. The purpose of the closure is to prevent snaggers with six-inch hooks bagging the big ones, hoisting them up onto the bridge, without a railing, without a sidewalk, with only one lane and logging trucks like huge prehistoric insects.

So, I'm leaving my river and backing into Christmas. It is 1 p.m. and my day is done. There are miles of rain, sheets of mud, and potholes grow so quickly, graders cannot keep up. My wheels slip the big circle around the swamp with its beaver dam, past the gate with the big rock in its bright red saucer. The Kissinger Lake gate is meant for guys like me who think nothing of cutting a chain with the hacksaw blade from our 50-pound tool boxes. The gate has an inch-thick metal finger reaching out, enclosed in a hood of steel so no saw can reach the lock. Someday, I'll add a reciprocating saw to my fishing equipment, for these gates made of steel.

But the gate is not closed on this soaked-to-the-armpit day when trees are mud-covered ten feet high. Ferns are drowned peacocks in Lake Cowichan valley. Then the ka-chunk of Little Shaw culvert, the radio point, then forest and stream on the right, chum like moles, tunneling upstream. The car slews to a stop, and my arms struggle into my very wet coat. I walk, looking into the deep water, sunglasses cutting surface glare, and there, the sway of fish, waiting, I'd like to think, for me.

I'm back to the car, lifting gear where rain gets in and leaves two inches of itself behind the driver's seat. The purple elastic is taken off, ferrule put over butt, green, plastic case of spinners stuffed in my chest pocket. Steam grows on the inside of my sunglasses. This is a difficult spot: a side channel that flows only when river is at its highest and dark limbs droop a little lower in heavy rain. The slick ends in a clump of willows with a frosting of water at their feet.

I step from road to seasonal creek, teeter on the edge where it falls into the channel. My next step ends with me not only slew-footed but within a twig's thickness of the top of my waders. The alder I hold snaps, depositing me, branch in hand, on one foot into the flood, where I stand, yanking my back-bent foot from behind me.

My rod cannot be held above my head, only sideways, a couple of twig's thickness from the surface, under long, tired cypress limbs. Their tips drag downriver, then swing back, where they drop and get dragged again. My arm is in the water above my bicep, sleeve full of water. I dip the spinner in the current, free-spool line, then click the drag.

Rain carries on hitting my face, the lure bleeps until it disappears and I wonder what ... until the rod bends down. A red fish long as my arm frames itself in the briefness of air between scrolling water and feathery green. Then it turns down and away, around the tail end of willows where mainline winds so perfectly, the weight of the big fish pulls until the line snaps with the sound of a wet shotgun. Then I'm standing in chest-deep water, holding a root with my foot, pulling another spinner from its green case struggled from my wet pocket, tying a Palomar knot, pulling it snug with white, wet fingers, tag-end yanked by teeth.

Again, the drop of lure from rod tip held flat to the surface. Again, dark water pulls the happy, bleeping lure. The click of drag, pulse of lure on my finger, then rod and my arm bury in water. The river sways me as if it would, in indifference, take me down. Branches move above my face like a hat of wood. Then pull and snap when I cannot stop the 20-pound red fish. Then, holding my breath, trying not to spook the rest where they skitter like horses. Then the green plastic box, lure between my teeth, pushing the box back into wet.

I repeat my drop of lure and my stash slowly dwindles. On my last, glow-in-the-dark, Mepps Aglia, a Palomar is snugged, tag end snipped, and lure charged with my flashlight. Another click of drag on my final blade, before a fish graces me with its open black mouth that closes completely on the little bit of curiosity it has left. My arm follows it downstream, so I am in some wet yoga pose, arm and rod straight downstream, other arm and toe stretching out behind, the other rubber-footed toe looking for purchase in the dark where my eyes cannot see.

Can I be so lucky, I wonder, on my last, little lure? The fish is held within the tailout, my rod and golden reel assigned to the water. Hand over hand, mainline is pulled up to me. I had accepted a skunk earlier, one that would be with me for a year, but instead I land and release my first December coho. Its black jaws are lined with red, opercula opening in the too-thin fluid of life. So, this goal I didn't think I had is reached.

With a snap of its tail, the fish streaks back to its life. I am wet to my armpits, pulling ferns to haul my wet, sore body up the muddy shore. My jacket is flung with its weight of water in the back, boots unlaced. Neoprene waders with a million holes from climbing over and under logs, its smell of sweaty body, are plonked over the seat and hatchback closed. My little engine chugs up over late autumn cool. I pass potholes I have come to know intimately, swing round Maple Grove Recreation Site into a clear-cut.

It is here my day is filled with elk. A good lumbering crew takes over the road. I stop and they pass as though I am not here, legs of horse-sized males high as my eyeballs. I could reach through the window and touch the great engine of their hearts, fur that smells like honey.

Mud? What mud? My car is so often covered in mud that I don't see it anymore; but which I take care of on the way home, picking up gas in Mill Bay and running my car through the car wash.

Chapter 13

HERE'S THE THING

My car slides round the big loop that circles the bog, with water up alder trunks chewed off like popsicle sticks. Moisture from the beaver dam rose in the night and fell in masses of droplets smaller than humans can see. My car swings to one side, then the other. I cram my foot on the brake and this sends the car on another skid fully broadside down the frozen road. I brake again and it swings the opposite, so my back wheels are almost off the road, where I would fly and come to rest on my roof in the swamp.

As a last resort, I take my hands off the wheel, so I am not steering *into* a skid. The wheel spins and my hands grab again. Thankfully, the car comes clear, heading down the road through white alders in white morning light. I realize the problem: I am driving in wading boots and they are too big; when I have hit the brakes, the boot has also hit the gas, so I have been full braking and full powering into each of my skids.

Now the danger is past, and I hit the gas. I fly through white forest, thinking we don't miss things until they're gone. I take a leap to a foolishness of mine. Coho season in pouring rain, river rising and catching fish for a friend to take home. Knowing my river cold, I stand on a piece of orange clay in the boat launch above the bridge up to my chest and fling a spinner into the back of the back eddy, a foot from overgrown trees, standing in water.

I look at the windows forming on upwelling water; work out where, in each few feet, the direction is actually flowing, so I can move and cast and the lure comes back directly "upstream." The various shadows under willows are coho waiting for winter to come and let them leave their bodies. Life keeps them another month or two and they weaken and wait for the lining-up period to start their transition to death through the door of spawning and rebirth of another.

I see a 10-pound fish open its mouth and close it, then feel the bite on the rod and set the hook. It is one I know I will take, though there is a difficulty: the back eddy is beside the main current and swiftly flows over the tailout and its spawning gravel where dozens of coho wait for time to release them.

My fish does the coho roll and gets more and more trussed up in the line. As it swings by I cannot grab the line. In its little sack of mono, it moves out into the river. The current, taking it sideways, has it move round the first willows, where it will be lost, as I can't stop a fish pushed sideways on its entire body by current.

I can wait until the line snaps and lose the fish and lure, or move after it. I take the latter, moving out past the willows. The water is waist deep and more rapid than I thought. I am past the commitment point and have no option but to ride down the river. My feet fly on each step until both are lifting and I must grab something to save being washed away.

I don't realize I transfer rod from left to right hand, only know I grab willows with my left, and immediately my feet are whipped from beneath me. Now I am horizontal, grabbing the next branch, as water rolls me on my face. Now my left hand is across my face, holding above my right ear. My body is swept under branches and they knuckle their way up my back. Now the shock of freezing water in my waders. Facedown, I hold the last branch before the sweepers ... and then, I am swung into calmer water. Now I see the rod is in my right and the fish has broken off.

I have done a stupid thing: trusted my river, and it just kept being indifferent, and without thought as it bore me down. I rise with the hypothermic gasp of cold hitting hot, steam rising from my shoulders. As I stand shaking my head, I move backward some years, to fishing steelhead in the winter. In Big Bend the river has been busy, working on sand, clay, white alder on the other side. The exposed gravel wash in its hump makes clear the river has been 10 feet higher than where I bump against a log.

This tree, undercut, has fallen all the way across the river and 50 feet out onto the gravel bank. It is pinned by a big dead fir tree, eight feet in diameter. My boat nudges the fallen tree, and I haul myself up and out of my kickboat, wobble on the log in ten feet of water. Down-current is a tangle of trees, branches from water surface to water bottom.

I struggle the kickboat up and over to the downstream side of the log. I hold it there, Spey rod jammed under a strap, packsack in the clasped-down bag, lunch and camera in the roll-over, seal-up bag. Sifting flakes of winter move through whatever air there is, falling slowly. They do the same as when we are in a warm place, watching, mesmerized, out the windshield as chunks, of air, it seems, touch our faces, then peel away.

In trying to get into the kickboat, I place my foot on the nearest bladder. The boat moves out from under me and I fall fully spread, face first into the river, and the gasp of frozen water. I come up, arm held tightly to the kickboat. Fortunately, someone is there and I take the arm-leap from boat to log. I hang on in water so fast I can't get my legs up to my arms stretched out to hold the log.

I release one hand and grab a little higher, release the other, move it up, holding onto indented bark. My legs are out straight as though I am flying. I lever my arms to the upstream side of the log, and kick both legs in the dolphin stroke. I kick and kick and slowly gain my chest, my belly and finally my hips. I stand heaving on the log, fully soaked from toe to head. For the first time I feel fear of my river. I am no longer strong enough to save myself. I am so fortunate someone was with me, because the kickboat would have moved out and bobbed past the other logs and been lost, leaving me standing on a log in ten feet of water with no option but to leap for it and swim as fast as I could to the shore before the sweepers swept me under.

I wear no lifejacket. My feet are in boots. I have three vests on, a shirt and undershirt, sinkable Goretex waders and wading belt. I will sink like a rock. I have been stupid, made an error, thinking: this is my river, so it cannot kill me.

Behind this belief is another, small, quiet one: if my river killed me, it would be okay. *Take my ashes and throw them off the Nitinat bridge. Which bridge, you ask? Ah, well, that's easy—there's only one.* And then shoving off down the many miles of water for the car, because I have an hour before hypothermia sets in and makes my mind lose reason.

Later, driving through snow, I sing softly in the green light of my dash. My socks drape heating vents. I am sitting in only a shirt, no long johns, no socks, no pants, no vest. It comes to me, I am singing a song famous long before the Central Park Simon and Garfunkel reunion. Yes, I'm still crazy after all these years.

Winter has begun. White among white trees and black pains where limbs have broken free. Along the stretch of alder before the loop in the road are ones who cannot bear the weight of snowflakes landing imperceptibly on trunks and limbs. Alder shoot for the sun 30 feet in two years and are so flimsy you can break them in your hand. Snow in its beauty gives death to alder, broken trunks in the road. I press the brake pedal; think I will have to get my saw out of the back.

Instead I head over far ends, in only my shirt. Trees give and crack beneath my wheels, rake my exhaust system. So it goes, for hundreds of yards. Only me and my headlights, crunch of wood, passing the beaver swamp in the lowland. There, as though unintended, are two swans, large but not too large, white when there is only white, side by side, heads down for bits they root off rushes and drowning plants.

Such anonymous beauty. We think of swans in connection with man, but here, and for millions of years, these swans with hourglass necks have stayed side by side. In the beaver pond in the alders, dying in the swamp. Around the great curve I go until I am looking into swamp from the other side and beauty is swept away by the miles I will travel before I sleep. All things go together, though I don't quite know how.

Chapter 14

WHERE THE STEELHEAD HAVE MET ME

I also keep my fingertips in contact with the line. The human hand has more than seventeen thousand touch receptors. Sometimes I sense a trout before I know it's there.

Trout School – Mark Hume

This is my story of steelhead. In the past they grew greater than 20 pounds. Now there may be one or two, for winter fish number less than 150. So few it is not worth going to fish, when other nearby rivers, Cowichan and Stamp, both have so many more steelhead, and hatchery steelhead, it makes the Nitinat not worth doing.

But not for me. I have spent my days on the Nitinat in winter, in high flow when only I am here in the lonely valley where even trees seek companions. And in the spring when summers return, it is the same, 150 at best. But it is worth my time, because I think of this river as mine. And I make it more difficult, refusing to fish with gear for fish so pure, you see their shadow on the bottom before you see the fish above.

My first steelhead came accidentally, swinging a Courtney Bugger through the Stump Pool below the bridge. It yanked away from me and lifted its silver hologram so clear I could hardly see it. And had the worry of six-pound tippet—I was fishing cutthroat trout, a fish that hits a fly so hard the shock breaks four-pound test though the fish is small. When at last the wild doe lay in my hands, she wore the faintest blush of pink on her gill and the rest of her was so ghostly I could not hold her in my hands. She melted through them. So, I met my first steelhead on my knees in morning sun. My hemostats turned the small bronze hook with its golden eye from her jaw.

As she swam away, I did not realize my fishing was changed forever. I have always fished cutthroat, and they have their private ways, living in softer, farther-down water, among trees, not ruffled runs. On this day my conversion began, and fishing became more complex. This is because cutthroat and steelhead habits differ; fishing for one means missing some of the other.

Steelhead, summer or winter, are found in ruffled water, even absolute heads of runs only a foot deep. Then in runs two to five feet deep, dappled, tan water where I would have walked in and cast to the opposite side for cutthroat; they seem to want the fly within a foot of the bank, perhaps to see it swing from one eye to the other and then the follow and take. Times that feel like scraping bottom turn into cutthroat biting before they secure the hook. But not from steelhead runs with ledges or runs with large boulders. More cutthroat lie in woody debris, though neither species will lie in water much off the main current line.

Another time below Stump Pool, I push through water growing deeper, holding onto roots until armpit deep and hauling my body up the bank into the green world of rainforest. Green so deep I cannot see my feet, cannot see holes deeper, and then fall face-first into one. There in the green is a broken-off branch so jagged it would have gone through my neck had my hands not spread before me. Then, at the edge, I literally fall from green onto a steep bank of strewn alder. And there, in one foot of water, are twin summer steelhead, 10 pounds each, I spooked as I hit.

Shit, I say and a whole lot more. I am still, watching the fish slow down. When they are above me, I climb back into forest, push through branches, pulling my rod when branches catch its fly. Downstream, I slide into the water, grey mud coming away in streaks like paint. I cross 50 yards below them and walk the opposite shore, lowering my head to my knees, back into sunshine. I walk above the steelhead and sit, eating a tuna sandwich, sun on my legs on an early June morning. A can of Coke—one of my few vices.

I wade above the pair and, because I need back casting room for my single-handed rod, find myself once again deeper than my waist in my quick-dry togs. I cast and strip and move down, casting two feet behind the first—a pattern more useful for cutthroat, as steelhead will come as much as 20 feet—until the cast into a snag I think will be the first chance and there, in late morning sun through shady trees, the fly stops confidently, and the clarity of water shatters.

The fish hangs in trees, shaking its head. When it comes down, it runs all the way up to Stump Pool, pulling and turning me. Then it turns and runs toward me. I wallow backwards, reeling at rocket speed, to not loosen the hook. It shows me more than once the small black bugger with chartreuse, purple and Schlappen red hackle, its Glo-brite black chenille.

When it comes to hand, it is a full 10 pounds of summer, tan and silver fish, one of the very few that call this river home. And I am satisfied, for if I catch nothing more this day it is the second largest steelhead I have ever captured. I sit on gravel in sun and let it warm my bones.

I have learned many things since then, and here are some of them: for fly fishing, the months of April and May above the bridge are the best months to catch a winter steelhead. They are few in number and the water sometimes lower, so wading the river is possible. For summers, though you may catch them above the bridge, your better bet in warm months is downstream, in August, before salmon come home. They are very few, too, and if only one person is ahead of you on the river that day, you will catch nothing, for the Nitinat is seldom 100 feet wide—sometimes as little as 20—and is a soft, little river. Once the fish are caught, or merely disturbed, by prick of hook or fly-line shadow, you will catch nothing. So, get out of bed early.

I am the only person who regularly fishes them, and I can say, while I accept a skunk before I start, I am usually rewarded with at least one steelhead a day, April through September; then salmon swell the river, pushing the steelhead aside, until November.

From the top, let me tell you the story of my steelhead in my river. I have taken steelhead from Parker Creek run, where its water joins the Nitinat and from the tailout of that run. And don't simply race the rapid through the trees, for water of even knee-deep on the close or far side can hold a steelhead or trout in this cool, shady spot. It is terribly slippery for footing and terribly close for a rod. Most fly anglers do not fish it, and that makes a good spot for undisturbed fish.

The best-looking opportunity is the pool below the rapids. I have never caught a winter steelhead here, though I am told those with pencil lead bounced along the bottom take fish. I have caught many cutthroat, many coho, and a few summer steelhead. I have come to know the back eddy on the right and the brown water where river plunges into a pool, and two brown eyes look up.

Then there is a barren half-mile to the corner of Diagonal Pool. Where the water drops on the left is good for the odd large cutthroat. This stretch bears the unusual nature of the centre being shallower than the sides, and you don't discover this until you are so deep it's hard to turn and move up-current. I find this out first time down and have no choice but to swim across to largish rocks demarcating Diagonal Pool—missing that the tree root to the right often holds a fish. And behind it small gravel—a spawning spot for winter steelhead. In other months, slide in a fly—a Badger, or Beamer, or tri-colour bunny in wild, bright and contrasting dark colours—and they may move to investigate.

Diagonal Pool fishes best in October when the river has risen a few feet. A boat is necessary, as water falls quickly over largish rocks lying left to right where the main channel crosses down, giving steelhead water. Take special note: this left side is always the absolute top of the run, in brown water, knee-deep or less. I will tell you this once more, later in this book, and you will remember. If you do not, you will not be lucky enough to hold the most number of the most beautiful fish in the world, with your fingers and eyes.

The river you own has many moods, and so much of my own has been autumn, when a million fish are dying. But there is later, after the river has leashed its fury; both the pool where you step into nothing and the pool below the diagonal rocks can be spots for coho in soft, deep, shady water. In summer when sun is behind the cedar on the far shore and mist is in treetops like stubble on a face, you may stand long enough, understanding wilderness, that a cutthroat will leap into your eyes and show you its fine brown vest buttons on a golden chest.

I landed my first winter steelhead—ever—in the Diagonal Pool, having seen it jump, and in two casts laid my fly 15 feet above and was rewarded by a minty doe of 9 pounds, recently spawned. I held her long enough to be sure she had the strength to shove away.

Below the dark opposite shore, the pool becomes a tailout of boot-sized stones. It is not a spot for steelhead, as brown algae is evidence of the hours it spends in sun, and so no good for fishing, though in shade, swing a fly through. Do remember the tailout of the Diagonal Pool is deceptive. It is always deeper and more slippery than it looks.

Next, you must be ready to commit to Tree Island Run. This is best fished moving down slippery rocks that make for difficult wading. Stray not from the right-most branches of the left-most fork—they must be at your right hand—and cast quick swings from halfway down. I have taken steelhead from here in one foot of water, to the water that falls on the left-hand side. It is far fishier, though it does not look so, than the right, where the river streams around the bottom tree and falls into the main run that deepens into seven feet of aqua-green. Only few steelhead have I caught in this water that looks the best, though I have claimed many just above, from the brown-bottomed water under the willows on the far left, which is deeper than it looks. You will see the image of the 18-pound summer I caught here one May, so fish through methodically.

Where the tailout tumbles into the next run is a small patch of good water, browny—and less than knee-deep—but hard to cross in rising water. Once you have plumbed the left, turn your attention to the right bank, where aquamarine stares through large pink boulders that provide space for steelhead to stop your fly. Fish this section in five minutes, as it looks better than it is.

Do not be quick to cross the tailout as the far side can be six feet deep, though it hardly looks deep as a summer knee, and a place for fish to stop among boulders having lifted themselves above Crossover riffle. The end has an unusual feature better fished from the right side, though I have taken winter steelhead beneath willows on the left. It's a very difficult place to wade when water is running fast.

The best water is on the right. You must cast from the left to cover water under far willow branches. This is an odd run because the main current passes down a ridge of boulders and thence to a long, right-hand bank that fishes better in higher water. For the next half mile, though there are few spots five feet deep on low water, a good big, cedar tree halfway down provides cover. I have only caught steelhead in November when the river is up two feet from summer flow.

Switch, where the river changes its flow to the left bank, it can hold winter steelhead even in the ill-defined centre-of-river run, so do not tread before casting. You can miss the only fish of your day if you do. On the left where it begins to curve down, work the run. The twig where water deepens is where I caught my second winter, then discovered I had to wade in the middle where the river is shallowest, but only traversable on lowest summer water. I have seen winter steelhead spawning here. If you see them, please pass them by to provide more fish in future.

Fish this run from top into and under the tree, on the left bank, with rocks jutting out beneath the surface; this is the best spot, then down to and below the next dead head. You will be up to your elbows and a back eddy billows your fly line, so you have less connection with your fly. On summer days, in shade, fish farther into thigh-deep water before moving on, practising casting as you wade to Glass Run. On deeper days, wade back up to where you cross to the right bank for wading down.

Glass Run is glorious in afternoon summer sun full on every stone, every blade of plant. Cast for the far-side rock wall—aim three inches from it, to improve your casting. The top under the wall is best, but fish the whole run, though you would think no fish could be present in such clarity. Then from the invisible, a 10-pound steelhead spikes the fly. Fish to the end of woody debris. One day, in 10 feet of knee-deep water I cast my fly and, while stripping, a three-pound fish jumps and I cover it immediately, taking a 16-inch steelhead, then a 15-incher on the next cast—but not the biggest of the three. In 2018, a new stump fell into the water here; it is good for fall coho and a summer spot for both cutthroat and steelhead.

The riffle above Rock No Rock can hold winter steelhead on the right in calf-deep water and you are strongly advised to fish the riffle before you move into it. As soon as a fish sees you, you are out of luck. Years later, from knowing my river well, and remembering the three, small steelhead, I cast in where no one would cast and caught my largest steelhead, longer than my arm to middle of chest, which is more than 34 inches. It took me six hundred yards downstream before the release.

I have landed only a few trout in Rock No Rock Pool despite what a pretty pool it is, and all the way round the corner through the back eddy into the next run. I haven't plumbed it in coho season but expect a major place for them against the left-side rock wall. If you can, cast in summer all the way across, where cutthroat stop.

The unnamed run below, all the way to the river dropping into right hand willow, is a major place for spawning winter fish. Think April. It fishes best one foot above summer low. You must cross high and fish a long line; cast farther downriver than you would across, as fish take when it swings to almost straight. I have spooked a dozen over the years. One year I will smarten up and take them before I see them. Fish a line 80 feet or longer on a flow only half that wide.

Big Bend begins where the river is its narrowest in 20 miles of fishable water, seldom more than 10 few feet wide in summer. All along the right-hand bank is good for trout and steelhead. Most steelhead are halfway down the run. Cast to the opposite side above the branches, feed line in so the fly is carried down under branches, then stop and let it swing. This is the hot spot.

In 2006 a half dozen trees plugged the bottom of Big Bend. This is where I almost drowned, falling in after lugging my float boat across the log crossing the river. It is 10 feet deep and you can dangle a line, but you are not going to pull a steelhead from the snags. Do note where any new log comes to rest, anywhere in the Nitinat, as it scours out the bottom, deep enough for cutthroat to stop.

I have never caught a steelhead in Coho Alley, though I have seen several bruised and spawned-out fish recuperating on the right bank—please don't fish intentionally for such fish; give them a pass. Where Worthless Creek empties into Worthless Pool—a son of a bitch to get foot access to from upstream—you may find a winter fish lying in 10 inches of water. Hence, fish from well upstream in a boat, tied to right-hand branches. For gear, the high season is February/March. For fly, that can extend into June.

Worthless Tailout and Run are the least likely looking steelhead spots, but I have taken many, even from where the tailout rises from the pool and up into a long section of lovely boulders almost to the far bank at the lip of the run's tumble. The run fishes better on higher water, and both winter and summer steelhead hold here. On water so high you have trouble crossing the seasonal channel on the left, steelhead hold just below the big cedar branch that sticks halfway across the river. A boulder creates a soft spot for them to hold. From where you stand, run your fly into the left-hand bank, as I have taken fish on high water within a foot of shore.

Fifty yards below the branch there is another. Send a few probing casts, and if water cascades from the left-side seasonal channel—you are in the middle between it and the rest of the river—it creates a good depression where fish might hold before moving up.

1906 Railway Grade. One of the nice things about getting to know a river well, is finding the hidden gems in its valley. This is the original railway grade from clearcutting the Nitinat valley at the turn of the last century. The steel tracks have been removed and this bit of history behind Big Bend has regrown with alder. Also of interest is that where the grade passes over small streams, it reveals the huge timbers they used to make the trains pass over.

Second Creek, below, has a good seam and the highest end, less than knee-deep, holds cutthroat. This pool has a very strong back eddy that threatens fly fishing. The key is to keep walking down the river, deep and muddy as it is on the left bank, until it runs true, and cast your eyes to key on any stump deposited down the right bank. It is also a good spot for coho and Chinook.

Corner Pool, just above where the boat launch used to be, where the massive tree fell and almost ruined my day, has never offered me a steelhead, though it is good-looking water. From here, past the back eddy, hard to the road side, the river flows down through sequential runs that in summer are a tad shallow and in winter too difficult on foot.

I have taken a summer buck from the riffle above the Bridge Pool on a low-water summer day. Even though this spot is surrounded by campsites and other anglers, you can get "first water" all day long, as moving fish must crowd into this small space before moving up. Then cross the river to scramble the brush to the bridge abutment. The right-hand bank gives access for an outstanding caster to reach steelhead lying in the tailout, a good 100-foot-long cast. Those with usual skills plumb the snags on the right, for the occasional cutthroat calls them home. Note the seasonal fishing closure in this and other pools before fishing and being embarrassed.

Nickel, just below, is where the hatchery people like to find winter steelhead, a small bit of good water that carries on knee-deep and fishy down to the Stump Pool, of which I have written. The river hits the rock wall, turns to the left and sluices around straggling willows with good clear boulders that provide a run to hold fish on higher water—though that leads to a problem in wading. New Moon occasionally holds a steelhead, though it is good slow water where cutthroat like to stop. One day I took a dozen, but that is the exception, though that illustrates the rule: fish all good water, as the fish may be there and nowhere else on that day.

Just below, the river runs through boulders and under willows. Right below the bottom willow on the left side is a spot that often holds a steelhead. Cast above, let the line sink, and connect when the fly is under the branches.

The Road Pool below holds steelhead in its tailout but is difficult to fish unless you come from upstream—the road side allows the fish to see you long before you inch into casting position; this is a major pool for all species year round.

The Hatchery Pool, closed year round, is next, and you will sometimes find steelhead lying in the open portion where the Little Nitinat River joins. They are resting and tasting the water. In September, stand below, on the mid-river island, and cast up into the Hatchery Pool. In the dawn you may be surprised by a fish held there overnight under the first of the harvest moons.

Shady Run, on the right hand, often has a steelhead lying in June to deepest August when the run is totally in shade, sometimes all the way back into knee-deep water. At this point simply turn left and probe Subway Run, the centre of the river. It is a deceptive bit of water that looks out in the sun, shallow and unfishy, but it is deeper than it looks and ruffled enough for steelhead to stop after the long flat run of water above Red Rock Pool below. In afternoon Nitinat wind, plumb the shallow riffles on the half mile right side for summers, down to Red Rock Pool.

To fish Red Rock Pool for steelhead, resist moving in above the drop-off. Start casting a good 50 yards above. Steelhead rest above the drop, in knee-deep water, and you simply scare them by walking in as you would for cutthroat that wait below the fall. Most commonly, trout are on the left in slow water. If you see fish early but can't catch them, come back when wind blows your cast into a silly thing. You must cast all the way across to the rocks to catch them; you will, once the wind-skinned water has rested them.

I have been unsuccessful in catching steelhead between Red Rock Pool and Cutt Corner, though on years logs are on the shore, many cutthroat inhabit this stretch. I have taken many steelhead in the half mile Corner, especially in the tailout among terrific logjams. Logs are thrown on the outside of curves, when the river turns but the logs do not. For the past decade, dozens of stumps have piled on the left bank, and this is how you know where the tailout is on years the river mangles the gravel to suit its purposes.

There must be a cool spring, as three-pound summer steelhead like to stop, having swum the pretty red and brown rocks between the tailout and Eagle's Nest Pool below; this pool is difficult to fish because there are sunken logs with branches poking up and you are always having a problem getting your fly far enough across and keeping it above the snags, where of course, many fish sit.

Most anglers scare fish into submission before they start casting at Eagle's Nest. Most years, the southwest bank is a few feet above the pool and thus your image and shadow fall across the water. Many times, I have walked the other side, the right bank, and seen steelhead cruising the waters, but by the time I spot them, they have long since seen me. Try cunning and the long line of success. For stillness add a flat trajectory that lays the fly out before the line kisses down. This stretch can vary dramatically, depending on whether there are logs deposited that scour out a pool. The year this book was published, for example, there was no Eagle's Nest Pool; that is how much the river can change.

Steelhead Run, below, is one where I have only taken trout, though one winter or summer day, river one foot higher than low water, I will take a steelhead, for there is a good 400 yards of the best water—knee- to waist-deep, brownish, ruffled, usually at the pool's top or right, beside the main current line. Interestingly, there is a first-growth stump cut down a century ago—it appears they had to try several times, as there are many saw bites in the cut. The Nitinat has swollen around it and now it sits in the middle of some great steelhead water.

No Fish Pool has, in recent years, held lots of trout, particularly in August, just before Chinook enter the river, and steelhead May to August. The run—or should I say, very rocky tailout—below is the most deceptive on the entire river. It is deeper and faster, with bigger rocks than any other crossing. You want to be on the left bank, looking down. Where it flows over rocks in its mouth is the best water, and you want to cover it into the brush on the right-hand side, through the boulders and thence to where the current runs into the left-hand bank.

From here is a lovely half-mile, summer-afternoon walk, Nitinat wind coursing through trees and making them complain of various ailments. You don't fish here unless the winter has deposited a big stump that will eat out a pool around it. When you have come to Glory, start casting above the left-hand logs, a very consistent spot. Where the stump sticks out, steelhead and cutthroat sit before continuing, and so their beauty may surprise you.

Glory Slough proper, on the right-hand side, dips into a gentle glide. You must be a good caster for, as I have said, cutthroat like to see a fly go from one side of their eyesight to the other, and the bank is 80 feet from where you are belly-button-deep. But cast and step, cast and step, for the glide is populated by good branches and old stumps for 1,000 feet. This is a prime spot for fly fishing for Chinook in the fall, and where, as I will tell you, the bear drank my Coke.

Then you arrive at Sturgeon Pool, where the river has its way with gravel and will, in every rain, rearrange the bottom to suit its grand indifference. In September, this is the low reach of half a mile, where people come and take tyee and then, in forgetfulness, fail to realize they have a full mile to carry and then drag a great fish home. (And note that after 2014, the Hobiton

Main was fully decommissioned, and you must egress by boat, or the very long walk up to Red Rock Pool).

And when the snaggers, who do not realize they are snaggers, fill the water where the river bears a little right, and the black they see is a wall of salmon flesh, I have stood above, among logs strewn in green. I seduced a summer buck beauty and counted myself lucky to receive its rareness when fish were being ripped from the river so audibly I could hear hook through flesh a hundred yards below me.

And that is some of my evolution, from no knowledge, to catching cutthroat, to catching the big boys of September, October, and November. Then I become a steelheader—the days, as I have said, when I accept a skunk and then am happy when the unlikely happens. You may progress from probing with a single-handed rod to the reach and precision of a double or switch, their ability to handle difficult mends and cover distant lies. There I am today, looking for more steelhead waters. The first winter came to me in 2005, an important step in a river with only 150—I received a hand's full of fingers that year and startled more than the digits on both hands.

Now I am learning each rock that bends water from Parker to Poison Slough, where few boats come because the crossing at day's end means broaching afternoon crests on blowy Nitinat Lake. I will fish them more often and will be rewarded for my willingness to catch nothing and be satisfied the river fished well, that my cast was long and straight. I become proficient and the river rewards me more than any other, in my trembling hands the fish emblem of this western island: *Onchorynchus mykiss*.

Evolution keeps on moving. There are other rivers in the area to love: the Klanawa and its canyon; the Sarita, with steelhead I've seen leaning on shore; the Pachina, Gordon, Harris, San Juan; the Franklin along the gravel to the Port; and, the Nahmint, where they dry fly for the Ghosts of Summer. Then, further afield, the White, the Salmon, and a dozen more.

If you come to my river, having read my words, I will see your footfalls on my banks. You will not see me, for I will melt into the distance. I want to be alone. Don't know why, know only that I do.

Chapter 15

INUKSHUK

Patrick Stewart, the ever-commanding Jean Luc Picard, gets stranded on some alien planet where he and another sentient being are trying, given their mutual strandedness, to get along. The problem is the "universal translator," by which we mean a nonexistent machine doing a nonexistent job of translating nonexistent languages of nonexistent beings into English, and vice versa (we'll forget the translator is on the ship, and not stranded along with them) into ones that sort of make sense.

The other biped—strange, every sentient being in *Star Trek* galaxies has two legs—holds out a log and says, "Timber." Jean Luc's intelligent, shrew-nosed, bald head lacks comprehension. The other fellow repeats: "Timber" and adds "is arms open wide." After a few times, a match lights in Jean Luc's face and he says, "Yes, timber is arms open wide."

What he has understood is that the language doesn't work the way ours does, its verbiage describing things that *have been*, *are* and *will be* happening. It speaks simply in metaphors, and the fellow is offering friendship, the good will of his people for a positive working relationship with humans. And here is the pithy connection with fishing: fish are arms open wide. Sorry, couldn't help myself.

Now, the parable of Hobiton Main: I always thought inukshuks made by non-Indigenous were in bad taste, not realizing this is reverse racism. When the road behind the river was decommissioned past Sturgeon Hole on the lower end, 13 dips were put in, along with culverts, so the road above could not be washed away.

The government blasted a hill and used the sharp brown rock to line the dips. My tires make the sound of rubber on glass each time I go through one, car jolting and exhaust scraping so hard rocks are busted and I give up trying to fix the exhaust.

The Hobiton Main begins over the Little Nitinat River bridge—please note that this road has been decommissioned, sadly—in a canyon where water comes between two high wedges of rock and turns the corner into a strew of gravel and rock. Deep in their soundless world, steelhead, as if mesmerized, fin slowly to stay beside a rock the size of my car.

There is also a little bridge where one day I miss my footing and end up face-first among rocks the size of basketballs. When I land ten feet below where I stood, I think I have broken my leg. But I am graced with a small good thing: neither I nor my fly rod that I have fallen on are broken. A little further from there I stop one day and, for no reason, gather blasted brown rock to build a little man. Two rocks on one side, two rocks on the other, a broad rock for a trunk, resting on the two legs, another for a chest, and a longer rock, sticking out on both sides to form arms. One with a strong chin for a head. I find the dynamited rocks among small frog voices in spring, when bear scat is black along the gravel from eating shoots of clover and fiddleheads.

I take my camera next time I bump the overgrown trail in the rain. I come in Chinook season when the day might leave me having caught and released 25 huge fish. I am anticipating fish satisfaction. There he is in the rain when I bump past, thinking of camera angles, en route to commune with fish. Later, when I come to the rock on its dip, my little brown man is no longer there. In the time I have fished he has disappeared. Rusty Subaru chugging through its holey exhaust, I remember the little scene from *Star Trek: The Next Generation.*

It doesn't occur to me to be disappointed, though I wonder whether the desecrator has been angered. Is it because he—I assume it is a he—doesn't agree inukshuks should be made by white people in an Indigenous area? Is the man an Indigenous person? I have no way of knowing, so I get down in the ditch, search up the rocks I used before and make my little man again. With the remaking is a small satisfaction in rain: this is the way things should be. Across the Little Nitinat I go, river dirt-thick and risen six feet in the day I fished in trees shrieking in wind from Nitinat Lake.

Next time I return with my camera will I also find my brown, dynamited depiction of a man kicked or beaten or shot off its flat rock? Now the dips have orange Dayglo circles painted on each side by the Ministry of Forests so that people will notice the drop they would fly off and hit hard on the other side, had they not seen the Dayglo circles. Such nice people.

But the man is gone again. In the poor, gruelly light of morning, rain streaks down my shirt as I search out the various rocks and put them together again. And here is the thing: isn't symbol the way of men? I want to leave a little bit of recognizable humanness on this one flat, blasted, five-foot-across rock.

I go down into the forest, across land where the mother bear and two cubs live, through the backwater in the giving-way soil and up the river with wolf prints and bear prints prominent in the sand. At the end of the day, I slither through the mother bear's territory without her charging, cross the stream and hot-step up the hill to my car. I bump back with forest closing in until I come to wave at my little man and ... he's not there, again.

So, someone, some mushroom picker, fisher, hunter, camper—ones who leave two dozen beer cans in their fire pit, as though they will disappear—presumably the same person, is angered so much or is so destructive he will knock the man to pieces. Still, this does not anger me. I go down among broken branches, black and falling fern, foot-wide yellow maple leaves, and retrieve the brown rocks to set up on the grey rock again. And so it goes.

I have no anger, no real feeling any which way, but each time the man is broken, each time he is killed, I get out of my car in the rain and put him back together. It comes to me there is destiny in this and it is that the angry one will lose because of his anger. He will never, ultimately, destroy the man, because if he breaks it, I will rebuild it. I will always build it one more time than he destroys it.

Perhaps this is a metaphor: anger is its own hand grenade, its own Fat Boy, its own Enola Gay. And then another thought occurs: I will build another inukshuk, a little farther down the road, just in the place they blasted the quarried rock, where elk in their effortless perfection rise up the steep, slippery slope into the forest as though it is flat ground. Ah, the beauty of their muscles.

It occurs to me that, were he to bring this one down, I could rebuild my inukshuk and then another, in the forest, that the person will never find, and it will be there long after the last time I beat my way back through the second growth. And should I leave him a note? Should I scribble: *There is one you will not find* and leave a line of faces staring out from behind trees along the roadside rocks, the broom in bloom in June, its bright yellow making it reach beauty for one moment in its ugly life.

I'm thinking this one day as I stop the car up from the Nitinat T-junction at a little nondescript bridge. It does no inviting unless you heed the pull of your own intuition. Below the little bridge of logs laid a hundred years ago is an ankle's worth of water flowing down. I push through dusty roadside growth, work down rocks into the little bit of water that flows into a pool in the rock and then from it turns to another bowl and flows, creating a miniature waterfall beside the rock and its bit of juniper, the toe of its root almost as blood vessel-streaked as a writhing summer foot.

The 50 feet of stream in the middle of nowhere is so beautiful it is as if some god has granted a Japanese gardener life for all the eons necessary to make this one small spot into perfection. And when perfection is achieved, the gardener can give up his life because he has done his thing of greatest worth: he has fulfilled the promise and fate that he had to grow this little stream, its small shadows of fry with orange tails among rocks in dappled shade where sun cannot fall harshly.

Not long after, I am past my man, in the river when wind from the lake has lifted into its daily torment of treetops. The tops are faces, now awful, now haunted, now frightened. I turn and find an eagle feather being blown up the river to me. It is actually moving against the current. I am struck by a need to get out of its way. But, when I step backwards, it changes directions, to come at me straightly. When I move forward into deeper water, it alters course again, until, with me retreating upstream, the feather finally comes up like some small thought I should understand and touches my leg. So, I pick it up and save it in the buttonhole of my fishing shirt.

What I understand is: this is the same as the little man; same as the nameless creek I am told by hatchery workers is named Useful Creek, though they asked me not to say why. And it is the same as the small toads I once found myself within and unable to step out; same as the female elk who turned to look at me though I made no noise; same as the fish who look up into my eyes and I feel their understanding; and is the same as the inukshuk broken down and built back up.

I am the student sent to rake sand all day around the rock like a mountain lifting through cloud in the monastery. On Useful Creek, the fellow takes the petals and he takes the leaves and he rakes all day. And he is not hollowed out when night wind softens the edges of his furrows.

So, I build my little men and cannot remember where I put them. Perhaps someday, I will drive Hobiton Main behind the fish hatchery and find someone else has made a little man. All things go together if we can figure them out, or don't even bother. Inukshuks, our little men, are arms open wide. Make it so. And I do.

Chapter 16

WHERE EAGLES HAVE MET ME

Where children leave no footprints

The whiskers I never see, but on river's edge
where time is my companion,

I have smelled the tracks. The round lion tracks.
I have seen them filled with water,

have wandered the killing fields of fall,
the carcasses of salmon, fungus folding

gentle as flowers. First the trillium,
then the salmonberry. Then

the mountains of strawberry jam—
what the bear gives back to summer.

Water holds my fingers until the drops
have dried a little diffident. The elegy of me

is my children, murdered a score
of years ago, and a burden

I try hold not closely anymore.
My winter sickness leaves even me

a summer day and the round paws of predators.
How I move in them, berries bruising my lips.

These Elegies – DC Reid

Notes:

1. I lost my children through divorce and it has been the sadness of my life.

2. Strawberry jam—bear scat in summer.

An eagle falls from high trees lining the dusty road. I push bleeding brakes, and wings wider than my windshield lift a body above my bumper. The eagle flies in the Douglas fir canyon of road ahead of me. When the pothole road bears left, left pinions lean down. When the road drops, white tail feathers flick low. So, we go, great bird not lifting from the moist forest floor, from no-see-ums looking for blood.

Locked in our speed, we rocket along, eagle on smooth wings, I in a car splashed with oil from shocks that can take no more. My roof complains where spot welds have been pounded apart. What the eagle has to tell me, skimming so close I can count its feathers, I do not know. When trees bend away, the eagle rises out of darkness and is gone.

Shortly, the car locks four wheels like a reined-in horse whose legs can't stop their cantering. My Subaru comes to rest sideways at the T-junction on the Nitinat road. Dusty signs point left, and dusty signs point right. It is summer, and so much greenery has grown from the wet coast it obscures their messages.

I know where I am going: the bridge on the Little Nitinat, where river issues from canyon and spills into the present. A rock the size of my car lies below the bridge on the left-hand side. Beside it, sometimes you see them

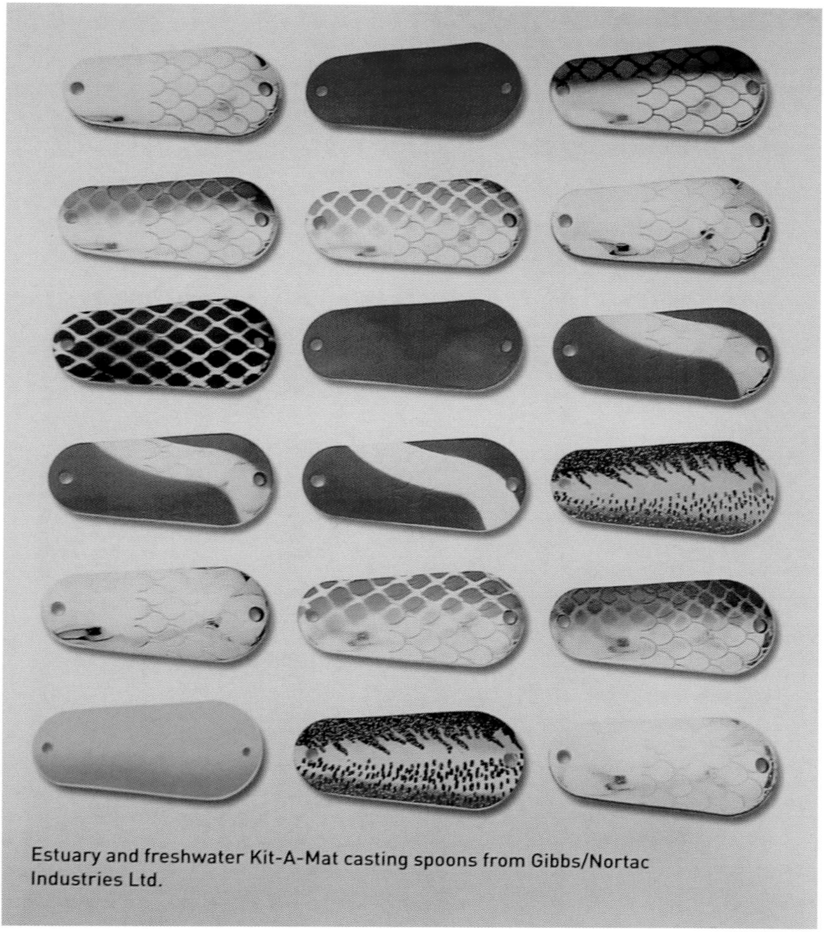

Estuary and freshwater Kit-A-Mat casting spoons from Gibbs/Nortac Industries Ltd.

Spoons

Gibbs Nortac spoons have a wide variety of patterns and colours. They show advantage in higher water and broader rivers as they cast farther than spinners and sink quicker. The red one is good on many rivers on Vancouver Island, particularly for coho later in the fall. The same can be said of gold models particularly in muddy flood water.

Spinners

Number Five Blue Fox Spinners. These are the largest Blue Fox Spinners and they cast farther than lighter, smaller models. Similarly, they catch more fish, particularly later in the fall. There is a colour progression in the Nitinat, from early sun days of September to late November. It is: red/orange early, then as the rains begin and the river rises, you move to pink and finally chartreuse, being thoughtful enough to try different colours if the fish won't bite what they are supposed to.

The blue model is a Cowichan River favourite, while purple and white fish better in tea-coloured rivers; gold in mud-coloured rivers. Also pick up a Mepps Aglia Glow model and try it early in the year. If it works, it will work for the rest of the season.

Tuned Spinners

Add a split ring to the lure's trailing loop, then a black crane swivel, then attach a black hook. Done this way, the fish bites on the lure, ahead of the hook, and thus is well hooked when it snaps down. After squeezing the hook eye to the swivel with a pair of pliers, take the hook between point and shank and introduce a 15-degree bend that makes the barbless hook even more secure. Add a bend to any lure that comes with a straight hook, and an extra black split ring if fish are still biting short.

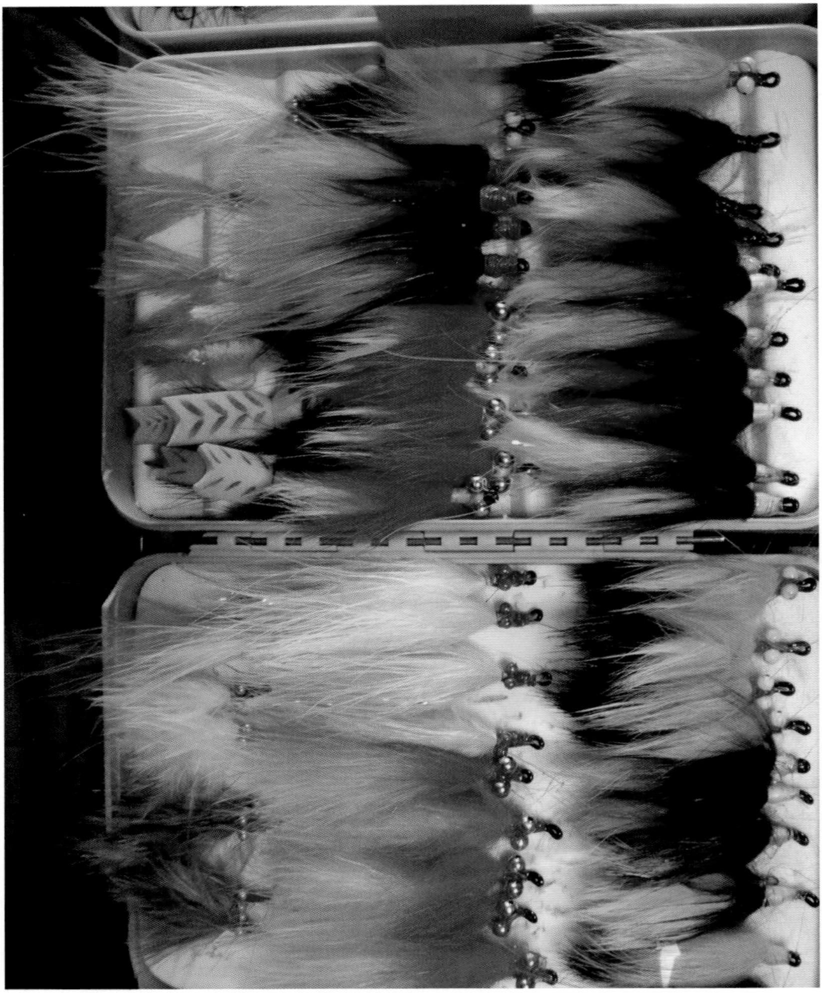

Killer Steelhead Flies

All these bunny and marabou flies work well, mostly for winter steelhead. The issue is contrast in the colours, for example, the red over chartreuse over black is the best, even though to a human eye it looks an ugly combination. The point is that flies are easier to see with contrast. As well, the best marabou combination is red over orange over yellow and catches more summer steelhead. Make some of both styles with or without bead eyes, which are both a visual cue to the fish, and make the fly sink quicker. On the other hand, if you are using a full sink line, eyes are not as useful. Also note in these flies that silhouette plays a role in effectiveness on any given day. Add a pheasant rump tail feather to some, for a gorgeous silhouette, and you will get the point.

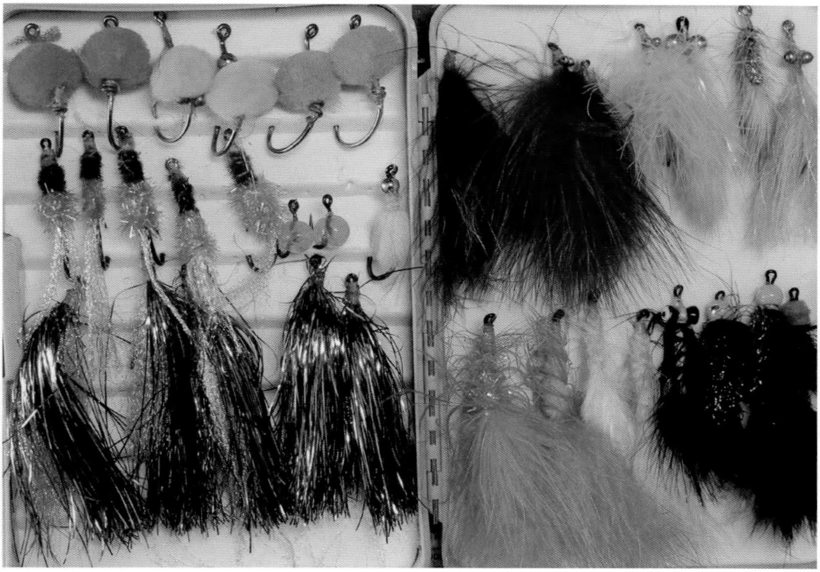

Chinook and Chum flies

The balls on the top left work well on Chinook, along with the simple, pink yarn, with bead just below. The second row on the left works well in multiple systems on chum. Just below them are some rapid ties for chum on days when they prefer a large, flashy fly, as simple as they are. The chartreuse flies on the top right work very well on Chinook, and the two beat up ones work so well that I still use them as scruffy as they are. A fly that works is worth saving. At the bottom right are several versions of egg-sucking leeches, also a chum pattern.

Two other patterns, the Nitnook and Needlenose, which are leech knock offs, work well on Chinook. White as well as chartreuse ones work well first thing in the morning, when light is low. Then switch to darker patterns through the day, ending with the ones you started with. My patterns are in *A Compendium of Canadian Fly Patterns*, by Jones and Mariner, also a good source for many of the other flies in this plate.

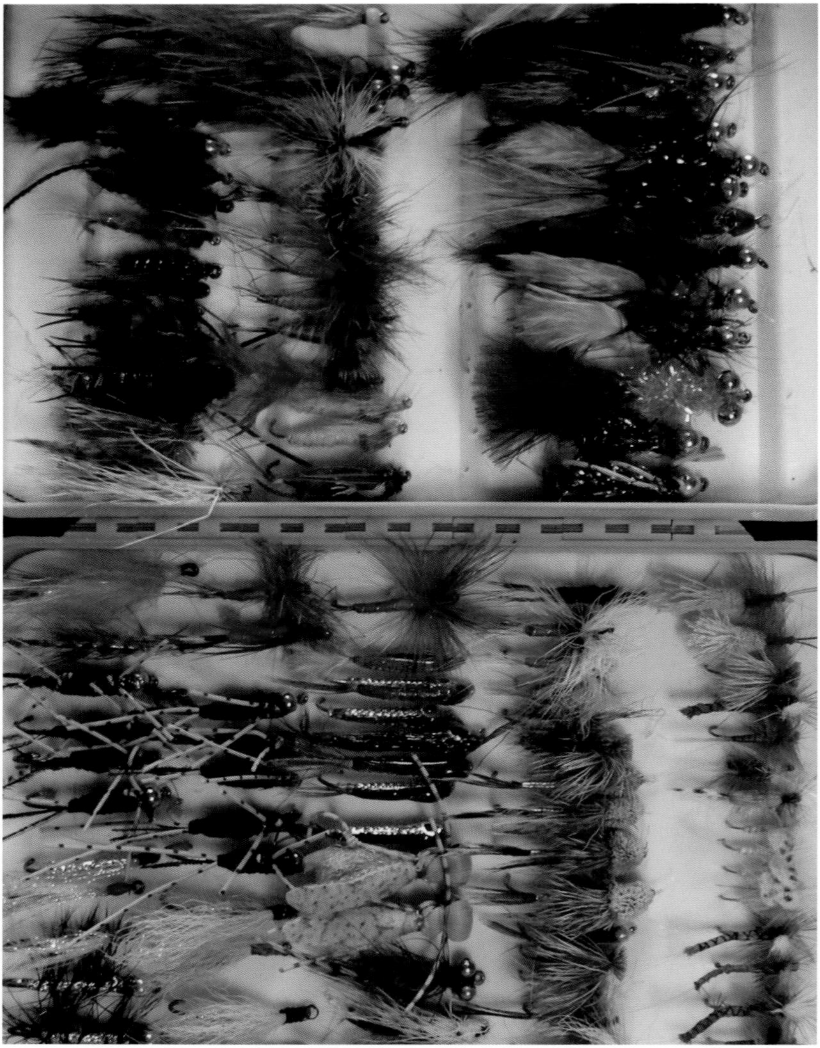

Trout and Steelhead Fly Box

An example of many types of flies that work well in the Nitinat – and other rivers on the Island – mostly on trout and a few for steelhead. Top box is variations on woolly buggers, including the yellow tail that took my first summer steelhead. There are many nymphs, minnow patterns, along with dries, Muddlers, Mickey Finns, Goddard Caddis, Tom Thumbs, etc. Note the simple nymphs on top and wriggly legs on the bottom. If these don't work, move on to stoneflies, which are larger flies, and much more visible.

Stoneflies

Stoneflies are particularly sexy during the summer. However, stonefly hatches end in September and the fish go off biting them very quickly. Keep checking the bottom of the river to find when the last stoneflies hatch from nymphs. Note the different patterns and different colour leg patterns. Make sure to use Hard as Hull to bond the middle of the fly to the hook.

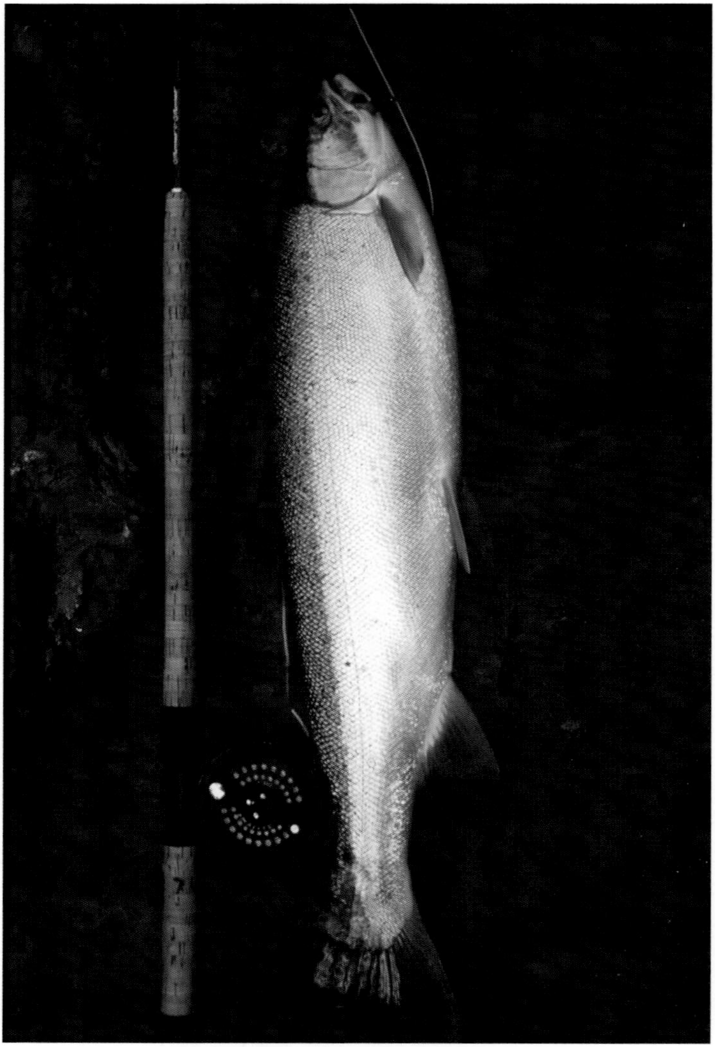

Winter Steelhead

A very large winter steelhead taken on a multi-coloured bunny fly that makes the fly more easily seen as it sweeps across the eyes of the fish. This was taken on one of my favourite rods during the Skagit era, a dark blue Thomas and Thomas DH1308, made in weights 7, 8, and 9, with a total grip length of 24", making this fish about 30".

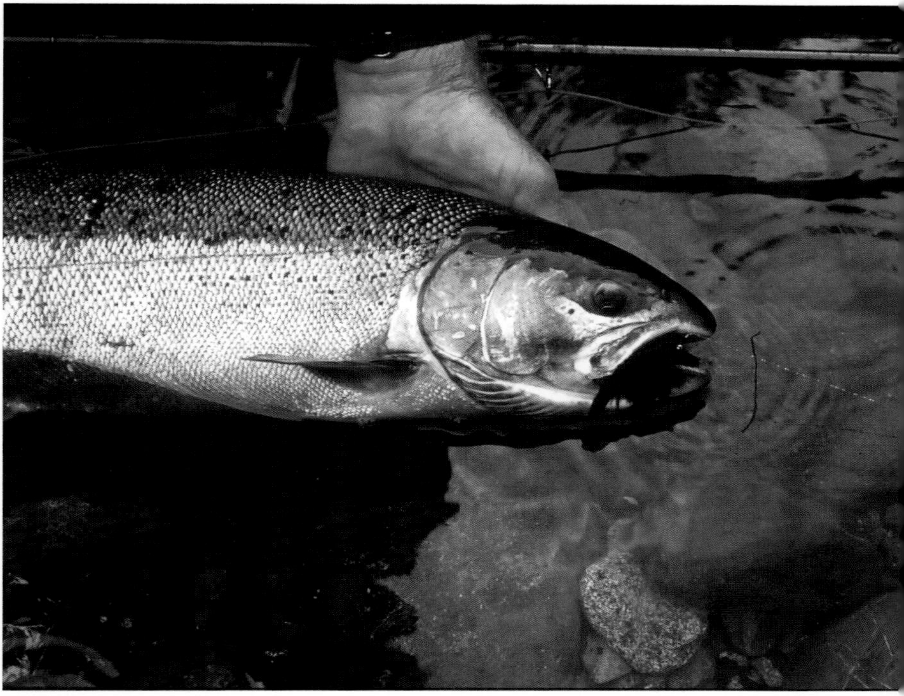

Winter Steelhead

A 10-pound winter steelhead taken on Worthless Run with a black bunny bugger with silver bead eyes. It is tumbling water with only one or two rocks to rest behind in 100 metres of run. In higher, or coloured water, steelhead sometimes lie within two feet of the near side, or left bank, as you look down. So, swing your fly all the way to dead below your rod tip.

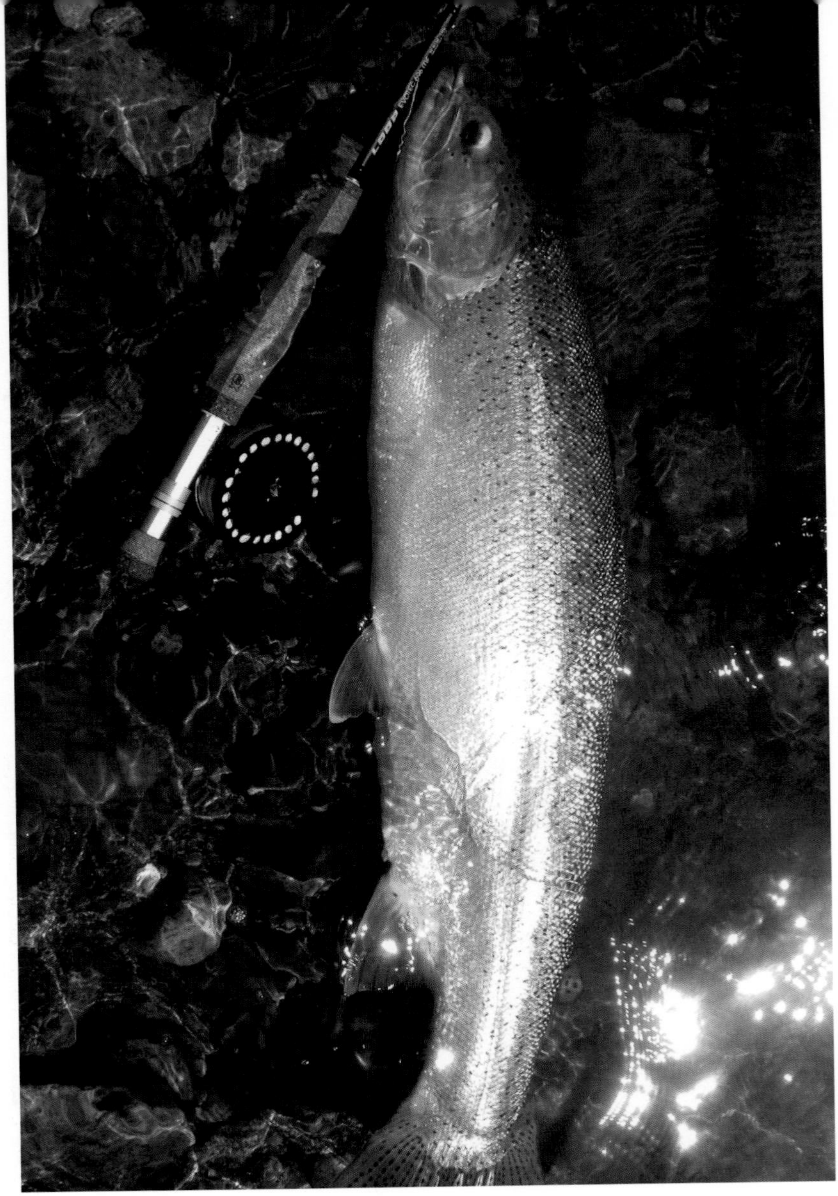

Summer Steelhead

A 20-pound summer steelhead taken at Tree Island. The cork on the rod is 1 foot from butt to top of cork, showing that this fish is in the 36-inch range – taken on my out-gunned 6 Weight, Loop, 696, Evotec rod, with a simple, killer fly: red over orange over yellow marabou with silver bead eyes. This fish is phenotype 1, and the most common, of the three summer steelhead types in the river.

Summer Steelhead

An example of the second phenotype of summer steelhead in the river, taken on a simple nymph with wriggly legs.

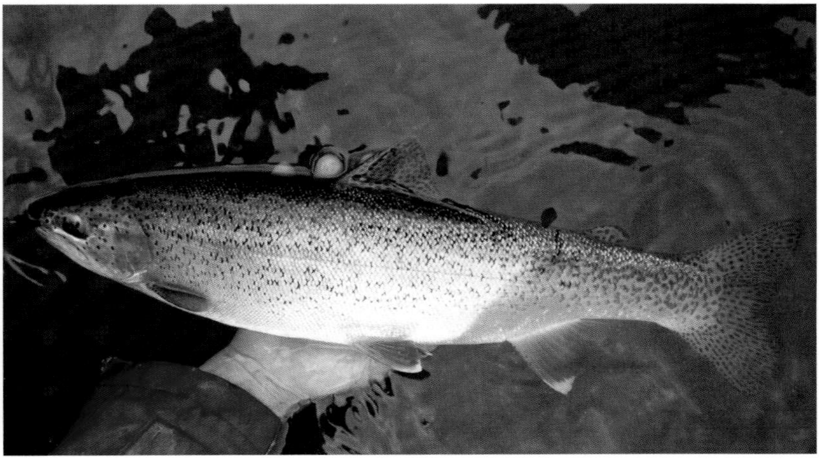

Summer Steelhead

A lovely example of the third phenotype of summer steelhead in the river, a blend of pink and spots, taken on a large, heavy nymph to make it sink into No Fish Pool.

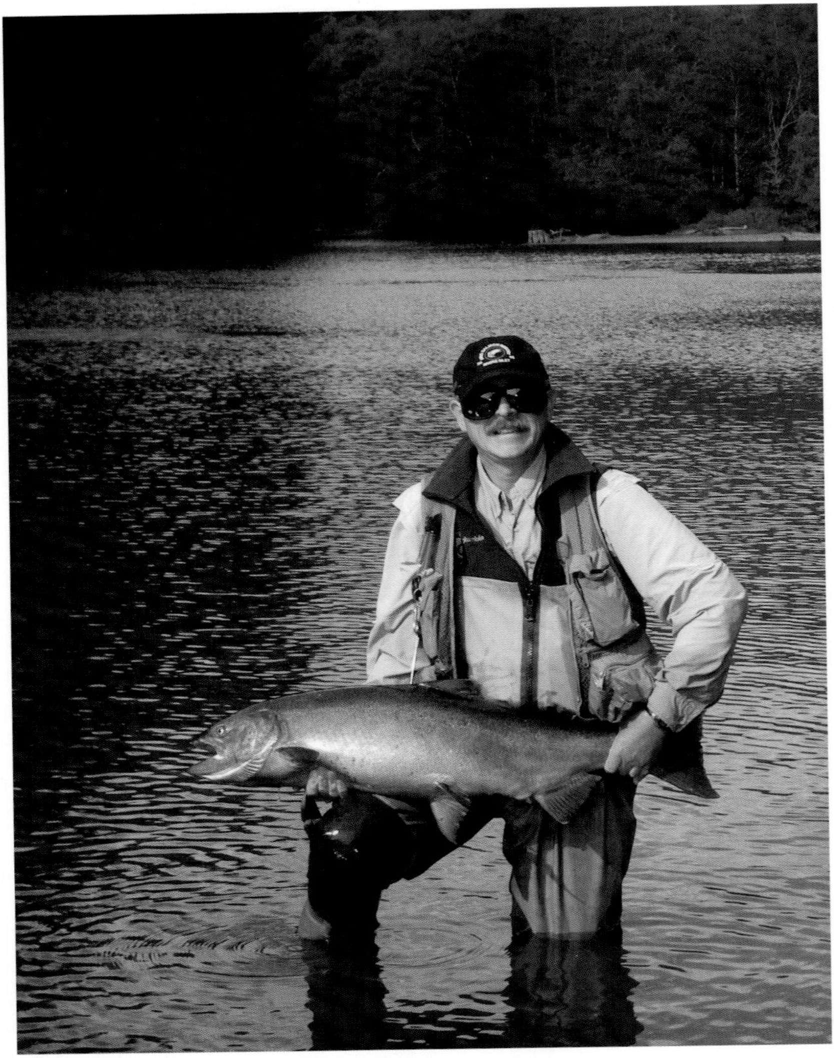

Chinook Salmon

Me and a +25-pound Chinook taken at Gary's Pool in September, just above where they enter the river from the lake. This image shows the high tide that pushes into the bottom end of the Nitinat River – about a vertical foot at the rock wall end of Sturgeon Pool. Note the in-river maturation of the fish. Taken on a Chartreuse Nitnook fly.

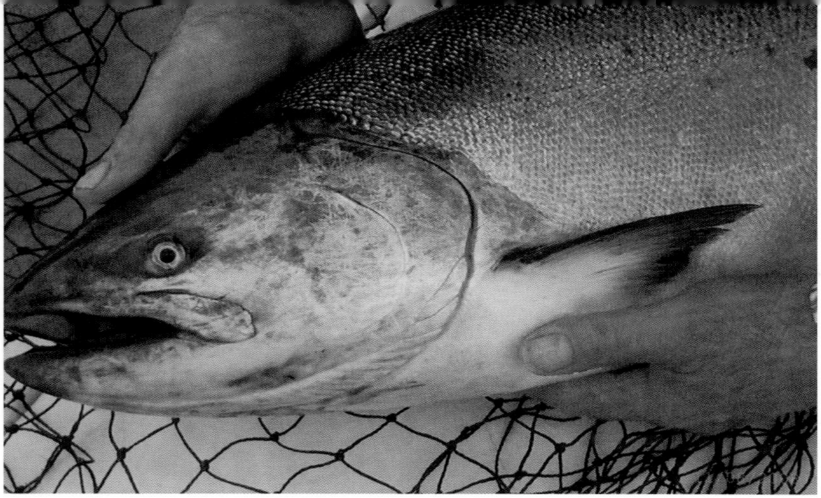

A fresh, seagoing Chinook salmon of 25 pounds, taken on the saltwater bar in front of the narrow Nitinat Lake entrance. This is a place to fish early in the day and then move on, as the combination of river, bar and wind often form dangerous combinations.

School of Chinook

A school just below Glory Slough, in the 1000-foot run. Note the detritus, bubbles and scum on the surface. It moves in a circle where Chinook stage in soft water and you can see it moving up, across, down, across and back up again. Fish these when they are in shade, to receive the most bites. This is a small portion of the 5,000, 20- to 30-pound Chinook circling the run.

Jimmy

This is a one-year-old male Chinook in No Fish Pool, that didn't stray far from the river entrance, perhaps to the Bar, during its short life. These have sharp, sharp teeth and the unmistakable armpit smell of a Chinook. Note the fly. When you see Jimmies taking dries on the surface, put out a generic Tom Thumb with floatant. Keep fishing until you have caught them all. Then switch to a sinking nymph with legs and take all the rest that were not on the surface.

Coho Salmon

A dime-bright coho that must have beetled up the lake and into the river, as it retains its saltwater colours. It was milling with the Chinook at Glory Run but was the only species that would bite once the fly was changed to one with a metallic sheen: a pink streamer with a single silver bead eye.

Male Coho

A mature, yet silver, male coho later in fall, before the species turns bright red. Note the kype on the upper edge of its mouth. Both of these coho images are of 12-pound fish. The latter taken on a number 5, Blue Fox spinner in pink, a late season colour.

Chum Salmon

A male chum salmon sporting its mating colours, before this species degrades so quickly and painfully. This prime fish was caught on a slim egg-sucking leech in pink and purple. While the occasional chum will venture down to pick up a fly or lure on the bottom, Chinook will do this much more frequently.

Cutthroat Trout

A lovely cutthroat trout taken in the summer with a large, heavy black nymph. Note the red 'glove' on the angler's rod hand's second finger. This vastly increases the sensitivity of the finger to a strike and thus catching of a fish. Similarly, wet fingers often make the fly line bump in your hand, and thus a false strike with no fish. Make them out of spandex. Wrap it around your finger, add a quarter inch of extra fabric, sew a seam 1/8th of an inch from each border, turn it inside out, and slide on your finger.

wavering, steelhead in ones and twos, doing the dream of waiting, "pooled up," s-bends passing down their bodies all day long. In fall, when the river rises three feet an hour, thousands of coho in festive red fin into autumn. You sit on rocks and cast into the back eddy where they wait. When the silver spinner lands, a fish turns, moves positively and connects with the blade. You feel the adrenaline of connection before it happens.

Then I jolt down the decommissioned road, passing my inukshuk, crunching through potholes. I bear left down the Y trail, push trees aside. Limbs scrape my car in protest. Then the muddy pool and creek of free stones. It comes from nowhere and goes nowhere, crossing the track three times before it bears into jungle and is never seen again.

There is another Y farther down: left for Cutt Corner, right for Steelhead Run. I pull into side bushes gingerly, having had sidewall-punctures from branches stomped down by elk the size of horses. This track no one knows but me—well, the local Ditidaht know; they have a small reserve in the wilderness—Wokitsas—where they seldom go. I step over and under white alder reaching for sun. Many fail because the plop of rain is enough to break them off brittle trunks in their early years.

Beneath my feet, the flatness covered in growth was a grade of strength. Narrow railroad engines pulled logs wider than themselves. My boot knocks something metal and my hand moves through leaves to find a muddy spike. They made them by hammer a century ago when they clear-cut the valley. It is put in my pack for my mantel. A trophy of the disappeared. I push through willow, push round blackberry, its inch-long thorns, move down Lonesome Pole, through a fretwork of branches to Cutt Corner.

As I cross the wide gravel verge, I see the tip of my fishing rod is gone. *Nuts*, I say, and more colourful words. My pack, my vest, the butt of my rod, my water bottle get dumped. I plunge back, thorns poking legs and arms. How many branches are in a forest? How many leaves? Where does one look for something thin as a straw? My Diamondback, fast as they come, could be used as a pole-vaulting cue. I stand in quiet trees, heart pumping. In a branch, in front of my face, is the tip of my rod. What are the odds of pushing through wilderness and finding something so slim, so black, so easily missed?

The cedar I lean against has a yellow opening in its bark. The trunk rises without branches higher than several humans. As mentioned, Indigenous women come and slice the bottom. Then they pull out. Up the tree shoots the cut until it breaks off a long yellow triangle. I remember now their belief that everything is two things: the spirit of the thing and the thing itself, which my novel *Execution Rock* delves into; this dualism of rocks, bent-wood boxes and men. I have found these ceremonial trees in many hidden places. Chapter 8 notes another.

I emerge from vegetation to Wokitsas beach. This was where I spent that magical day alone in the sun, landing Chinook from my toes to my waist. Dennis's Pool, I called it, but it is no pool anymore. The trunk, five boxcars long and just as high, has been scabbed from the opposite bank by the long arm of winter water. Where it once lay and made river scour gravel instead, is a simple bottom of small stones, less than knee-deep. No more snorting Chinook, when sun refuses to leave the land to winter. Now, all is shade, from the high cedar at Cutt Corner, so named for the many trout it holds in summer. There is safety in shade.

I haul my body from water onto a gravel "street" that leads into forest. I surmise it is a seasonal creek that flows into the river in high winter flow. Where water has gouged gravel between rocks and stumps are little bodies of coho, hundreds in shady pools, small orange tails distinct from other salmonids. The gravel must lead to Ditidaht road, the town of Ditidaht First Nation.

I turn round ... but there is nothing behind me. I have mentioned one has to come to terms with feeling watched when alone in wilderness, or you'll never feel safe. It happens several times on most days. I walk to the next stranded pool, in the lee of a stump. Hundreds of coho flicker like thoughts that barely occur. They wait all summer for winter to fill the stream and let them escape. At the same time, adult coho push in to begin the cycle again. I resolve to fish here in late fall, hike in from the road and take the coho when flood has come. Only, there is something wrong: as I walk the gravel, it drops into forest, turns south toward the lake rather than river at Dennis's Pool. Along the way, there is more shy beauty, handfuls of water, small anonymous eyes no one but me will see.

The seasonal creek flows *from* the river to Campus Creek and thence the lake. This is counterintuitive, because if a channel flows from a river rather than into, soon the entire river flows into the lower track, but that is not happening here in deep Douglas fir. The absolute highest water of December must be when coho spawn, when the river is so high it spills its banks. I recall I have walked this street before.

I once stopped on the road to Ditidaht because the river spread hundreds of yards into the forest and crossed the road. The Indigenous people parked their cars and waded down the road to get home. So, there can be no access to fish when coho "line up," waiting, opening mouths, taking in water, then mouth closing, and gills opening. All day long, every day, waiting months for water to fill up the forest.

A large noise startles me, and vegetation shakes. I fall over a log into a terrible smell, then scramble backwards on hands and knees. Then silence. What has it been? Wolves? Cougar? Bear? All big enough to kill me. I pick myself up and move forward into where the animals were, bear spray in hand, bear banger in pocket, whistle in mouth.

Moving through trees making great noises, blowing my whistle, I come to swamp filled with whirly-gig mosquitoes. Soft ground comes up my knees. My feet teeter on fretwork roots, in my neoprene, to my waist and deeper—it is always deeper, for me. When I am chest-level, still feeling for roots, my hands reach up for branches. The swamp is not far from taking me in the forest, where death is unnoticed unless it is a meal for the day. I would not be found, deep in soft ground beneath the yellow proboscis of swamp cabbage sending suckers for my flesh. Such a thought, such a death.

I wind tough red branches round my hands and pull. My feet release suck sounds, the size of elephants. I fall into the dusty ditch, the ordinary road, my ordinary life. I kick gravel up to The Seam, cross the river and receive a cleansing of mud. In all, a three-mile walk to get back to where I started. Then another river crossing, a non-compass walking of trees. Hidden stumps, where loggers cut holes to stick in planks a century ago. Then they climbed up and took the tree on for size. Hundreds of cedar stumps. I am eerily marked by this day of history and danger.

Back at Cutt Corner, where winter washed away the struggle of chum in Chapter 8, I see, in a half mile of gravel, a white cross; it is an elk vertebra, white as tusk of elephant, placed with its crest of bone sticking up. No one could have put it here, other than some friendly god, for no tracks lead to or from the spot. And here it rises from winter, a rare bit of luck, for me to find.

I remember some history from the provincial archives. *Chee-hah,* Indigenous called the spirit of the common man, less than royal chief. The common chee-hah rests on a bed of nails and wails, in painful afterlife; it cries for someone to break its plates and spears, so their spirits may keep him or her from suffering. Only when broken apart is anything readmissable to life. I take up the perfect white cross, spirit of warm, dead animal that was the thing itself. The other sacred thing for coastal native peoples is white feathers, those of swan and those of eagle.

Shortly, climbing up, I turn on a bluff, and look across wild land few other than I have entered. Somehow this makes it mine or, better put, I am part of it. The land, the river, the water. Across the blue valley, a small object falls from forest heights. I am high over a pool with sun on steelhead, nosing into tomorrow, the smell of their future. And, yes, once again I did see their shadows on the bottom before I saw them above, truly the Ghosts of Summer.

I look up and see, having covered the valley, the great bird coming home. This is the Eagle's Nest portion of the river, and perhaps it was cracked from a yellowish egg and brooked the wind, chaps on shaken legs. It is making for its tree, and from below me is the curve of flight, spreading wings twice as wide as I am high.

With the tear it rips in wind, the great bird reaches up yellow talons. Its arm-tip brown feathers sculpt what we cannot see but allows the magic of flight. It hangs on sky so close I can smell the air. I lean back, arms wide, holding onto nothing. Then, chest wide as my own, the bird with yellow eyes touches me with its own chest on the high bank where alder moan in afternoon wind.

We hang suspended in sun, ancient sawing of insects too numerous to be counted. I am in clothes of afternoon mist shed by saltwater, Ditidaht Lake. My thinking jags, and in my facial skin, sun tells me I will be cancerous before I die. I now know this. The eagle and eye, grasping what we cannot see. A cross, an arrow, whatever.

Chapter 17

THE DOWNSIDE OF SPEY

Within the fluid beauty of Spey, waiting for line to extend its loop, orange running line over stripping fingers, there is a world of danger. The rod moves so the fly lands beside you, then you cast the line, fly going along for the ride. The longer the line, the greater the speed. So quickly does the fly move, if you cast before the line has gripped water, you will snap it off every single cast. Like a line of kids on a frozen pond, the last person goes flying.

As I have mentioned, every afternoon, wind rises from Nitinat Lake. Early in the morning, an exhaled breath moves to meet the sea. Sun continues trekking over water and land, warmth making the invisible fluid rise, so cold soon blows in from the ocean. It blows so hard, tops of trees get ripped off. Foliage litters the land.

My bad habit is forming a loop on a snap T or single Spey so it sets up behind my head. Added to this, is laziness, sending the rod tip diagonally across my chest. I discover my error one rainy day in a 30-mile crosswind. I have, off my wrong shoulder, landed the fly below me with a snap and formed my loop on the downstream side on a right-handed bank. As the loop is pushed forward, I move my face left because I know how fast that hook will be moving. Unfortunately, in bending away, I launch the fly in a curve around my wrong, or left shoulder. Wind pushes upstream and a rocket-speed fly homes in on my face.

Then my right cheek is smacked and fishing line crosses my nose. I rub my right glass to clear away the rain. Then I feel a line of blood down my right cheek and hook buried up to the bend in my face. In this time of barbless hooks, I hold the fly and back out the hook and back-hand blood away.

I wipe my glasses again, but water will not clear. I take them off and find the right lens is not covered in water. It has been shattered by the impact of the hook. In other words, the hook burying in my face has been the lesser injury. Had I not been wearing glasses, I would have lost my eye. That's how fast Spey flies move—they shatter glass.

This pair of glasses now rests on my mantel with other trophies of my fishing life: a chartreuse Clouser Minnow that took 15 black bass in 15 casts at Langara Island and is little more than hook and dumbbell eyes; a tiny, size-6 glow-green fly with miniature eyes—a Chinook pattern for river fishing. It is bent and twisted from the 45-pound Chinook it landed; and a purple and white bucktail so beautiful with its load of iridescent Peacock Herl, I cannot use it for fear of its beauty being destroyed.

Other lessons of Spey have taught me to wear sunglasses and Velcro straps between the earpieces. One day in fall below Bear Island, I am using a 60-foot intermediate sink tip—a pre-Hardy Mach 1 line—that will reach five-foot depths where brown arrows of chum blanket the tan river bottom. As always, I am belly-button-deep and swaying on my heels in current that seeks to sweep me away.

Cast and swing, cast and swing, mend to the outside, mend to turn the fly. Chum are responding, bucks moving to push the fly from their territory. Not having hands, they carry it in their mouths.

I bend with the line in its downstream swing and fish are coming freely, as they do in the rain when it stirs them to carry on the blood line. Wind ruffles the surface and calms the fish. A snap of green line. A fly lands to my right, then the loop and coming forward.

Something lifts from my head and my eyes blur. The fly has taken my expensive new glasses, with their Nikon lenses, and my favourite black hat, and tossed them in the river. I'm so short sighted I can't tell there is a bear in front of me if it doesn't move. I am two miles from my car, through a forest of bears, branches in the face and dips and high spots. Blackberry and salmonberry thorns I cannot see.

I yell to my fishing partner a quarter mile below, but he doesn't respond. Then I see gold twinkling up at me. I know what this means: when you are up to your belly button and need to pick something off the bottom you are going to get soaked. I move my foot and my glasses disappear. So, I stand still until the gold comes back to me.

My hand in reaching the bottom touches the frame, but the gasp cringing my body prevents me from picking them up. And the river takes me downstream, where, chest deep, I have to force my way upstream to see the sun glint on the bottom and try my dive again.

The sun does its part between the clouds, and this time, already wet, my body does not tighten into a ball. Glasses secured, I resurface and wade to shore above the pool that bears my name and put them on. On my back, legs in the air, the many gallons of water I shipped, gush from the top of my waders. There is still something wrong. I look clearly from my left eye, but blindly from my right. The hook that took my glasses also took the right lens. Now it rests on the bottom of the river, never to be found again.

Later, having fished soaked all afternoon, I look up and see the day is leaving. Bear time is coming. In the day, bears grant you time on the river, but as the light softens, they become impatient to be with their fish. They will do damage unless you go. Bear time occurs every day in the falling light of autumn. It is a time I do not transgress, for the attitude of bears changes and I can feel it in the air, like some pheromone we have forgotten in humanity's rush to civilization. We have pushed evolution away and killed all the bears.

Now I am blind, bush hitting my face, down bear tracks running both sides of the river from top kilometre to bottom. My face is hit and I cannot see where my rod has caught its line on the many waving branches. I might as well close the eyes that have always let me down. I've had glasses since ten and have watched the world move farther and farther away. My correction now exceeds 13 diopters. Only a spot the size of a fingertip in the middle of the lens gives sight. The rest curves reality into blur. I cannot look out the side of my eyes. I must move my head to look at anything.

Though I usually fish alone, I am fortunate this day to have a partner. I cannot see with one good eye added to one blind. I am led two miles from Cutt Corner, past Eagle's Nest Pool, past Steelhead Run, also known as the Meadows—a name from when the gravel river bottom shifted from one side of the valley to the other and in so doing killed everything in its path. But nature returns from its ruins. It filled the meadow with willows and alder, now several times higher than my head.

Added together, my "sightful" eye is as unable to see as my blind one. We traverse three seasonal streams, ones that hold chum and coho in the fall, scenting the weary land. Then we intersect the track to Hobiton Main, with its ruts only a truck can pass. We walk through complaining alder, pungency of rain, scent of mushrooms, orange fungi flesh like steak on fallen pine. We pass where I fell into the herd of elk, pass the cut-block sign, the hidden path, cross the little stream in the trees three times, up to the Y in the road.

I sit in my car, wet to my neck. I peel off neoprene, shirt and T-shirt until I am in only my boxers. The Columbia shirt I put back on. It is one of their PFG material that dries in minutes, ones so thin they surprise with their strength, and cut the wind even when soaked. The glasses from my glove box I wrap round my head. But they are old, old, and do not clear the murk. I bump down the decommissioned road, not seeing my inukshuk, not seeing large black dumps of bears, not seeing birds, nor individual trees.

At the T-junction past the bridge, I put my glasses back on and drive with my right eye closed. When it opens I have to stop and pull electrician's tape from my red toolbox with its 50 pounds of tools. In afternoon rain, steam building on the windshield, I wrap the right lens frame completely. When I open my eyes, I see from my left but the right is black. I can drive, slowly, but come so close to hitting things I understand depth perception is from seeing with two eyes, not one.

I traverse the forest full of rain on my muddy slip from Nitinat valley. Past the sprinkling of houses that is Youbou. Past the stop sign near Lake Cowichan, the 100-kilometre highway to Tansor Road, back door to Duncan, car doing its best to heat its engine out of control. My new—well, newer—Subaru station wagon, a white one, without four-wheel drive, that I treat better than my maroon trooper, is growing its own list of atrocities; these injuries from driving full blast have begun to spray a hiss of water from a hose. Every few weeks it must be refilled. I notice this, when I notice it at all, by the temperature gauge slowly climbing to death, on the long slope of Malahat Drive up the mountain to Shawnigan Lake. I don't know, seeing with one eye, whether it will blow on the uphill or hold until the five-mile downhill where the gauge comes back from the brink.

I left with two eyes, return with one. Just enough to get me home. Just enough so the old glasses, which I also broke with a Spey fly, can be worn with their shattered lens, for the two weeks it takes the Japanese to make a lens for the one I lost. They don't trust anyone else in the world to fix them. I put a gallon of water in the holding tank. And my little car will, provided I also add a quart of 10-40 every couple of weeks, take me and my new glasses to the beauty that is Spey, and the river that is my home.

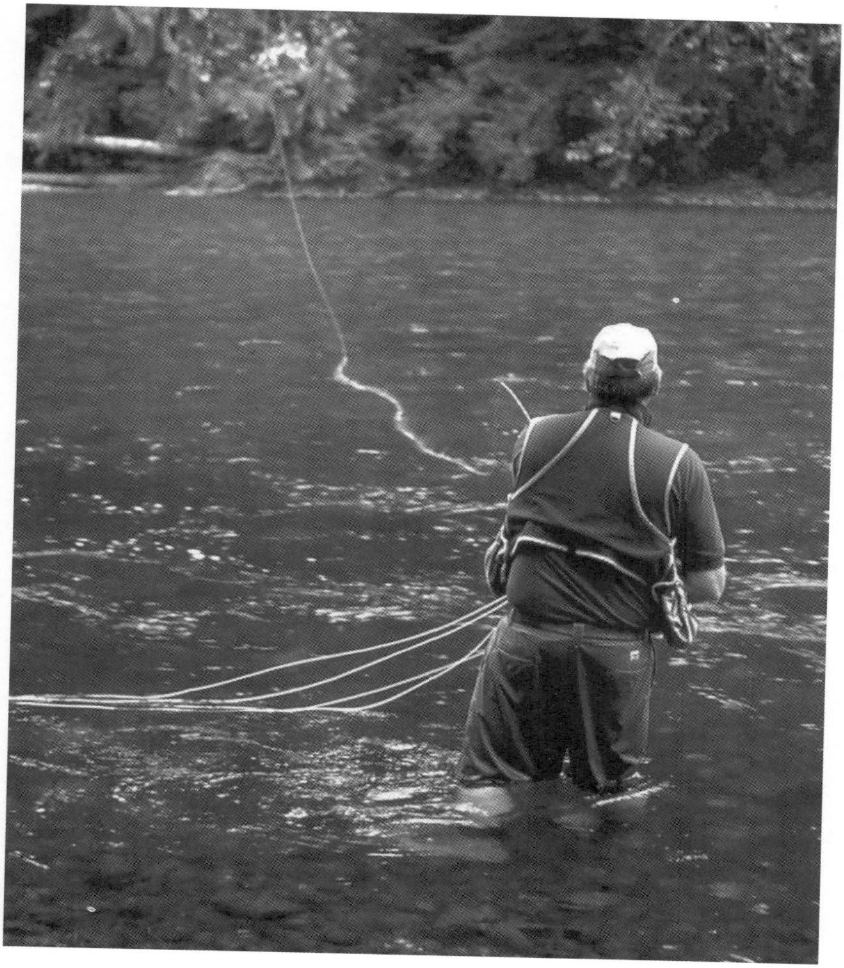

The first time you achieve the long, long cast of a Spey rod, you immediately understand why you need to learn more. Once you can reach out another 20 feet or more, the river becomes a different river. And this shot shows how long and how smoothly a cast will reach out and land your fly on the other side of the river. The other advantage of Spey is that it needs far less back casting room than a single-handed rod.

Chapter 18

SPEY AND WORTHLESS RUN

About halfway down the top end, a very large boulder lying just below the surface held up currents and caused unnatural drag. It took several casts to work out the mends, after which a very forceful upstream mend would eventually give me a proper presentation past this obstruction. The first time I was able to swing the fly into the downstream end of the boulder, I saw a flash and felt the steelhead take the fly.

Steelhead Fly Fishing – Trey Combs

I am fishing a middling fast 14-foot rod and, as is my custom, place the butt and reel in the crotch of a tree branch while I string the rod. If I don't, while I shuffle forward, bending a loop through each of the 15 guides, the rod will bend lower and lower, until the reel is sitting in the sand. Getting grit in expensive bearings, ones that would slow a fish, is not something I want to happen.

The Skagit head I am using has so much body, it must be bent into a loop early in its tip or in the slime-line tip I put before it. But one cannot make a loop too close to the beginning, because if it is dropped, the fly line slips back through the guides until the entire thing is sitting in the grit, and my face is unhappy. All anglers know this one, just as they know landing a fly in a bush; just as they know when making a Martingale, using figure-eight loops, you sometimes put the wrong end through the loop and when you throw the tip out—and I have done so with many expensive tips—you throw it right off the line into the river and it is never seen again.

Sometimes in pre-fishing nerves, I tie the fly on before I have connected the tip to the line. Then I am stuck, trying to get a figure-eight loop over a fly. The alternative has one trying to get the fly through line guides where it inevitably gets stuck. This is just one annoyance every fly guy experiences. But the river is not one of them. Worthless, for instance, named for its lack of gold, is not worthless at all. The tailout is 90 to 100 feet on diagonal and filled with large boulders. In water's green clarity they are red, green, brown, black and orange, thrown large through the lens of water. Then the river breaks over the edge into a good rushing 100 yards of quality run.

I stumble through boulders larger than basketballs, each tipsy, my feet moving with water's push. Noon sun covers the rocks with slippery algae. After 2 p.m., it sinks behind thousand-year-old cedars on the far side. As I have mentioned, one has a long arm of branch splayed over the river. Below the branch is a slot between boulders, two by six feet and two and a half feet deep.

This spot holds summer steelhead on their way up, and winter fish, too. Each run, each fish has no connection with any other fish or run. So, the behaviour of a fish with a life of maybe five years, brain the size of my pinky fingernail, will make it stop, for the cover broken water affords in shade. This life is much more controlled than ours by its smidge of DNA.

It dawns on me, running a bunny leech point across my right thumbnail, a *behaviour* I consciously repeat, to check for sharpness—that our lack of instincts, our frontal lobes, set us apart from all the plants and most of the animals in the world. We don't live in a river; we appreciate it.

The line of willows at my back prevents an overhead cast, what a single-handed rod would do, along with catching the fly almost every back cast. I am using a Spey of robust butt and trying to drill into the shadow of the branch, so my fly will slide underneath and come under connection just as the magenta creature with its bead chain eyes zips through the holding water.

If I am wrong in the weight of fly, tippet or tip, a tree will be caught and a great amount of tugging will result. Whatever fish may be there will melt into its shadows. I could change to a heavier tip, but I am too adrenalized. And I am having difficulty walking slip-slidey boulders. I hold my rod like a great big saxophone, right below my knee as though making music.

The purpose is to lower the rod tip, bring the cast from 16 to 13 feet, so the space into which I need plop the fly can be more easily reached without catching the fly on the branches above the branch that sweeps the water. Then it occurs to me I can achieve the same end by tipping the rod tip forward so the loop forms closer behind the rod tip, but also higher—and thus not catch the willows behind me. And if I stop the tip quickly, it will shoot a tighter bullet under branches across the way.

Then it occurs to me—and this is easier to do—to land the fly higher in the river, where there are no branches. Then another, better solution: put the rod tip beside me, horizontal with the water. Do the snap of a Snap T, land the fly above, extend a loop behind, followed by the push, firing bright lime line in a bullet a foot above the water. Most Spey anglers will know this is not a true Spey cast, as it does not depend on a roll cast loop, and touch of water, rod tip high. Finally, I bring the fly from downstream, in a semi-circle loop in the air and slingshot forward. No touch.

I congratulate myself on the wonder of fly landing in dark shade of polished roots, like claws of some great, slow-moving beast. It crosses my mind that life becomes what you do. Such as stopping the rod high to drill a tighter loop, tipping your body forward to drill it down, holding the rod lower to drill it down, tipping the rod sideways so a loop forms sideways rather than over the top.

I connect with the fly below the branch, and am chagrined, as it traverses the tiny spot I have worked so hard to reach, that the fly gets stuck on the bottom. I swear several times, and yank the tip here and there, disgusted. Then, oddly, the rock moves, in fact it moves out of the holding spot, and just as I understand this rock I am reefing on is … a fish comes from the water, cartwheeling its broad, square, silver tail. I have been too asleep to know a brainless steelhead has deigned to pick up my crummy fly, and I am far more stupid than it is. "Expletive deleted," I shout, with veins in my teeth, and—as you would expect—the

10-pound leader goes *plink*, and I am separated from the fish for which I've been working all morning long.

Even with Stealth Bomber Kevlar in my expensive rod and 747 brake materials in my drag, I lost the fudging fish because I'm too fudging stupid.

Hands unmanageable, I tie a new fly with an Improved Clinch knot. But the knot wraps round the fly and I have to cut it off. Ten minutes go by while I cut a new piece of leader, tie in a Figure Eight knot, clip the tag end, and put the loop from the flyline through and etc., so I can continue through this nice stretch of steelhead-attracting boulders. On the very next cast my fly swings—I can see this happening before it actually does—around a stick sticking up from the water and I am for Christingly-sake's stuck on another insensible material object. And it, with nothing for brains, is beating, easily, evolution's greatest creation.

Incensed, I sidle out into the river. No piece of stick is going to take my fly on the first cast after I've retied the entire works. Water presses on my knees, then presses on my thighs. I am rocking on rocks and the tip of my 14-foot rod can't lift the fly off the stick. Now I'm close enough to grab the stick, yank it clear and find the river has a mind of its own and it wants to take me there.

So, I'm holding on, wondering how I can be so stupid after being so brilliant, to a stick that will catch every fly that comes after mine, and now I need this stick to help me back out of the river. I tug and tug until I realize the stick is ten feet long and stuck under a 200-pound rock. Another solution: the boulder is round and the stick is a lever. I move the rock each time I pull the stick. But, each time the rock shifts, the stick pulls from my hands and the rock settles back down.

Then it comes to me: if the rock dislodges, it may roll down over my leg, breaking it, and pinning me under water. I push and pull like a fiend to dislodge the stick and, as I do, the boulder rolls with the current like an oversized quarter, just past my leg. It clunks downstream with the sound of heavy glass. Smash, crash and then no more.

Sweat from inside my body slimes the inside of my glasses. Sunglasses I keep on my head with Velcro straps slide down my nose along with my glasses, which, you will recall, I need, from the time I lost them in the river. My chest heaves. I drop the stick. My line slips back through line guides until the fly stops on the tippy tip. Brilliant.

Well, at least there is one thing. I have come to the point I have been trying to get to for 30 years: making my living writing books. I resolve, when my parents are gone, I will move from Victoria and buy a property on a river. When I can't stand being at my computer any longer, I'll take the fly rod leaning against it and walk across the lawn and let my fly bullet the morning waters. I resolve to be awake to possibilities. I won't lose any more fish because I am asleep—oh, sure. I resolve to bring a shorter rod next time, with a springier butt for side casting.

So, I am moving through life, now writing only books, and thus can fish every day of the week. And then another image, I remember my daughter, Vanessa, at 16 months and riding my shoulder in her little red and green plaid jumpsuit. I can feel it even now, her little hand holding my shoulder for balance. In my hand her little calf—at the time she was so small her ankle to her knee fit in the palm of my left hand. And then I need to move on and not get trapped at that point of pain some 20 years ago, which is still there if I let it come, having lost my kids to divorce.

I climb through swamp, the suck of each foot. My car bumps pot-holed gravel. The tip of a black tail, a back of brown, crosses Worthless bridge where steam donkeys pulled logs to the railroad grade. That is all I see—20 years of bush and the first cougar I have ever seen, a whisp of it moving away into whatever land there is in the valley of a river that has rocks that glow from the cavern where time and gravity were introduced to one another.

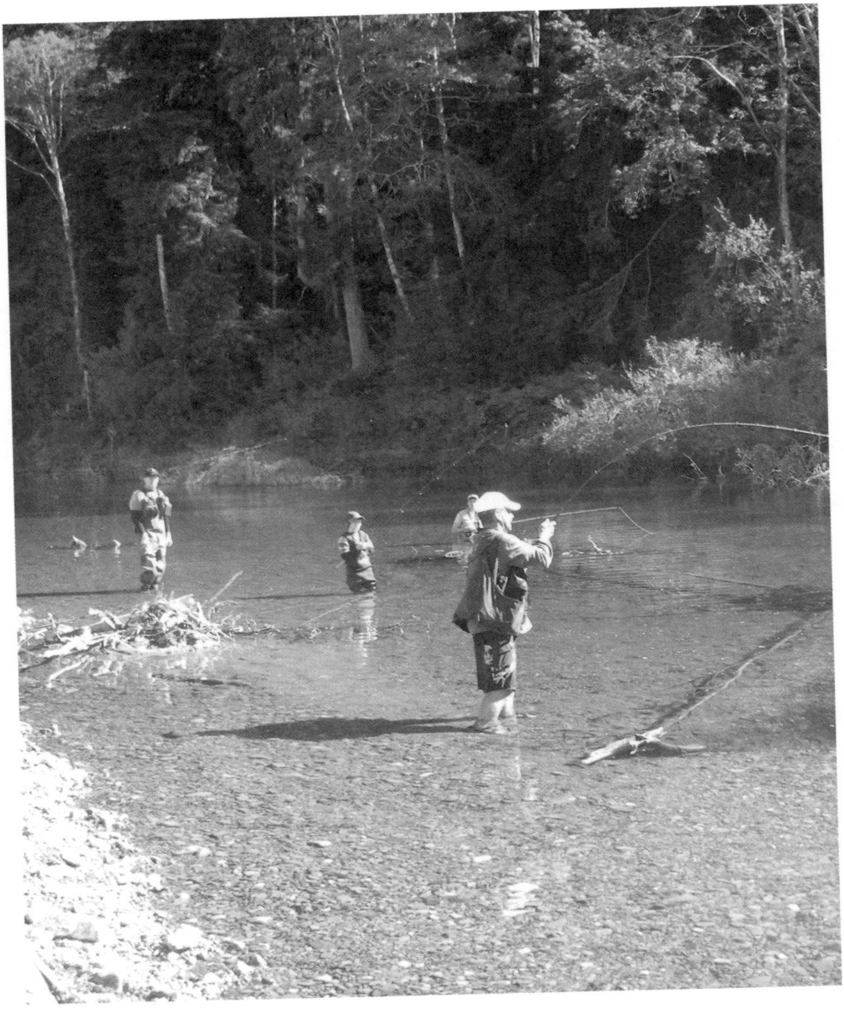

Chinook fishing at the bottom end of the river, Gary's and Sturgeon Pools, where the salmon first spill into the river. This is the high September fishery for Chinook, on nice warm days, for both fly and gear anglers. In the past, this fishery typically lead every angler to take home at least one huge fish. However, since the Hobiton Main was decommissioned right from the Hatchery entrance, this is considerably more difficult to reach. One alternative is to bring a boat across the bay so you can return with it. Note that you must contend with the Nitinat wind that typically blows every sunny day on your way home, so take care. The alternative is to lug the fish upstream, a very long way, to the Red Rock Pool area and your car.

Chapter 19

THE MOUTH BITERS OF STURGEON HOLE

Sturgeon Hole is the last, slow, deep pool before the Nitinat empties into the saltwater lake of the same name. Chinook, in coming from the tidal lake, rise completely into the mostly freshwater pool. On high-tide days, it rises a foot up here, and access to the pool is too deep—for humans, that is. Not for fish. Not for bears.

Today a wave spills over the tailout of the pool, spills upstream, a wave of fish, so many, I cannot stop myself backing out of the river out of fear the fish will mow me right down. The electricity is so strong I cannot tie a fly to my line—nor can I cast. I stand on the bank, concerned large fish will somehow come right out of the river and take me.

I have never felt frightened of fish before. The wave moves right on by, several thousand 20- to 45-pound Chinook. Had I remained in the water I would have been knocked over. That is what steroids do to fish en route to spawning. They become unable to resist their own hormones, become more than fish, in September sun that warms their day.

I have learned a thing or two about Chinook. In the early hours, in rain, they prefer pastels, bright, primary colours, and I make them simple flies, the Nitnook—a chartreuse and holographic tinsel fly, a Woolly Bugger knock-off. And, the Needle Nose, in chartreuse, peach, or white. I wrap 2/0 saltwater streamer hooks with chartreuse chenille, then two marabou feathers in the same colour and a rump of chartreuse wool, the kind gear fishers use. The cheapest is often the most effective thing for hooking Chinook and chum.

Among the five types of salmon bites in fresh water that I discuss later in this book, the most common is the passive bite. The fly or wool is floated downriver at eye level. They lie on the bottom and mouth whatever floats down to them. And then they let it go. That is why it is passive; the fish doesn't move and so the bite is registered only as a diddle in the float or slowing in passage of fly line. This is the first thing I was taught, on my first outing so many years ago, more than two decades.

I am halfway up the pool, at the spot where most Chinook come to rest. The wave that rushed past me will turn at the head, 200 yards above, and disperse, bodies of fish flowing back into this deep, sweet, yielding crease on the opposite side among many logs where the river makes a subtle turn. This spot does not look any better than any other in the deep softness of Sturgeon Pool, but this is without doubt the hotspot. And, I suppose, there must be a cool spring come up here that changes the water's taste and temperature. Changes it enough to make them stop and line up together, waiting for rain to carry them forward.

I have developed the Tutu, a white Woolly Bugger with a bell of chartreuse or pink or peach wool. Get this one wet and you will see its gorgeous shape, its simplicity, the reason a Chinook will touch it. And the bite of Chinook, like that of pink salmon, is very slight. The fish stops the fly but does not move, and you strike up hard.

Across the way, a male black bear comes down the bank toward me. He looks at me and his front legs disappear into the river, then his head, his body, and I am backing out of the river when he reappears, dragging a 30-pound Chinook in his mouth.

As I have mentioned, contrary to the ballet TV shots of bears catching fish in the air, real black bears are clumsy. Sure, they can catch fish, but they prefer dead ones they drag out of the river. Eat the meat behind the head or brain and leave the body to rot a couple of weeks before it smells tasty. In between, they have been hauling out fish all day long and placing them in the forest where I come upon, next spring, the bones, all that is left of flesh that has made the transit back to soil. Calcium in the bones, the cartilage, keeps them from disappearing for years. I find them in dark spots among mushrooms. I pass the same white pick-up-sticks bits of ribs, jaws and vertebrae many times over the years.

The bear backs up the bank, hunkers down and tears a lump from the fish's back. And watches me, across the river, where I believe I am safe, because invisible fluid separates us. The bear watches me and my rod, sloshing up and down, pliers in my mouth, drool coming down my chin. Its head actually moves to watch me frothing the water in chase, as though I am its entertainment while it eats dinner, like TV for the forest.

When I am down on my hands and knees in the water, hand barely closing around the waist of the anal peduncle, the bear rises as though cheering me on, and of course I wave, like a gladiator, for, yes, I am a warrior questing after noble prey. I'm almost getting misty eyed when it claps for me and puts its thumb down. I shake my head and, instead, take my drool-covered pliers from my mouth and turn the hook out of a mouth that is large enough to hold both my fists. The fish turns its head like Stevie Wonder, and its body follows it back to the black anonymity that is cheek-by-jowl Chinook salmon. The black there on the opposite side is 5,000 to 10,000 of them, side by side, finning and waiting. Tons of flesh, stopping my flies.

After a few years of fishing, I have come to understand it is easy to snag a salmon in such circumstances. My fly drops among them and the river moves it through. Among so many bodies, a wall of flesh, really, the fly and fly line contact many. The feeling is transmitted up the fly line to my rod's stripping finger with its red spandex "glove." I feel instantly a fish's touch and strike up hard.

The fight can last half an hour, fish moving downriver, stealing my expensive fly line, stealing dozens of yards of backing—use no less than 30-pound, because a fly line is 20-pound strength. And when it begins to tire, I retrieve three feet. But then it takes three feet. Then I take three feet. But then it takes three feet and so on. This "bite," the one hardest on both man and beast, is the dorsal fin bite.

Here is the concept: all fish are biters, they just bite with different parts of their bodies. There are mouth biters, fin biters, tail biters, dorsal fin biters and so on. The fight I have just had is the dorsal fin biter. And it goes on far too long. When, finally, the fish is subdued, and the man worn out, the fly is found in the flesh in front of the dorsal fin.

The dorsal fin bite is the most common of the non-mouth biter bites. This is because the dorsal fin sticks up higher than any other part of the fish, and when the line rasps over the back and the hook is set, or sets itself, it does so right at the dorsal fin and the struggle between man and beast begins. After many such fruitless struggles—the purpose in fly fishing after all is to get the fish to bite the fly, not foul hook itself—I begin to understand.

With a wall of flesh before you, you can foul hook—and it's against the law, if you do it *intentionally*—a 40-pounder every cast. But that's not fishing, that's snagging. The method for taking Chinook that bite, in slow water, comes after many days of handling as many as 25 foul-hooked fish and 25 properly-hooked fish—"processing" fish, almost a ton of weight a day. It comes that I have to find a method of telling the difference between mouth biters and fin biters.

Instead of striking every touch, I stop and begin to feel in my fingers, when the rasp of a back or whatever has occurred. When I feel flesh, I do not strike, and this saves many foul hooks. And I start stripping in short, few-inch pulls. My fingers begin to feel the stop of Chinook on the fly, and when it doesn't. *Slippery fingers* is what I call it. If a body part is touched, I let my fingers be so light the hook slides off the fish.

After another year, I start using circle hooks. Circle hooks were developed for conservation purposes, but I begin using them to reduce the number of foul hooks; the hook point is so curled around it will not sink into flesh anywhere near as often as a regular hook with its pointy point. When I use these, my foul hooks decrease to almost zero. And the opposite, fair hooks, increase, so virtually all the Chinook are cleanly, fairly hooked, not flossed (line insinuated through the mouth, so the hook hooks the outside of the mouth on the far side of the fish, from the outside, through the gill plate).

Somedays gear fishermen, those with pencil lead and peach wool, dink floats or no floats at all, push me from the main part of the pool and I look around for other options. They can easily cast 90 feet to the other side—a greater feat with a single-handed fly rod—and begin reeling slowly. When hook contacts flesh, they yank their rods and chase the fish up and down the bank.

When, finally, the fish is subdued, hook taken from dorsal fin, the proud angler holds his catch for a photograph, perhaps the first 40-pound fish of his life. There's nothing wrong with his appreciation of his good fortune to have captured such a large predator. What's wrong is he does not understand he has snagged the fish, and, more importantly, hasn't really been fishing at all. It does not register when he is smiling, or groaning at his fifteenth fish, that when you cast across a wall of flesh and reel in, you will automatically foul hook a fish. There is nothing illegal about this, because most of the anglers are not intending to foul hook the fish, it just happens, and they think that in the fish's clumsiness that it has missed the hook in its mouth. After all, chum in freshwater are the clumsiest fish when it comes to biting a fly or lure—most hook-ups in the chin or nose or shoulder result from such clumsiness. Why not Chinook, they may reason, if they reason at all? But at the heart of it, the issue is the angler doesn't understand the fish is snagged. He thinks he has, as a great angler, caught a great fish and that is all.

And sometimes, smoking their cigarettes and bending their rods, they look over at me, as at a poor relative, someone who does not quite get it. And perhaps, they think, they should say something to me, so their good luck can be passed along.

Well, I just continue casting my fly to the other side, and feeling it drop. And I find, if I resist striking, I sometimes feel more than one bite as the fly drops through the zone. Occasionally, three or four Chinook touch the fly passively, and let it go. And only when I set the hook do I do so, knowing it is in the mouth of the fish. The trick is to feel the stop, the small stop that is Chinook taking a fly.

My understanding of technique goes unnoticed. "Ah, ya finally caught one, did ya?" is offered to cheer me up. And I nod my approval—every fish I catch is hooked in the mouth. So, I *catch* a dozen 30-pounders in a day, that I have actually caught, not snagged. But I don't offer my opinion. These people are in an earlier stage of evolution in their appreciation of salmon fishing in freshwater; each fish stuns you right off your feet, and you spend your year waiting with images of huge fish, September sun and October rain.

Oh, and there are those who use 12-pound test and think it sporting. That is another stage in evolution, when they scowl at me, using 20-pound leader. What they don't see is: they are breaking off big fish when a couple of hundred feet has been taken. Then they sit on the gravel, knees splayed, pull the remaining line from the reel, dump it on the ground and load another 12-pound line.

This isn't sporting. The fish trailing the line sooner or later snaps it off and it wraps over the river bottom or ends up on shore, where guys like me put it in our pockets, take the mile-long trail to the car and the 100 miles to the garbage. Low-pound test is not sporting, because it breaks every time. Use 20-pound as standard and, if you break off at all, you break at knots or nicks close to the tag end.

I keep my opinions to myself unless I become friends with the angler, as happens over a few years of us both showing up at the same pool in the same month of September, and then, once the person will not take offence, I point out the flaw in thinking 12-pound is sporting.

And of course, there is always the biggest fish. It's particularly nice when it happens to leap right in front of the snaggers and leaves a splash the size of a Volkswagen Beetle—my car of the '60s. This fish makes all the anglers back up as I race after it in the shallows and then race back upstream again. And finally, when I have the fish at my side, the size of a wolfhound—60 pounds, the largest salmon I have ever caught—I cannot get my hand around the wrist of its tail. Hell, I can't get my hand spread as far as the width of its peduncle. I can only push the fish against my chest. Then I find I cannot lift it from the water and have to drop on my knees and hoick it up to sit on my thigh. Yes, very satisfying to have all the anglers at Sturgeon Hole stand and give me applause.

I have had my own evolution. I have come to double-handed fly rods after 10,000 salmon. It comes when I have grown enough to wish for symmetry and beauty in the cast. When a Double Spey or overhead cast rolls out more than 100 feet and allows me to fish the tail out of Sturgeon Pool where most fishermen cannot reach. The gear guys want the "Honey Hole," as they call it. The single-handers need closer fish, too. But with the big double-hander and a few casts one executes perfectly, the line shoots right into the backing. Now, that is evolution. I can watch it and do it all day long. If there were a job classification for "sports fisherman," I'd certainly apply. I'd be willing to work every day. Do overtime. Seven days a week. You want it, you got it. I'm still waiting as my line unfurls to the farthest Chinook in the tailout. And the shy stop that is the greatest bite.

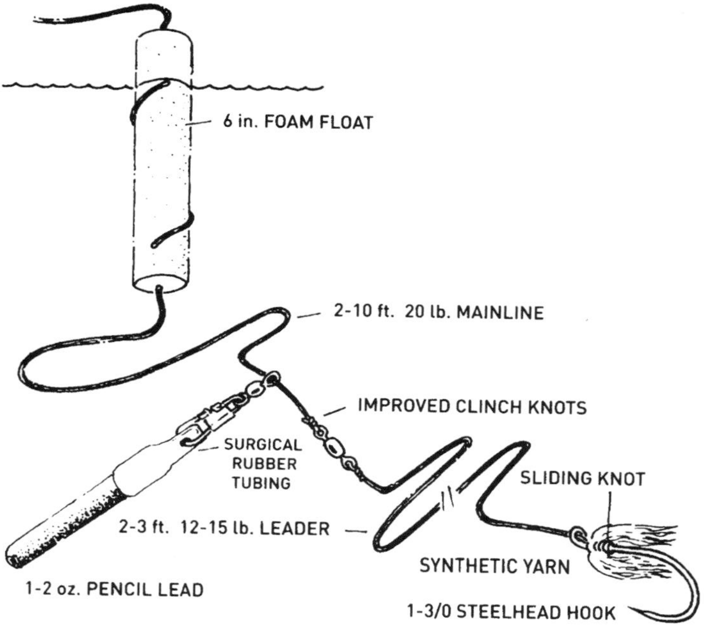

Dink float setup for gear fishing.

Chapter 20

BEARS

Fear nothing but one bear.
– adapted from Rollo May

There are days when I am alone. When leaves are golden in their dying. Spawned-out carcasses paste the trees in late September. Light comes later to my windshield and leaves a little sooner. These are the days when bears come. I walk the deserted streets of this river when it is sections Richard Brautigan took apart and left in storage for the freshet of spring.

Trout Fishing in America does not talk of bears. It has no need, because the rivers in their dusty fly-speck warehouses do not bear salmon. And thus, they do not smell of death. The bodies that were green are now softer than a finger's touch. All around me on the gravel of The Seam, Cutt Corner, Glory Hole and Sturgeon. I arrive before other human beings and leave a little later.

Where there is my car, there is a bear and her cub in the moving trees. Or should I say there *was,* because the story of bears is like wind; it moves through leaves and leaves only that as proof of passing. Or the one-and-a-half-year-old cub, on its own, at Worthless Pool that stood and smelled the air. Smelled the smell of me and came to water's edge to gauge the trouble it would have, having had no teaching in gathering meat.

On the other side, I saw the little bear should not be alone. It should be following a mother who would teach it. I tossed a little spinner it watched plop and whir away. It smelled me again, and my lure plopped at its feet a dozen times until it got the message: I was too much trouble to bring down for a meal or two.

Of course, there is lunch all around us. As I have said, salmon do not swim through trees, they do not swim in air. When found a hundred yards into forest, they have been taken to the kitchen of the bear that will eat them. And they are regular in their habits when the amount of death lying around exceeds their ability to eat. Eating kills what is eaten, whether carrot or clover. I remember the chum I walked through almost going under the year the river scoured the land. It came to me: the whole corner was 12 feet higher than it had been before Europeans came to carry away trees and let the mountains down hard. That much logging gravel over a century.

This is from a day a bear rifled my packsack, neatly took out my lunch, and ambled into the forest with me in hot pursuit. It plopped on its rump, lifted its head high, crunched the Coke can in his teeth and drank the Coke, proving that bears understand Coke. Looking at all the tooth holes in the can, I decided to take it with me on a quick retreat, and now it sits on my mantle above my fireplace.

In days when cool is in the air and sun no longer bears its strength, I have come to understand bears; they follow their noses to so much food they tolerate each other more than other seasons. I yell my "Hey" and "Hey-ah" to the valley, cross my chest with my fist and go down through mud and water, walk roots that take me through forest that ends at the river. Trees cannot withstand years of Nitinat wind. When one is exposed, it takes the beating it can until the wind, one day, turns its roots into the aftermath of galaxies.

I cross the stream that is bog, an old channel, and up through Queen Anne's lace that snaps with my passage. There is wild rose and its tousle-haired flower with a small yellow eye. There is nettle that stays on my skin, pulsing my hand all day. I remember it for the pain that tells me to.

I cross the wasteland where trees leave themselves in the seething that is living greenery. On the wet coast, they submit to decomposition, leaving skeletons I use to pull myself up and over and down, through holes in roots torn apart. It is 7:30 and the mother and two cubs are not yet in this little bit of undefended land. They will be later, when I return.

By the time I am casting, the big brown bear that follows its nose around pads the long, dead tree on the other side where salmon make rain fall up in their passage over shallow land. He does not bother me. He takes a rotten fish and his brown-black body into the woods. I will not see him before two jars of sand drain down.

There are other bears I have come to know. And they know me. I have not the temerity to put out my hand, as one would do to a dog. There is an injured one who comes from behind my back. She does so now when the zzt of chartreuse fly line lights the air with noise. A sow without her cubs, leg bent as though it has an extra elbow. She has survived the winter with her broken leg and is now behind me in the wind. She scents the tuna in my sandwiches, the sweetness in my oatmeal cookies. She edges closer, from log to willow, to gravel behind my pack.

I could turn and touch her nose with the end of my fly rod. And I want my sandwiches, my cinnamon and raisin cookies. I put on a special fly that drops among a thousand Chinook, rumbling their size and impatience. I can select the coho from among them. Only a few are there, but they dash past every Chinook to hit a tiny piece of metal, or Flashabou.

The fish when taken from her element is to be pitied. Her magic of flying in the invisible has been stolen by the man who hooks her cleanly, hook sharpened on the stone he keeps on his chest. Her head, when she wriggles into frenzy, feels the boot heel of sympathy. The snap of death and her flanks shiver in transit to death.

The meal I pick up in a hand with many scars. Teeth of coho and Chinook and most particularly chum, are the stuff of needle and make my autumn hand a pin cushion of pain. The blood on my fingers is mostly my own. I always say: fishing and my blood go together. In my turning, the broken sow turns away. The coho is launched head over tail, its 12 rays of black fibre. The fish hits gravel in front of her face, a bear so much smaller than she would be if able to deal with her life.

It is raining, and I should put my hood over my hat, so I don't get wet down my vest and white-skinned chest. But I can't hear what is behind me and don't trust the sow, ones that may follow from the trees.

I pass upriver, bullet of green passing backward, forward, and like a palm, turning over its fly near trees the river has pushed into the opposite bank. Hours go by, sound of line moving through air. The big bear has taken his nap and once more appears from the green, each paw secure on wet stump and log. He takes another carcass from the water and backs up the bank, footprints like those of chubby humans. Rain has been the only sound, but now there is the sound of flesh in teeth, meat pulling from brain and neck.

Then the bear retires to its rainy home. The next time I will see it is 1 o'clock and it will come from the top end of Sturgeon, where water deepens into green. It will thread the opposite bank until it finds another lunch and again the flesh will rip.

I am alone with autumn thoughts. My breath I can see like the end of words that were on fire in my mouth. Rain goes on blistering my face. My glasses are streaked with what comes at me. My rod moves forward, my hand tugs the line and the line is a tongue laying out its Needlenose fly. The weighted offering I let sink and feel in my stripping finger what is happening. The fly line is a small white cord resting on the bottom.

I need not fear the fly growing accustomed to the rocks. A circle hook holds its sting within its circle. When the line continues its journey, only then do I lift the rod. I know it is a Chinook before I see it. As I will mention again in the technical section that follows these stories, Chinook are the only salmon that will follow a lure or fly down—well, a chum may do this, too, but only very few—and when it reaches bottom, gently pick up the other-looking object and rise, steel between its teeth.

It does not do this to eat, because it has ceased to do so. Freshwater has told the fish behind its brain, there will be no more eating. And it is not out of passion, curiosity, out of aggression ... perhaps, like the magpie, attracted to something out of place. This behaviour is its undoing. Fly line zings water like a blade. In the deep, the circle hook finds its mark in jaw.

I sigh when this fish is brought to my knees and I bend in the river. Red pliers remove the sting from black teeth in a black mouth. I sigh because no one is here, and I have no reason to hold tight to my share of shore. I sigh because I am weary with this ... *life's work*: bringing never-ending fish to hand, the magical animal, and the hand letting go.

The head of Sturgeon is changed from its past. It was deeper than sight and 30 feet wide, a hundred yards long. That was before the river choked out gravel carried down from Glory, the next slough up. It is deposited in Sturgeon's head, 100,000 cubic yards of silt and gravel let down from mountains when finger roots let go.

Above me is a bear, head under water, searching the shallows. It searches with claws that hold a fish decisively, unlike the human, come slowly, eyes on the ground. To my "Hey ... hey-ah" the bear lifts black wet nostrils and moves into forest. I will see him again. He will sleep the sleep of those with green eyes in a month when there is more than all the bears in the forest can eat.

My feet scuff gravel and I have no thoughts. None are needed, and none come when I am doing Dennis. The coho, Chinook follow me, backs of silver, of black, leaving furrows like ploughs in the gravel. They plant their kind and water brings the next yellow eyes when winter passes away.

My feet take me the half mile up to Glory. When I arrive, the hard part starts. The river is slow but still moves deep, up to my chest. I cast into shadow, where windows of light show chum are moving. The river is always moving, with itself or life it holds, thousands of caddis larvae, stick-walking their lone, tan, algal world. Tick tack of little black feet and a tongue eats across a rock. So many I am not able to avoid killing, with each fall of the foot.

My pliers are in my mouth. When dog is brought to hand and teeth find a way through neoprene, wetness finds me there. Later I will find blood down my thigh, but now, I drop my rod, wrap line around my arm and pull the mulberry male to pliers. Pincers go down the shank and turn over the point.

I do not feel anything, and this is good. I am doing what animals do: living their lives. They need no monuments. Fish need not make long noses caress bones of ancestors. Each leaves its body and one orange egg. I am at peace, taking fish. No need to justify my existence because I feel it existing.

When I turn downstream, my eyes swing from fir, to cedar, to hemlock, to blackness in the river: bear and bear and bear and bear and bear. There really are five bears in front of me. They could kill me, but I no longer fear that will happen

"Hey-ah," I say and hold my rod like a cross, like the guy in *Platoon* who beats himself as the helicopter carries Sheen away to his grandmother, his war now over, though it will live in him a very long time.

My feet follow one another. One brown boot over algae-brown rocks, then the next. They keep walking, as though looking for the last piece of stream Brautigan placed in a special place for those who will move through point of thorn and blackberry sucker. The bears fall open and I flow through.

When I am with my fish at Sturgeon, the sleeping bear has again taken the rocks. He pads the opposite shore, foot for foot with me. I wait upon the tailout, where water is shallower than tails the shape of hands. He appears on his log, moves down to swamp that sends yellow penises and their skunk cabbage smell from leaves four feet long.

He walks his log. I walk my shore, fish on my shoulder. His nose can smell an atom of salmonberry, salal, and flickers through me. I smell of food. "Hey-ah," I say, passing in forest at river's end. The little bear is up its white alder in Nitinat wind, with a mother who almost killed me another day. I walk slowly, eyes down, away from the tree, through the Queen Anne's lace, and ivy, the thorn and nettle that burns my hand.

Across the swamp and through the mud, I pass with pudgy prints that slip until claws dig in. When I put in my finger, the hole is deeper. The key does its opening purpose. The fish is flung down, yellow eye staring at nothing. Slime keeps coming long after life has gone away.

My jacket peels wet from clothes, my waders roll down. I stand on a mat in autumnal rain in a forest growing old. I pull one leg up, holding down the waders' toe with the other foot. Pull, stand, pull, stand. I reach the point where I can neither pull my leg free, nor put my body back in. My eyes look up into a big black hulk of bear, walking his pigeon-toed walk.

He swings his head along the ground and looks at me. Stuck in my neoprene, I bowl the only food I have left, an apple, at its mouth. It curves down the track until the big boar vacuums the small fruit and keeps on coming. This is the time I climb into my hatch and close it. I am in my little piece of river bank propped against a dusty wall, listening for the sound of flesh, in its padding, walk past my own.

This big black bear looks close to me because he was – ten feet from my nose. The people behind me were pulling on my jacket to make me retreat. Of course, they kept me between them and the bear the whole time they were yanking, so that if anyone was going to get eaten, it would be me.

Bear Tracks – There are bear tracks everywhere in the woods. These were in the winter sand at Rock No Rock Pool, and looked just like pudgy, pigeon-toed human footprints.

Chapter 21

THE NAMES I HAVE GIVEN AND THE NAMES I HAVE RECEIVED

Over three decades, I have come to know my river better than anyone else. I fish it 50 times per year, a number more than it warrants. Yes, there are other rivers on my island in the ocean that bear getting known more intimately. But now I know the bends and character of my river that only long hours can reveal. Places where I can take a steelhead because I know not to step in and cast, or to go down and take a careful look, come back and cast, or stand above and run a fly into the water, in the correct spot that if there is a fish, it will bite.

I have looked for and found every access point on my river. This is best done in winter, when there is no foliage to shove your way through, and because, without foliage, you see the river far sooner than in the 10-foot jungle of second-growth, huckleberry, salmonberry and so on, in summer. Where you see sun, or clearing, is where the river is. There are a few dozen access points. I will tell you only one, because I want you to come to value the Nitinat over many years. Then your footprint in nature will be small. Purchase a topographical map, like the Backroad Mapbook, and pay your dues on this or any river you choose.

The access I'll point out leads into Rock No Rock Pool, just the Lake Cowichan side of Granite Creek Main, where road is slowly being eaten by runoff. Just a side track that can be easily missed. Keep your eyes open and find a pathway of beauty unlike any other on the river.

Behind the second growth by the road is a section of old-growth forest that was never cut down. You will hear the silence as you step over the edge. Old growth is dim and without growth other than moss and sprawling fern. It is easy to move around trees ten feet wide and so tall you cannot see their tops.

The trail passes down a 25-foot gulley and right back up the other side. This is an old railway grade, though it looks like a small ravine. Then slide down among great, old, cathedral trees that are so few, on the steep path I have worn over the years, walking up and down. Move to the river-side tangle where a spring comes out and muddies the bank. There, as though intended for you, is a riffle so shallow it seldom gets your thigh wet. Where you cross, you are just above Rock No Rock Pool and Big Bend. But, in summer, you really want to fish the run just above: Glass.

A drift boat is better in autumn flow and sometimes winter. The Nitinat is too shallow any other time of year. That's what I have come to love: its human size. You can cross back and forth on a day of wading, even as it changes almost every rain. I cannot say the same of other rivers of great change and character that I know.

Now, let me turn to the names of the runs and pools of this river that changes so much you will find many old channels from scores of years ago, here and there among white alder trees. From the top end of the river, the names:

1. **Parker Creek**—the top boundary of fishable water is where you drop off your drift boat, for your trip down the river. The access road is around the corner from the second bridge on the Nitinat Road, sometimes called the North Shore Road. The tailout at the top can hold cutthroat and steelhead. Always run a fly through it. The opposite side is a nice run that runs the entire corner for 300 yards. In salmon season, close to your

feet is also good for coho and Chinook. The bottom tailout, a beauty of multicoloured rocks the size of basketballs, sometimes yields a coho or cutthroat.

2. **Parker Rapid**—this is where your oarsman better be your best. This is the only rapid on this mild river, and a spot where the occasional steelhead/cutthroat may be taken. It is a dim place and very slippery, the kind most anglers pass right through without trying. As mentioned, if you make yourself religiously fish this and other shady spots you will catch many more fish, because they mean safety to fish. Fish will hold more commonly than they will in sun. Most fishermen know this, but most walk right through shade because it is cold, gloomy and spooky, and they do not want to fish in it. That is a great error, for there are untouched fish in untouched water.

3. **Teaspoon**—a neat little spot where the Nitinat splits into Parker Rapid, and this lesser flow, the shape of a teaspoon on the left. In years of high flow, when the gravel has been pushed through, it can hold a few dozen coho. Get down on your knees and toss across your spinner. Have the thrill of watching a specific fish chase down your lure and make it his own.

4. **Parker Pool**—the pool at the bottom of the rapid looks very inviting and holds coho, cutthroat and the occasional steelhead. It is difficult to fish because of the conflicting currents, back eddy, their speed and trees over the right bank. The pool starts far up and it is difficult to get yourself in the middle of the river where you must be to start plumbing the head, particularly the brown water before the drop-off, for cutthroat. It is easy to be swept off your feet here, and you will be carried a long way in deep water before you can get out. Coho sit to the right of the current line, under the tree branches into the deep water of the right bank—you will need a boat to reach the other side. When there are many coho, come back to the left side of the pool and fish the water from there, too.

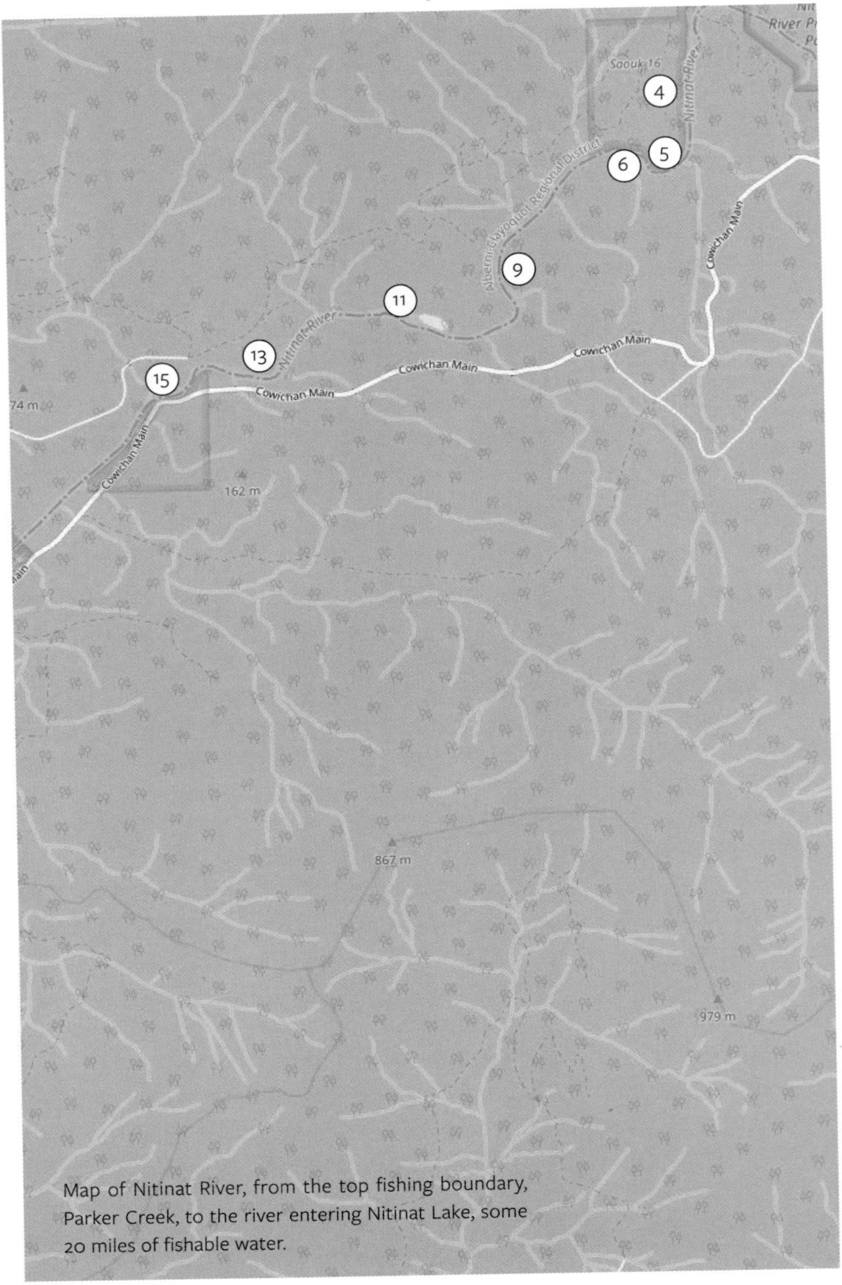

Map of Nitinat River, from the top fishing boundary, Parker Creek, to the river entering Nitinat Lake, some 20 miles of fishable water.

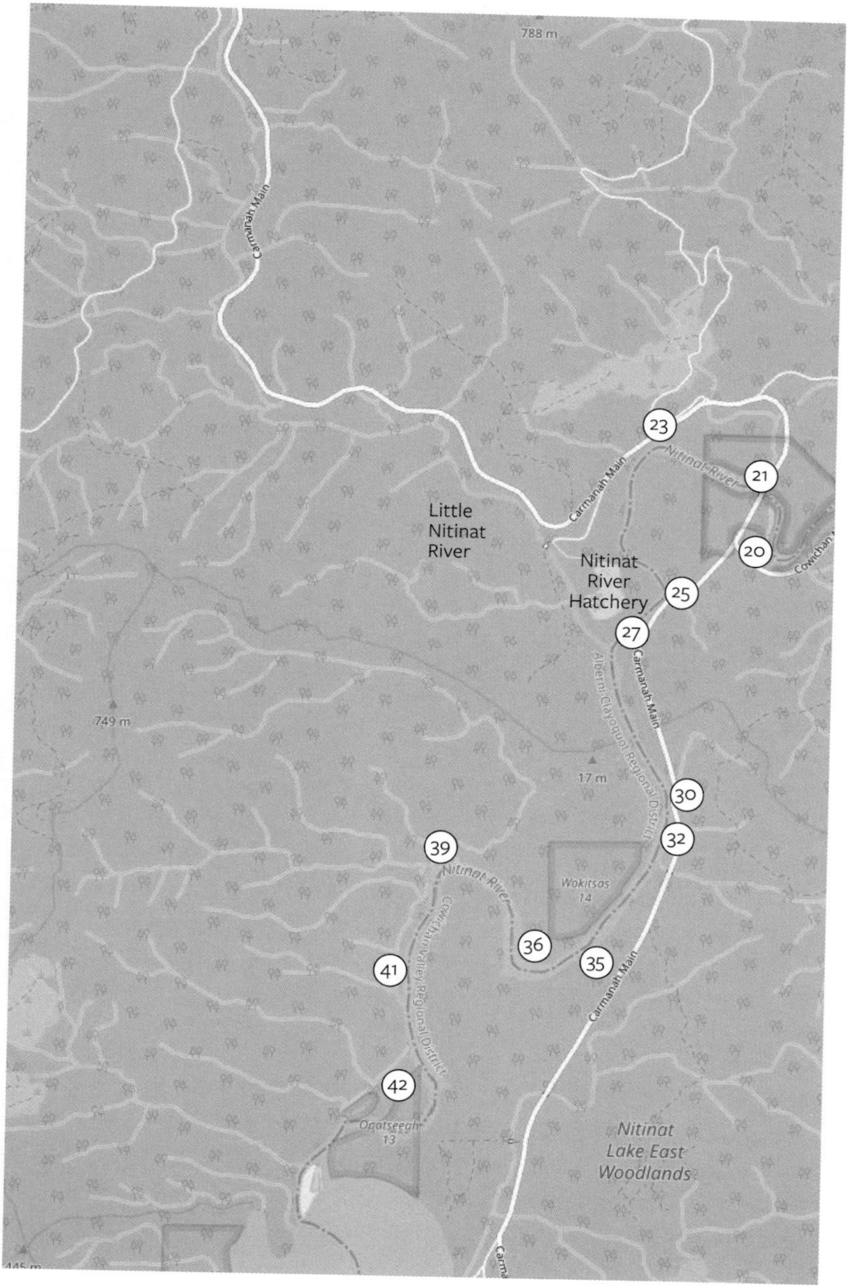
788 m
Carmanah Main
23
Nitinat River
21
Little
Nitinat
River
Carmanah Main
20
Cowichan
Nitinat
River
Hatchery
25
27
Carmanah Main
Alberni-Clayoquot Regional District
749 m
17 m
30
32
39
Nitinat River
Wokitsas
14
Cowichan Valley Regional District
36
35
41
Carmanah Main
42
Opatseeah
13
Nitinat
Lake East
Woodlands

Below the pool, the run moves down almost a half mile. All is good spawning gravel in higher water. If you are on foot don't bushwhack this section of river—left bank—down to Diagonal Pool. It is old-growth crud and new-growth crud and you will be covered in sweat by the time you decide to turn around. Also, remember: if you wade down, you will have to wade all the way back up, against the current—a hard thing in water the top of your thigh.

5. **Diagonal Run**—Just where the unnamed seasonal creek enters Parker Run at its lower end is a deep spot where coho hold on the left. On the right, good-looking woody debris ends in spawning gravel. Then the river bears right and flows over larger rocks, the backbone of which runs on a diagonal across the river, hence the name for this major coho pool. It is where I caught my first winter steelhead on the fly. Work this one all the way through to just before the tailout—for coho. Here you may spot winter steelhead in their twos and threes; the softest water on the right side is just the right spot of small gravel for them to spawn. You may miss them for many years and then spot them just as they spot you.

6. **Tree Island**—This is a good producer of trout, where the river splits around some alder and dumps itself into what looks like an exceptional spot for steelhead. It *is*, on the far left, but not on the right. Intend to fish the left channel, if you can reach it, then where the third channel enters halfway down the pool. Refer to Where the Steelhead Have Met Me for more thorough instructions. In the tailout below I have seen coho, Chinook and, strangely, sockeye spawning—so bright red they look, so out of place. The tailout of this spot does hold fish during spawning. And the deeper crease on the far right should be fished after the brown water on the left has been probed.

7. **Crossover**—The river bears left, and the far right shore occasionally holds a steelhead or cutthroat. Bear in mind, for wading, that the bottom end of this run is deeper than it looks, and the shallower water faster than it looks. Here, in a

short, fast run, the river changes from a right to left-hand bank and then back again. Run a fly under the willow branches on the left. They are growing tall now, and it is no longer safe on foot down the left. However, the river changed course some years ago, and there is a conflicted pool on the bottom right. You must stand mid-river to catch the right-hand water that is brown and boiling. This is easier said than done on foot.

Take a kickboat instead, a rubber raft style with a hole and seat in the middle. The back eddy on the right is a sleeper for coho, trout, and summer steelhead. Coho await the highest flood of fall to rise up the seasonal creek. You can tell coho fry by their orange tails, and thus, if you find them in spring or summer in a side creek, there will be a deep, soft spot in the mainstem close by for coho to wait in fall. Running the half mile below Crossover is a shallow, narrow run on the right, that can hold a summer steelhead in November. The rest of the year, don't waste time fishing this stretch unless the bottom has been gouged by a stranded log; this is good advice for the entire river.

This is a section, common on this river, where logging damage has occurred. Even though the loggers and their bosses moved on, what they did remains, and another 50 years will be needed to repair the damage. Added to this, the 2018 cut of second growth on the north shore will also deposit gravel in the river for years, and it will be a long time before it is spit out into Nitinat Lake.

8. **Switch**—This is where the river switches its flow to the left-hand bank. Keep your eyes open for winter steelhead spawning on the left in May. Steelhead sit just where the run spills under large trees. Switch is a difficult pool to fish; you must walk directly down the middle of the river, while each side veers down—like the bottom end of Parker Run—as you try to reach and plumb the left bank under the large cedar. If you clamber down the left-hand bank one day, a good thing to do on any river you intend to understand, you will find a ledge of rock right under the cedar that holds the occasional summer steelhead, with cutthroat in the woody debris just below. And then walk down to Glass.

9. **Glass Run**—This rock wall, half-mile run, on a warm summer afternoon, can be the most glorious place to fish on the entire river, with a 6-weight, single-handed rod, a good casting line and good shooting head. Alternatively, use one with a very long taper designed for maximum distance that will unfurl 80- to 90-feet, so your fly drops within a foot of the woody debris on the other side on a 45-degree angle.

You seem able to see every last sand grain and would bet there hasn't been a fish here in a thousand years. Have faith and don't drill the cast, scattering the surface. A fish will come out of thin, well, water, to become one with your Courtney fly, a tarted up Woolly Bugger, chubby, with a gold bead eye, #4 to #8 bronze hook, black Glo-brite chenille, purple, orange, yellow, black, red, olive, maroon, etc. marabou with similar colours in hackle and Schlappen. My favourite is olive marabou under red Schlappen. You will be surprised that where you think there are zero fish a trout will reach out and shake your hand. Also use rubber-legged, black, bead head nymphs in summer months. Stoneflies, too.

In 2005, an undercut, six-foot diameter Douglas fir was leaning so far the top was all the way across the river into the forest. Marvel at such things, but do not stand under them. They weigh 10 tons—or more.

Another odd phenomenon happens here some years. One day I was standing on the shore, among algaed rocks dried as though in tan paper pulp. I caught a movement in the corner of my eye and looked down, but there was nothing there.

I went back to looking up and up the leaning tree, so far I was almost falling over backwards. Then another movement, beside my boot. I looked down and kept looking down. Soon, a small brown thing moved. I bent over and picked up something so tender, I feared I would break its little bones between my ponderous thumb and finger. It was little more than a quarter of an inch. A little frog or toad. And when I bent to put it down, I could see, a few inches in front, beside and behind my boots, a dozen small brown creatures, sitting or moving.

When I looked up, all around as far as I could see were tiny creatures. I realized they were toads, because the egg mass I found here earlier in the summer was feet long, and not at all like the clusters of a frog (and frogs will seldom leave eggs in a river of rock—they would get washed away). I lifted one boot but couldn't put it down, as I would have killed something. So, on one foot, I slowly jumped my way into the river, finding so many black tadpoles I could not put down a foot without killing some.

For the next few minutes, as I moved downstream, there were more and more small brown toads. So unlikely, because the first heron or kingfisher or merganser that found them would make a quick meal, poking here and there. Perhaps that was why there were many hundreds of these tiny brown toads; so at least a few would be left to carry on the species. I moved out of the shadow of the leaning tree. It was not here the next time I came down. It had not just fallen over. It had been carried away.

By 2014, another tree had fallen, creating good cutthroat water; also coho, because they cross from a left bank to a right bank across a riffle into a scoured pool, and a good place to stop.

10. **Rock No Rock Pool**—Depending on how much logging silt and gravel the river is pushing through, you may or may not see the rock, which is 10-by-10-by-12-feet—in other words, a huge rock. In some years, the silt is so deep you cannot see the rock at all. Hence the odd name—it is Rock Pool when the rock shows and No Rock when it does not.

At this spot there is also a very old cedar that is mostly just a silvered spire, so prominent it could also furnish a name. While I have taken a few trout here, and way into the corner, the back eddy pool below becomes more prominent on higher water, a good bet for coho. I say this because the next 600 yards of river looks like fabulous water, nice and deep, good rock structure, shade, but I have never touched a fish in the whole length. But in the tailout water, which is knee-deep to thigh-deep, is good spawning gravel utilized by both salmon and steelhead.

11. **Big Bend**—This describes an almost perfect arc over the course of 500 yards. This is the narrowest stretch of the entire Nitinat River. In summer, it is seldom even 20 feet across the upper end. In higher flow, this is a spot where you must be careful when using any kind of watercraft. The current wants to push

you under willows at the top end, so take care. The entire run your fly should be landed in the openings between branches and then let sink as it drifts under sweepers. This is a good trick to know, and it allows you to catch many fish—on any river, really—that other anglers miss. As mentioned, perfect your skill of landing a fly within a foot of your intended cast, until you can do it every time. Do it with boldness, because you can never learn by trying to slowly make your way there. Accept that you will lose many flies over the years by your fly landing too far into the weeds on the other side. When you can put the fly right on the inch you want, you will find fish are so impressed they come to you more often.

The middle of this run, where you are trying to walk along a 45-degree angle slope in the water, and under the branches, is where most trout hang out. Winter steelhead, too.

12. **Coho Alley**—As the name suggests, this is full of coho in fall. This is the one of which I say the coho are "all lined up," in the story of Autumn Beauty, a foot or two from the sides. This stretch of river is almost dead flat, and in November you may walk down the middle, casting at coho that stage here for up to two months. This is one of the fisheries that draws me the most, because it is late and everyone else has gone home. The only sound is water running away from itself. The access will take you a year to find, but here is a hint: cross the bridge on the Nitinat before turning off.

In the fall of 2005, where the run bears to the left on to Toilet Bowl, a log ground to a stop, and the river dug out the gravel in front of the root ball as much as 12 feet deep; that's how deep logging carnage can be. Note well though, because it demonstrates that you must fish what looks fishy, even though it is structure that may only be available for a month before another storm washes the root away. By the next year, for example, this root was gone and the pool completely filled so summer water was barely calf-deep and too warm to stop a trout.

13. **Toilet Bowl**—I hemmed and hawed in naming this pool—for a number of reasons. It has or had three rocks sticking out on the left as you look down. Hence it crossed my mind that it should be called Three Island Mile, but that seemed a stretch, so every time I thought of this pool, and every time I came into it—it does not produce much on low summer flow, hit it after a rainfall, in coho season—it kept wanting me to call it **Manhattan**, so in my mind it remains.

Generally, there are prosaic reasons behind the naming of pools, runs and riffles, for gear fishermen who came long before fly guys have often done the naming. On the Stamp, it is Money's (even though he called it the Great Pool) for Brigadier General Noel Money, and Paper Mill Dam because someone built a mill there for making low-quality wood into rags, and there was indeed a mill with a wheel. So, while this pool remains Manhattan to me, it is better called after the well-developed whirlpool it has in late fall. In high flows, the eddy looks so much like the turn in a toilet bowl that that is a better name.

The pool is a bitch to fish on foot because, if the water isn't low—and in the fall, it is up to your ribcage in the shallows—you have to bushwhack up the right-hand bank and it is a bugger. But the lower part of this pool can surprise you in coho season; with them on the edge between water running one way and the other in the middle of the back eddy—*the deepest part of the soft water*. You will be surprised that even though you don't see fish you will catch them. And, of course, this seldom-fished spot is right beside the road, though few anglers seem to know this.

14. **Autumn Beauty**—this is where I developed the technique for taking "all lined up" coho in the story of this name. The first time I fished in fall, I looked up, in water to my waist that was shaking me the way wind does a flag, and realized this short stretch of nondescript summer river is the most beautiful I have ever seen in late fall, with all the yellow leaves gone and with the crystal wetness of pungent colour. If you read my poetry, you will know that one of my interests is pushing the English language to say things it is not supposed to. Pungent works for me.

15. **Worthless Pool**—For the first time in 2005 this pool was joined through Autumn Beauty and Toilet Bowl, creating a pool half a mile long. This temporary event was the result, again, of tons of small gravel and silt choking the bottom end of Beauty and making the river into a long single pool. I stood on the gravel pushed out of Worthless Stream one day and calculated that in the previous winter, 3,000 cubic yards of gravel had been pushed down from the clear-cut above this one little stream into one pool. Disgraceful.

In 2006, standing in Worthless Creek, I let my little red and white bobber and spinner (like in the story of The Seam on a memorable day), run and stop, run and stop for almost 200 feet before I contacted coho and then four 20-pound fish in four casts, though I landed only one. Four days later I came back and all the gravel at the mouth of Worthless Stream, those 3,000 cubic yards, were gone. In high water, the river sliced it all away and I was standing in front of 12 feet of water where it had been only calf-deep. This is the power of raging water. It also illustrates an important thing to remember: a river drainage does not receive rain or snow melt uniformly along its length. Thus, in one flood the stream pushes out a tongue, and in another, when more precipitation falls higher on the main stem, that flow slices it off.

But the pool itself is usually the best one on the river for coho, and best fished from the backside—the side opposite to the Nitinat main road. The coho mill deep water just as the river bears right at the top end. In most years, just below Worthless Creek it's 15 feet deep and you also see coho circling. Very seldom do I see anyone when two inches of rain comes down, but it is spectacular for coho. Don't sit home watching football.

16. **Worthless Run**—A gorgeous run starting from Worthless tailout, filled with big boulders in red, orange, white, and green. Fish the tailout before moving down. The run fishes best when you are struggling a bit to hold your feet among the boulders—and these are tippy boulders. The run is a definite bet for steelhead, as it is holding water in a pocket water spot. Don't ignore that the bottom end on the left side has water almost to waist-deep that you must turn and deal with directly and not simply walk through

while concentrating on the other side of the river. I have taken steelhead one foot from the left bank willows.

17. **Jasper Creek**—Under the second culvert above the T-junction, Jasper Creek flows most, and sometimes all year. This is a sleeper for coho that doesn't look promising because of the complex back eddy—100 yards long, with deep, weedy, muddy, shady water on the left. Uninviting for sure. And with the back eddy setting up halfway down and flowing back up to the run, it can be a very difficult to fish with a fly and even with a spinner. Remember: coho only bite facing up-current. If you keep this rule in mind and figure out the back eddy you will avoid retrieving downstream and catch many more fish. Sometimes the run at the top end can be black with chum. Walk in above the riffle for cutthroat at the absolute top foot of the run, above where the creek enters.

18. **Useful Creek**—This is the most beautiful little creek on the entire river. I suggest you go down beside the first culvert above the T-junction and walk down it—only 50 yards long, but you'll savour every second. Rob Brouwer, manager of the Nitinat Hatchery, coined the name for this one.

19. **Corner Pool**—The first time I fished this strong back eddy pool, the soft part had accumulated a drift of chum eggs a dozen feet long and a few feet wide, all eggs drifted down from spawning activity, the current dropping them in virtually dead water. A drift of dead pink eyes, it seemed. This is an interesting corner in coho season, as you often find bity chum and coho on the other side of the current line. Toss your spoon or spinner all the way across into the back eddy and reel only fast enough to feel the blade thump on your rod tip—the reason for 10.5-foot rods being popular on Van Isle. This is one spot where you need to keep an eye on undercut trees high on the bank across from you. They regularly break loose.

20. **Boat Launch**—the boat launch above the Nitinat bridge is one of the best sleeper spots for coho. It is absolutely specific about the coho rule: coho bite only when the lure or fly is moving against the current. I regularly take fish under the noses of other fishermen, who stand on the rock above the back eddy and cast out into the fast river, ignoring the back eddy itself. The reason for the number of coho is: this area and up to the Corner Pool can be mainstream spawning ground for them (chum too, but only a few Chinook).

Kickboat and Log. This massive trunk swept around the corner above the boat launch in 2006 and cracked pieces off the bedrock it weighed so much. The inflatable craft is eight feet long. Compare it with the log to show just how enormous the log was. Still, the river was stronger. It reached out and grabbed the gargantuan log and moved it downstream in 2021, along with much of the riverbank.

Once you have plumbed the back eddy, from the rock, the middle of the back eddy and from the boat launch below, trundle across the Nitinat bridge in your car, turn right onto the first track and find your way up to the Corner Pool. Right across from the Boat Launch Pool, you will catch more coho because the new side-stream scours the main stream bottom into a good deep, slow slot and coho hold here. Stay out of sight—if the coho see you they won't bite. It is surprising more anglers don't take this precaution, as not doing so vastly reduces the number of fish they catch.

The second most frequent problem is, unless you are float fishing, keeping the rod tip high in the air while reeling in a spinner or lure. Your tip should be low because you can't set a hook on a bite with a high tip, and thus will lose many fish that an angler who keeps his tip in the water will not. And a third thing: a bent, kirbed hook keeps the hook in the fish's mouth far better than a straight Siwash, particularly for coho, because they roll so frequently. And use your heaviest drag for coho, for their rolling behaviour.

21. **Bridge Pool**—Does it always seem the best pools are right under bridges and this makes getting down to the fish next to impossible? This pool must be experienced from standing on the bridge in sunny September watching many thousand Chinook of 20- to 45-pounds relentlessly circling and helplessly jumping and fritzing around because of hormones. This pool is closed during salmon season because people used to stand on the bridge and jig fish with big treble hooks. There is no railing on the bridge, and 25 logging trucks go across each day—not a good place to fish even if it weren't closed.

Stand on the bridge and see if you can see steelhead in the tailout below and fish accordingly. Steelhead stop just above the bridge, too, where the riffle falls into broiling water on summer's low. Completely plumb the water all the way back for cutthroat. A Spey or switch rod gives access to well over half the pool. If water height allows, cross the river and climb onto the right bridge abutment and Spey the river tailout. Check the right-side woody stuff for trout. Just below the bridge on the left is good for coho, when the pool opens for fishing.

22. **Nickel**—A small run below the Bridge Pool, on the left. Most years, a tree will be deposited and gravel scoured enough to hold trout. In winter add the occasional winter steelhead.

Note that if you are on foot, Nickel can be next to impossible to reach because you have to cross the right channel of the river, which is getting deeper. I've almost been carried away in this deceptively speedy spot several times—dangling on the toe of one boot like a drunken fool.

23. **Stump Pool**—From the bridge, a half mile down where the river turns left under a cliff. When you walk down, you will pass the end of the island where coho sometimes stage, because they believe the right channel is a small creek. And there is also a seasonal creek entering this stretch on the right.

The Stump Pool received its name because of the prominent stump that stood a good eight feet high for decades, evidence that in the time of logging and probably for hundreds of years before, the tree was actually in the forest. Generally, anywhere you are looking at white alder trees, as to the right of Stump, you are looking at trees less than 50 years old, and thus where the river shifted its banks, sometimes from one side of the valley to the other, as evidenced by the three sloughs down Hobiton Main.

This is a trouty pool, as cutthroat like woody debris and slower water than steelhead. Logs exposed on the right-hand side were part of a gravel bank a few years ago. The pool proper drops to a good 10 to 12 feet deep, with good boulders in the middle. Standing directly up-current and feeding in line allows you to plumb the top half of this pool without having to deal with a beauty of a back eddy that turns your fly line in funny directions. This is where I took my first summer steelhead and where I hunted my first 10-pound summer doe, after falling through the vegetation.

The Nitinat Hatchery has identified this pool as both the Slide and the Stump. I'll go with the latter because of the stump that used to stand here and because the Slide is a well-known pool on the Stamp River.

24. **New Moon**—After a lovely run of beautiful small boulders, the water deepens into a pool that curves to the left before dropping down a riffle. This is how the whole river should look if it were not damaged. It is about 10 feet deep, with good-sized

rocks and overhanging branches, a real sleeper because it is in shade. Casting a single-handed rod is difficult because your fly keeps getting caught in the willows behind. Some days it contains a lot of trout in June to August. Where water drops down to run into the Road Pool, toss a fly under the branches at the top left, because sometimes, exactly at the last branch, it is deep enough to secret a steelhead or trout.

25. **Road Pool**—Also a sleeper of a pool. One day after I fished through, I scrambled the left, road-side bank to see the water, stumps and boulders. It was 2 p.m. in August and this edge was in complete sun down 12 feet. I was astounded with the amount of life I did not know was there. Small coho fry, steelhead smolts, a bunch of smaller to larger cutthroat. The key with this pool is that you have to cast from the upstream side (the opposite side from the road) across the pool, one that requires at least 90 feet to reach the other side. As with most pools, you will receive your greatest number of trout the closer you can cast to the far side—within a foot of shore. For a fly caster this means being able to cast very well, on a single-handed rod. Try a double hander, here as it doesn't take long to be able to reach 90 feet.

In the fall, coho stage for as much as a month in the deepest part of the soft water. The river becomes too deep to fish from above on foot. It is best to anchor a boat from above and fish; this is pigging the pool, so don't hog the water all day.

Some August days before the Chinook come in force, early fish, only several dozen, will come into this pool. You will see them scurrying here and there in noonday sun once they spot you. These are one of the unusual runs on the Nitinat, as are a strain of August chum that, so I am told, offer up catchable numbers in Worthless Pool as early as late June, though I have never seen them until low-water August.

From the road side, this is the first pool you come to after turning left at the T-junction coming from Lake Cowichan. The tail-end can be one of the all-lined-up coho spots when the water is three feet higher than summer low. Winter steelhead lay here in late winter.

26. **Pumphouse Run**—This has slowly filled with gravel over the years and does not produce as well as the water looks good. In front of the hatchery pumphouse, it used to have cool inlet streams where cutthroat would hang in great numbers, but this is not so these days. This can be a good run for bity chum. Note that the bumpers in the air are the upper boundary of the Hatchery Pool.

The first time I came through here, in my little blue boat, freezing to death after turning over in the Stump Pool, water was being pumped out from 25 feet up, as though it was a waterfall.

27. **Hatchery Pool**—Do remember the Hatchery Pool is closed to fishing 12 months of the year. On the other hand, the bottom boundary gives you access to enough of the pool for trouting and salmon in a low-water year, until the monsoons settle in in October. The Little Nitinat River enters in the middle of the pool—the bottom boundary. At this point, where two bodies of water from different sources mix—and this is true all along the river—the fish stop and scent the water to decide where they want to go. A significant number of coho and steelhead turn left up the Little Nitinat, because the hatchery lets some of its fry go in this river—hence the fish come back here, all the way to the falls, before backing down to reenter the river. One year, 35,000 coho went up around the corner, and it looked like a disaster until one heavy rain brought them back down to seed the river admirably all the way up to Parker Creek.

One of the other small strains of salmon, spotted-tail sockeye, from Tuck Lake, will mass here in the summer. They number 200 and sit on the bottom waiting to proceed. If you don snorkel and fins, go down to the bottom and take a look.

28. **Shady Run**—When you stand on the island that splits the river below the Hatchery Pool, take the right channel first. It is usually in shade and cooler and gloomier for the angler but holds more trout and steelhead. It provides difficult back-

casting room for single-handed rods, with a bank of willows behind and because your fly needs to get under branches on the far side to land, again, within a foot of the bank. This run does not look fishy, but always fish this one. Once you have reached the end of the island, go back and give a quick fish through the left channel, in the two- to three-feet-deep water.

29. **Subway**—At the bottom of the island, the two river channels come together, and you get a waist-deep jumbled flow of water right out in the open, highly sunny, nary a branch in sight. But it is the protection of the riffly water and the many basketball-sized boulders that make the occasional summer steelhead stop here. A real sleeper. Don't miss it.

Below this run, the river runs south toward the lake for half a mile. In many years, this is just walk-through water no more than knee-deep in summer. Recently, though, a crease has started to be dug halfway down the right side, which represents a place to drop a few flies on the run down to the major pool below. Try it in the afternoon when the Nitinat wind blows and the fish relax—it is also in the shade. This long run is also a major place for chum spawning in the fall.

30. **Red Rock Pool**—After you turn left at the T-junction above, this is the second pool on the road to Ditidaht village. You will notice red rock in the road bed and bluff to your left. This pool is a major one and twice the size it used to be, again because of the huge amount of small gravel and silt being pushed through.

Start 50 yards above, to take any steelhead that are in the run, rather than just over the drop-off, where most trout sit. Stand back from the edge and swing a fly from each side to the centre of the river. Add another couple of pulls and cast again. Now, turn to your left and address the rocks on the left bank—laid there to provide a bed for the road. Start right up in the bushes and work your way down until you are once again standing on the drop-off, where you cast sequentially longer. Land your fly within a foot, because trout hang in shade most of the day. Practise your casting in a park if you can't reach the rocks. Buy a good shooting head fly line for Spey and you will find you can cast more than 80 feet. For a single-handed rod, Snowbee XS full float had a 60-foot head, and I bought several, the reasons being: the longer the head, the longer the cast; and, once they discontinue a line you like, have some new ones on the shelf for the next few years.

If you see trout but can't catch them or receive "short bites"—the mark of a pressured trout, tapping on the tail end without committing to a good chomp (and this is a pressured pool)—come back later when the Nitinat wind has come up strongly. You will be casting—if you can use this word—directly into the teeth of the wind and it will be ugly, but you will catch all those trout by overlapping casts every two feet as you move along the drop-off. Even when a good group of people have been swimming and jumping in the pool below for hours, you will catch fish, as they are pushed from their usual spots by the commotion and thus there will be more fish there than there would be otherwise.

The pool tailout has become more prominent, and longer, over the years. As the far side crease deepens, it becomes a better, brushy, trouty-looking spot. As mentioned, do look for opportunistic pools and runs. This may help explain why the trout population has both risen and declined over the years, but there are other reasons: the growing population of mergansers; the lake turning over in 2002 and killing all the fish because of its high sulfide concentration below 30 feet (and this will happen again from time to time); and Indigenous fishing in the end of the lake in April and May. On the other hand, in years of low flow, when they close retention, you will catch far more fish, and many more summer steelhead, too, because fewer are killed and retained—even though wild steelhead are not to be retained. A significant development occurred in 2017: three different phenotypes—see photo section—of summer steelhead.

One year in April I saw what looked like a big, red, dying penis on the edge of the drop. It was a lamprey, and I toed it out of the current to look at its prehistoric body, its shark-like gill slits and circular rows of glass-sharp teeth. Then it drifted off the edge and was lost. They say the greatest biomass in the Nitinat River is larval lamprey, pencil thick, six inches long. You will see them only in September when they rise from the mud, on their downstream run to saltwater. Some die and lie along the edge, like glass pencils with large eyes.

31. **Red Rock Run**—Identify the bottom boundary marker, a white triangle that is the limit for fishing Red Rock Pool in salmon season. On days there are coho and Chinook moving up, cast a spoon or spinner and let it bump down the run. The first time I fished this in the rain, I wasn't paying any attention to the rising river. I didn't know that rising means bigger and bigger logs coming down. This was the day the many-tonned tree swept by and the top tip touched my leg.

I almost had a heart attack. If it had knocked me off my feet, its pure motiveless efficiency would have rolled me under. Hand over heart, I went on to catch 11 coho up to 13 pounds in this run, which is far from the usual spot to catch them. You fish runs when coho are moving through. You fish softer, deeper water when coho are not moving.

32. **The Seam**—I have caught more coho and chum at this spot than any other on the river. You will see me parked here, staking out my water in coho season. Three things favour this spot: a good-sized seasonal creek for spawning; a good right channel of river—when looking upstream—in high water that joins the seasonal creek; and a good soft-water pool on high water.

In summer this is a gentle glide, as unfishy as can be—except for trout, if a log has been pasted to the left bank below—but add three feet of water and another three on high days and this is a good back eddy, formed by the river coming downstream and off into deeper water. With scented water coming in at right angles, this makes a good drop-off to 12 feet in monsoon season. As coho that spawn here stage and ripen, and those en route upstream come up this side (left side, as you look down) because it is slower and easier to swim, this can be a great spot. Chum can be so thick you need slippery fingers on your fly line to distinguish rubs from bites. The latter takes a few inches quickly, indicating a mouth. New fish come in waves for as much as eight weeks, and chum can be as snappy as coho.

On lower water, this spot also holds Chinook into early October. They spawn below The Seam because of the size of the rocks. Any spot that has stones the size of your fist will be a high-density spot for pre-spawning and spawning activity by Chinook. And the Nitinat wind comes into play, particularly for Chinook. This is one of the places they form a doughnut-shaped school of 500 to 1,000 fish that swim up one side, turn, follow the fish in front of them down the far side, before turning and following the other fish upstream again, and so it goes—a most unusual behaviour, particularly when you consider that in saltwater, Chinook are the least schooling of the five species.

I have come here with a double-handed rod late in sunny September, when gear chuckers have been pummeling the water all day and packing up, saying there is nothing to be caught, as the growing wind waves tops of trees and skins the water. I have run my Nitnook, chartreuse Woolly Bugger through and taken half a dozen 20- to 40-pound Chinook in the next few hours. It is worth remembering: whether you are gear fishing or fly fishing, once you have taken what you can, if you switch over to the type of gear you have not been using, you will often start off a bite that will carry on for hours. This is because the two types of tackle are so different in size and come down the river and go back up in such different ways, the fish don't seem to recognize the two are both methods of fishing.

This seam has changed dramatically over the years. When I started, none of the 10 feet of gravel where the seasonal stream pours in was there. The willows below were just shoots and the entire bank upstream on the right side was simply a gravel wash, not a jot of vegetation. The river channel by the road scoured a 12-foot pool in summer, and where the main channel dropped over the edge, pushing the seam over, the bottom contour was more distinct than it is today. The river was knee-deep along the edge, all the way across to the other side. Then, for years, it could be as much as 10 feet, because the river started digging into the opposite bank, creating a sleeper for trout in shady afternoon.

One winter, even more changed. The seasonal creek from mountains above, then under Ditidaht road, deposited eight feet of gravel 30 feet wide and 150 feet long. Then a greater flood cut the centre out of the gravel and took down six feet and 15 feet across of boulders—thousands, most about 200 pounds. A massive amount of rock.

The point is to get to know your river and be alert to its changes that will change the location of the fish.

33. **Bear Island**—500 yards below The Seam lay a little island that offered coho fishing on the left side. However, about 2012, the left channel was filled in with gravel, logs dumped on top, willows grown, so for many years the left channel did not exist. The whole stretch is fishable for chum and even below, all 500 yards to Cutt Corner; this is a major spawning spot for them, after the Chinook have come and gone.

I so named this long run because of the bear that likes to come in the middle of the day and fish the righthand side. I had to wait one day for him to finish jumping around and wear out a Chinook that looked like an enormous submarine sandwich in his mouth.

Below the island on the left, major erosion continues knocking down enormous trees. It is hard to believe, even as you watch it, a tree 10 feet thick at the butt and with a root ball 20 feet in diameter just moved down in high water. Later, at lower water, stranded trunks are witness to the strength of running water.

As above, winter high-water events have eliminated the left-hand channel and deposited up to 10 feet of gravel, almost 800 yards long, now covered with willow—millions of tons of rock. Expect change in the Nitinat.

34. **Lonesome Pole**—This is an unusual sight. A log has been inserted in the river bottom and leans out on a diagonal as much as 12 feet above the water. Sometimes salmon will rest in the slower water behind the pole that has angled here for more than two decades. From Bear Island to below Lonesome Pole, the right-hand bank was becoming more prominent just as this book was published; this improved chances for cutthroat trout under the willows, when for the preceding decade, the left of Bear Island was more prominent. Again, pay attention to the changes and you will catch more fish.

35. **Dennis's Pool**—So named after I landed those 12 Chinook one day, simply because I looked into the shade on the east side and saw big fish sipping air. This is another sleeper "pool," because, as mentioned, Chinook and coho hang sequestered

in the shade. It's only a so-called *pool* because in summer this is simply a glide little more than thigh-deep. Some people know this spot but most move on, passing up one of the great little spots the Nitinat offers. I assume coho stay right into December, when the river is finally high enough to lift them up over the lip of the dry gulch and into the seasonal creek that I have written about—one that flows out of the river rather than into it, a very unusual occurrence. Not so here. Maps indicate that in the '80s the river, as it does today, bore to the right and Cutt Corner.

36. **Cutt Corner**—So named by Curtis Myers, when he talked to me of it in the tackle store. It used to be the best half mile for cutthroat, June to August, probably because it is in shade most of the day, has good woody debris and probably a spring or two of cold water.

Again, land that fly inches from the far bank. This is an area where the river has eaten as much as 100 yards of the curve, making it tighter every year. One summer I came back to spot a tree trunk on the far side six feet wide. It had been snapped off 10 feet from the ground in the winter's high water. Presumably a log wedged against the tree and the force of water simply snapped the huge fir off. And whistled it away. There is a big tree on the beach on Nitinat Lake that bears the 29-kilometre marker triangle. Think how unlikely it would be for a plastic marker to still be on a tree that had been swept downstream and around corners for almost 15 miles, without being ripped off.

Stop and look at the gravel bar, which is 800 yards long and at least 100 yards across. This hides the fact willows have moved forward over the gravel a good 300 yards, too.

Logs are jammed on the left-hand bank, which used to have a lovely 12-foot pool with a wide tailout where trout and steelhead lay, but these trees are now gone and the area is not as good as it once was. But always plumb the bottom section, because fish often stop there, I surmise because of a cool spring. Springs are evidenced by fish being in a spot that looks ho-hum, but over the years gives up more than its share of them. Sometimes you can feel cooler water on Goretex waders. The pool on the last bend of Cutt Corner often contains Chinook in the fall.

This section is an important spot for wading across, and it is difficult because the rocks are the size of plates and, at thigh-deep, the river runs quickly. But you need to cross over to the left bank to fish the next half mile of river down to No Fish Pool.

37. **Eagle's Nest**—So named by the hatchery people because there was, wait for it, an eagle's nest in a tree. The tree is history, but the name remains. Some years, the scouring can make this a great spot for trout. It can be 10 feet deep with good brush on the far side and bottom structure with many trouty branches that rise from the bottom, their logs having been buried in gravel. Some years, the logs are moved.

Few people catch fish, because they do not understand how their behaviour affects fish. The left bank can be steeply sloped and difficult to wade. So, most people walk along the gravel bank casting across. They are high up, and their shadows pass long across the river; the trout see them and clam up. So, get into the water to catch fish. Surprisingly, fish don't seem to see you under water, though they react immediately to the part of you they can see above the water. This is another spot where, if you see fish early in the day and can't catch them, come back once the Nitinat gale forms in the afternoon. The wind makes for strange casting, but the surface ruffle makes the fish feel secure. And this is a spot where several steelhead can hold in low-water August.

Keep this spot in mind for coho in October, because three seasonal creeks enter. Surprisingly, one starts opposite The Seam and snakes through forest floor almost a mile before dropping into Eagle's Nest. I fish mostly on foot, so I stop in autumn only when in a kickboat and the river is high.

38. **Steelhead Run**—So named because, some years, it looks like the best, classic, winter steelhead run on the entire river, though I have never had a touch. Again, the issue is getting across the river, by boat, to fish it properly. Probably because it is out in the open sun, trout swim right on through. But this

looks good for winters when four to six feet deep and green. I remain confident I will one day take a winter steelhead here.

In addition to the stump in the middle I have spoken of, there is one on the left bank. Stop and take a look. Even a century after the tree was cut down, you can see they had to start the bucksaw cut several times, because there is a saw plane for every time they restarted. I surmise the tree sat on the blade and they had to start cutting from another angle, and so on. Think of them, sweating in the jungle of old river bottom, scooping cool water from the green river, propping-up a cork boot when they took a wedge or roll of tobacco, as it was once sold. The river runs west here until it hits the rock wall on which the Hobiton River Main was built.

Local guide Kenzie Cuthbert called this run The Meadows, which means the river must have shifted to its present course less than 25 years before publication of this book. I mention this, as willows take over in a few years and soon grow to 15 feet high, in a tangle. Then alder take hold, and as they grow 10 feet per year, choke out the willow.

39. **No Fish Pool**—This is one spot I couldn't catch a fish for so many years I called it No Fish Pool. It looks wonderfully deep, and gear fishers do well on Chinook in fall, but it has a strong back eddy that makes fly fishing next to impossible unless you can throw a very long cast—up to 90 feet. Start at the top, fishing the woody stuff on the far bank. Cutthroat, cutt-bows—a cross between cutthroat and summer steelhead—and steelhead inhabit all areas of this pool, sometimes even right at your feet.

In 2016, I came to the conclusion there are residualized rainbows, meaning a steelhead that doesn't go out to sea, but stays close to its river, probably in the lake, and then appears in the river in late spring. No Fish Pool can be a classic in June, and again in late August, when cutthroat precede Chinook into the river, looking for eggs during the spawn. In 2017, Jimmies, as one-year Chinook males are called, when they re-enter the river, are as bity as any fish in the river, and you will catch every single one if they are there. You cannot mistake their smell:

a ripe armpit, i.e., the normal smell of Chinook. And do they ever whack dry flies.

Just below No Fish is a river crossing that is the most deceptive on the river. It looks shallow and slow, but it is moving quickly, and the depth is soon above your waist and among rocks that are really boulders.

This is one place to look up and see the two trees leaning against the other in the dry wash of the seasonal creek. One day they will come down. In addition, behind the pool is the first of three sloughs—old river channels—that enter the river from here to the bottom at Nitinat Lake.

Where water feeds out over the deceptive rock bottom, it falls into a deceptive run that looks like nothing, but on the right side, if there is a log there, it has good potential being five feet deep in summer and below, again the brown broiling water up to waist-deep that spells steelhead.

40. **Long Run**—As the name implies, the river runs in a straightish line. In fall it is stuffed with chum. Though difficult to fish from shore, as trees are right to the water line, put a 10-pound barbell on a line from your kickboat and you should catch many chum in this crease water, reminiscent of the lower Sarita River, about half a mile long. Your take outs were Glory and Poison sloughs, before the Hobiton Main was decommissioned. Now, add a windy crossing of the lake to the parking lot by the hatchery nets. Fish for trout if a log is stranded in Long Run.

41. **Glory Hole**—The second of the three sloughs received its name because at one time guides could run up the river from the lake and, on every pass through the spot, pick up a big Chinook—or so I'm told. If everyone waited their turn, each would receive a fish each time through. That is the dependability of the Nitinat River. It is the only river on the lower island, including the Stamp—a more noble river of far more interesting character—that you can count on taking a salmon home: Chinook in September, chum in October after the closure, running to the 15th in most years, then new coho after that, into the third week in November.

At the top, anglers key in on the five-foot glide on the left side of the river for trout and steelhead in their season. In salmon time, Chinook sit most of the day in shade, as well as below on the right, which is more difficult because, in even average water, you are walking down the river on a ford that has water to your belly button. Even the most seasoned angler doesn't like standing deep in the shade for long, even though Chinook and chum are thick in there—it's a good place to fish in the glorious morning suns of September and glory in the fish you take. It can be the best spot to fly-fish for Chinook on the entire river, often 1,000 feet of calm water. Fly fishers fish here, while gear fishers fish in Sturgeon Pool below.

One day I grew tired of watching gear chuckers at Sturgeon (so named because a sturgeon was pulled out of here once, having swum all the way from the Columbia River!) throw wool flies across a black wall of Chinook flesh and hook them in the dorsal fins. The fish were hauled out of the river, angler backing up the gravel, then putting a knee down on the head, taking out the hook and kicking the fish back into the water. These lardy louts should suffer the same fate in their next life, if life be granted at all.

As I moved up to Glory there was a bear above, jumping around in the stumblebum fashion that is black bears. It's a good thing they have sharp teeth, or they would never catch a living fish, head under water, snapping around like a linebacker. I gave a few grunts and the bear, 40-pound Chinook shaking its face, stumbled into the trees, and I passed up to Glory. I spent the afternoon catching chum that made the river look alive where sun patches showed through maple trees with leaves so large they reached from one side of day to the other. There must have been 50,000 fish.

When I espied a seal, head like a coconut, I turned to go—in the bear story I have told—and found five bears jumping around like big black kids after grasshoppers in hot summer grass. Fourteen bears I saw that day. Fishing means bears every day on a salmon river in the fall. And that bear banger you carry costs $17 a shell. An Air Bomb firework costs a buck. Just don't let it rip so it shoots beyond the bear before the bang, as the bang might send the bear right into your face.

Another day in another year, I was standing around, knee deep, rod over my arm, jawing, when a banger went off so loud the three of us guys had heart attacks. The three bears—there really were three bears—just down from us didn't flinch a muscle. Hmm.

42. **Sturgeon Pool**—The best spot on the Nitinat to catch a 30-pound Chinook in good shape in September. A very popular fishery for meat, and it delivers better than any river and any pool on the island. Just remember before you catch it that you have to carry that great big fish a very long way to your car, particularly since the Hobitan Main was decommissioned at the Little Nitinat River bridge, near the hatchery. Alternatively, you will be crossing a windy lake to the Ditidaht side.

The first time I fished this pool was a Labour Day weekend—which is usually a few days before the Chinook enter. I was about to walk in below a log at the top end, when I said, *no, walk above the log because it's woody, there's less current and a good spot to be a sea-run cutthroat trout.* That decision landed me five cutthroat trout I would have missed if I had not made myself do the right thing. On that day I landed 15 cutthroat trout in the 800-yard-long pool and saw schools of 15 and 20 that saw me before I saw them. The timing of the later cutthroat entry reflected their being in for opportunistic feeding on salmon eggs whose presence was a week or two away.

In the past, the river had its greatest number of cutthroat in January. The hatchery guys used to go down on Saturdays and fish spinners at Glory and Poison sloughs, because that was where the fish spent the winter waiting for spring. Not anymore. And the biggest lake-end fish for them was May, but that is lesser, too.

In September you may find the biggest school of Chinook 200 yards below the rock face that juts out to start the Sturgeon pool, it being an immoveable object that even irresistible water cannot wash away. The black among branches on the far side is Chinook. This is the best spot on the entire half mile and beautiful for a fly, in years when no logs have come to rest. Cast the fly in and let it drop into the fish, sensing flanks and fins until your slippery fingers lose a couple of inches that marks a Chinook bite and stop the line.

Behind the snags that form along this pool can be a wonderful place to catch chum as the season progresses. A 110-foot cast from a Spey rod will put your fly on the other side, though you hardly need cast out 50 feet, into this wide run of five feet deep. You can fish all day, moving up and down to get the "that moment" biters. At the end of the run, there is a good flat riffle before the river runs down into the next body of water. On days when it seems the sound of water increases and decreases, it is not wind blowing over the high trees; it is the sound of hundreds and thousands of salmon coming up the riffle. The latest chum are small females in December.

43. **Gary's Run**—This is so-called for one of the hatchery guys. This is a good bet for trout all summer long, particularly the absolute end of the willows on the far, left, side. In the middle is a difficult fish, because of logs lying there. But do not pass it by, for coho can sit on the bottom in their hundreds in September and October, completely invisible, in shade. The salmon count guys were the first to tell me this, and they are bang-on. You won't see a fish, but you will catch them. This is often a back eddy and you must always retrieve, as I have said, your fly or lure up-current.

The river is tidal from this 1,200-yard section of two pools that join at the riffle. And the river changes its course dramatically every year. I have seen it on the left side of the depression and 75 yards to the right in another year and right down the middle in others. Amazing. From here down I have taken few fish, presumably because it is tidal. Fish seem to want to swim right through the misty saltwater that rolls in underneath the fresh into the freshwater end of Gary's Pool. On days of very high tide, water will push right up into the riffle and beyond to the head of Sturgeon Pool, a very long way.

44. **Poison Slough**—A major slough just below Gary's Run that you cross to fish the lower end of the river, and thence to the river mouth. Around the corner is an old recreation site where you can camp, accessed now by boat.

I have seen the Slough calf-deep and 10 feet deep, because of scouring and tide. This used to be a major Chinook spot before the

Hobiton Main was decommissioned. One could drive right to river's edge. But the road was decommissioned in two places—the ministry did not want the expense of keeping the road up, so they had to do it twice, I guess, each 20 feet deep. Not even an ATV or motorcycle can cross. Thank goodness.

The only people who like ATVs are the people on them. Guys with big treble hooks snagged big fish and dragged them out. One day I looked down and saw an orange line streaming by. When I picked it out of the water, it was attached to a six-inch-long, three-inch gap, Siwash hook, clearly used only by a snagger—for meat, not for sport. Fortunately, those days are over.

I don't know why the slough is called Poison, but believe it is because great three-foot-thick layers of leaves drop in the stillness of the two false streams. When silt is dropped on them, they begin to rot and ferment. You will smell the rotting even before the salmon come to make the river smell of death. This is the last freshwater part of the river, and, of course, rotting things in saltwater seldom smell.

Please Note: The Hobiton Main Road Has Been Decommissioned

The road down the back side of the lower Nitinat River from the hatchery road was decommissioned about 2010. You can no longer drive across the Little Nitinat bridge and access, by car or motorcycle, the lower end of the river from the hatchery pool down. You can walk or bicycle until the road becomes impassable for its alder growth over the years. Take clippers and clip them back, if you intend to fish from the west side of the lower river. Count on a half hour cycle. Note that the road has been decommissioned in three places, two noted above, and the third at the bridge.

The three main bottom-end access routes are: 1. By foot (takes one hour, 20 minutes of walking and 10 river crossings, each way) back to the culvert below Red Rock Pool; 2. Boat from Red Rock. Do note there can be log jams anywhere and a boat will have to be lugged up, over and down on your way down the river. While this is difficult, do remember that when the rains begin, you can go under the logs and never be seen again. Take care. From the bottom end, you cross to the Nitinat Lake boat launch and pick up your boat; and, 3. Park your car at the boat launch on the end of the lake and motor/row across to the river mouth. You walk up and access Poison, Gary's, Sturgeon and Glory. In September, you will find guides with parties of up to 20 people with lunch and beer for all. You might want to get there early or avoid this section of river altogether. If you decide to launch on the lake, do note the lower end of the river is tidal, and the Nitinat wind blows every sunny day, and most cloudy ones, so take care on crossing from river to boat launch later in the day.

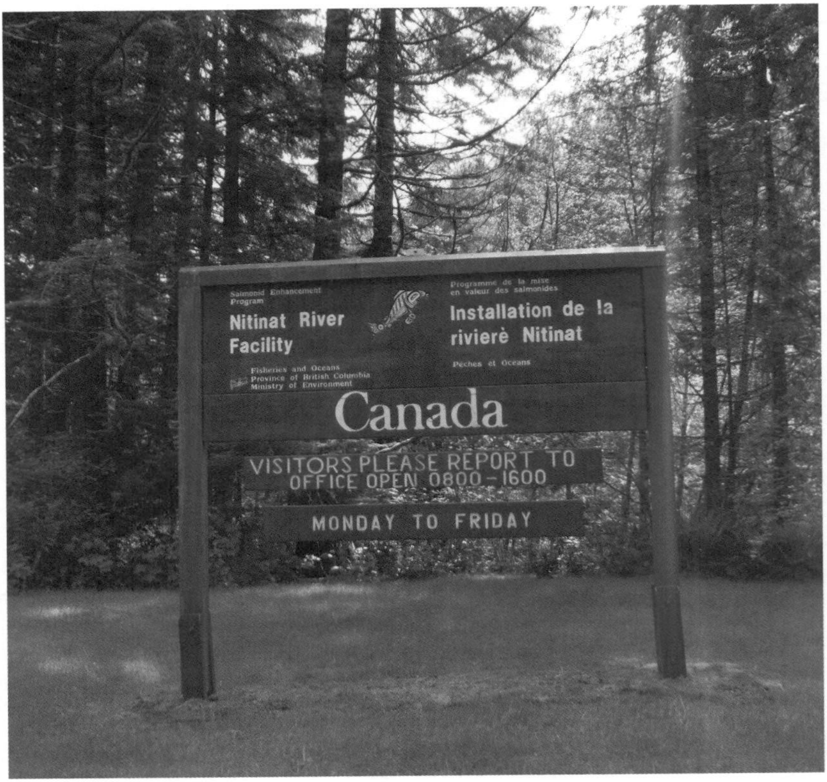

The Nitinat Hatchery Sign near the Little Nitinat Bridge. At the T-junction from Cowichan Lake turn right, cross the river and around a large bend you will find the entrance to the hatchery and then this sign beside the Little Nitinat canyon and decommissioned bridge. Please note that you should check on the boat take-out being open to all boaters. This is Ditidaht territory, and thus they may, should they choose, close/open the launch and parking.

Chapter 22

A RIVER NEARBY

The Dipper

Only we see death. The animal is free
and carries his death behind him,
just as before him, he carries God,
so that when he moves, he moves into always

Duino Elegies – Rainer Maria Rilke

Only we see death. The animal is free.
My west coast totemic bird cheeps
amazement at the wonder of its own
existence, anonymous in cedary
canyon bottoms wet from water
falling. I found a skeleton once,
a folded down animal. A mink, otter,
I cannot tell, though I keep its bones to
let me know it closed its phlegmy eyes
and shrunk into death. The dipper dips

and carries his death behind him.
And above the falls I have slid under slim
branches until my head was just above
the breathless water. The balsam kingdom
could kill me with vast and beautiful
indifference. The love I am always in
sees not the rain that aches with clarity
on the territory it washes into beauty.
The granite, criss-crossing green and white,
is an eroding checker board. Dip and

just as before him he carries God,
without the pre-frontal cortex prod.
The bone above my right eye, scarcely a
metacarpal tip beyond conscious I, awed
by my 11 second existence melded
into my next little bit of edited animal
world. So I have the memory
the brainless log would have robbed
were I not to have slipped its unthinking.
The dipper blinks and is on the other side

so that when he moves he moves into always,
as streams do. Anonymous vertebrae trays
make the way to escape unlike the way we came
crowded by womb and doctor faces,

their oblong, mirror, forehead faces ablaze
with looking into the future of us. I slid
the rim of waterfall among the dipper dips
where water curled me into the birth
of losing me. I was and always am a part
of nature. It's man I can't stand.

The Spirit of the Thing and the Thing Itself – DC Reid

After many years coming to my river, I found another in a canyon close by. Into its anonymous green beauty, I dropped a stone from the bridge. It took a full three seconds to splash into water of a green I have seen only in dreams.

Downstream, the river was a deep, silent pool. The only way downriver was to swim from where the stone went plop. I looked up and another creature looked at me. It was a bear with a white mark on her chest. We both went, "Oh," and beetled to our respective ends of the bridge. She to charge off the right and me to drop down the left, holding bridge abutments until I realized run-off from never-ending winter rain had made a natural set of stairs. I casually descended 90 vertical feet, to a large black rock toqued with moss and bulging with water.

The track lead me to a log that smudged my chest as I squeezed underneath. Then I waded in my pants and shirt. I looked up the side the bear had gone down and was looking into thousands of droplets of water, catching liquid sun, and I leaned against the wall arms spread, drops of light hitting my face.

Above, the far side was too steep for the bear. And there were no fish, on this day. I have looked at the map and when sets of contour lines make it almost black, there is cliff held within the forest. A bit later, on the bear side, I took the car up to a locked, red gate, took my map, and kept looking back as I walked the overgrown road. Old-growth forest has this silence, like a presence is watching, not with interest or malice, but there and untappable.

I went looking for black canyon walls that lean over and fall. Steelhead rise safe and protected from human beings. Chest heaving, I looked for the edge. I had been told steelhead move at night and stop where the first squeeze in rock occurs. I had been warned to tread only with ropes and carabiners. As I stood in the forest, my right leg went through the floor and then I was stuck in the ground, all the way to my hip. When, finally, I pulled my leg free, I ran from the forest, down the afternoon track with its small waving green life that cannot leave. I ran all the way to the car and slammed the door.

Jittering out the gravel washboard, I knew I was coming back to this river within its canyon. It was waiting for me, its liquid afternoon air around rocks like mist, taking land to sea. To fall here is to fall out of life, and I am not easy with that.

This river is not like my own, where I have stood everywhere and we are so acquainted, we are friends. I came back in the locust heat of September, sawing insects in my ears. On an access different from the canyon river past Ditidaht, and whose name I am not mentioning, I followed bear scat that told a tale: "No one comes to this river anymore." A bear chooses the easier path, and squats for its business where it feels safe. If it is in the middle of the road, like right there, no one comes to the river. The scat was three fingers wide and evidence of a huge boar.

I bore left, on a thin track, clear-cut falling away from me. The trees had been gathered downslope hundreds of feet below the yawning edge. Then a black shape moved down the access road. I turned off my key but heard no sound. There was no bear among the bugs that moved from my feet, drill of legs on dusty wings. The blaze of their yellow and red. I kicked a stone on the edge of the valley laid out in vegetative afterlife. Jimsonweed blaze was evidence of only one year since the forest was cut.

I wondered, hands in pockets on the edge, "Where did that bear ..." And from less than 10 feet below, a bear in full flight gave me a heart attack. It sped far down the slope before I could pull my hands from their pockets for protection. Pretty useless. That slope would have taken me an hour to get down.

There was nothing to do but get back in the car, drive around log ends rolled on iron oxide soil to the road edge by a D9 cat. My wheels picked a way down the naked hill. Its jutting stumps were bones of a dead forest. Where the switchback started, I parked my car and pushed through green, broken slash, scaled green rocks the size of cars, slipped the anonymous roots.

The snap of a twig and its dust in the air so slow it was loneliness come from far away. That was the feeling of this valley where I hoped no one else would come: loneliness, out-thereness, not for human or animal. Do animals feel lonely? I don't know, but the Aboriginal people would never have had a reason to come down into the canyon. I spilled down walls, climbing like a backward spider, to the valley floor, where the river was only three feet wide in some places. The rock beneath was green granite, laced with white, like a chessboard of nature that took ten thousand years to be revealed. Boulders in the valley, from ones that could fit in my palm to much larger than my car. My hands touched the smallest daisies, growing from rock clefts, gravel wash the size of bears.

Where the river was loud, I looked up and realized it made the rock give in, for it would never stop coming. Above the falls, I chose to cross into the dark wet rocks in shade. This shelf of slippery rock gave way to a pool so deep I could not see the bottom. Twenty feet? Thirty?

As mentioned in my poem, I came upon an animal. It was a mammal of some sort that had come to this difficult spot to die. It simply crouched down on all four feet and passed away. The entire animal had been consumed by time. Only the skin of moldy fur, tight over bones, remained. Maybe a small wolf, too large for mink, a large otter with no more play? This was such a deserted place that nothing other than putrefaction could find it. Usually wolves, cougars, bears, even crows and seagulls find everything, and flies reduce meat to maggots.

The forest had secreted this one small death and sent out small roots of filamentous fungi that slowly sipped the body away, making the hide a deflated balloon. Two femurs, perhaps they were, I put in my pocket and buttoned it closed. I shivered in summer shade, broken rock above me, the ledges from which logs hung down.

I returned another year. To the steelhead from the switchback road. No bear this time, no hoof of elk, no deer. Only the least lonely of all animals—the dipper. These birds are endlessly happy, in a life no one ever sees, dipping on this rock, appearing on the next, across the river, up, down, and dip and a single chirp. Getting down to them, my right foot was placed on a root, then my left, so far down my right knee came up to my chest and I had to turn sideways, left hand seeking purchase in the air. Right upon an alder too thin; it cracked, and I hung from a root. This little climb of double my height placed me unseen in the willows. The river was so clear I could see fry come from bottom to kiss the morning.

I was the predatory face blending with leaves. In their flight that goes nowhere, three silver streaks wavered in the invisible. I was the hunter they could not hear or see, moving among rocks and crispy leaves. On my knees I moved from forest out upon the rocks. On my knees I took the line and loaded the rod. I scraped the point on my thumbnail, then sharpened it.

The river was clear to the point of not being there. I landed a light fly on a straight white line, 40 feet above them. The interested fish saw the fly and moved forward—think of how good their eyesight is and how motivated the steelhead must have been—to inspect the fly, then another 50, to where I was hiding behind a daisy. It looked up at me, and said, "Nice try, turkey," and drifted back 90 feet, to settle among buddies, all of whom were informed not to come forward. Hmm. I pitched a rock in my exasperation, and the pool exploded, with the steelhead I was after and a whole lot more I couldn't see. Summer steelhead are indeed the Ghosts of Summer, so a fly fisher had better be clandestine.

On another day, below the major falls, in river barely wide as I am tall, I looked down 20 feet to the cut rock bottom. Hands on my hips, it came clear there was a big steelhead lying on the bottom. It was actually lying on its side and the only thing moving was its finny hand thumbing its nose at me. So, imagine my frustration, when I plopped in a stone to make the steelhead move, and from under a ledge beneath my feet, an 8-pounder moseyed out and whacked the stone! Grr.

And then it tried, gills flaring, to engulf the stone and make it food, which didn't happen, so it choked out and the stone tinkled to the bottom. It was not going to take my sexy fly and came to rest beside the rester on the bottom. Cheesed off, it looked up, staler, warier, "all pooled up," as the expression goes. They snooze to save energy until rainfall triggers them awake.

On another summery, 85-degree day, I was leaning on creosote planks of a bridge a bit higher in the system. Ninety feet down, in a granite elevator shaft, was a long pool that wound out of sight. It led, though I had never been there, for it meant swimming downstream, to the major falls of the upper river.

Out of 2 p.m. sun, on the only day of the year sun could shine up the canyon, materialized a smudge from the deepest part of the pool, beside a rock larger than my car. It turned into 50 steelhead trapped by summer—falls below, and fingers of water above too narrow to slither round green boulders rolled smooth by the sandpaper of ten thousand years, the silt of ice ages.

Once again I spidered the cliff, rod in one hand, securing boot holds in clumps of fern, to the foot-wide ledge at water level. One of the unexpected good things about a canyon is there are no trees to catch your fly on the end of an errant cast. Back the fly went in a straight line, and forward in a straight line. The fly touched the right wall and dropped in the green. The school exploded and disappeared.

It came to me that a fly cast within canyon walls in early spring would yield a bite, but these were late summer fish. The only way to catch them was to float a piece of wood, with a line and bait attached by slipping the leader under an elastic band. When the fish bites, the poacher strikes the rod and the line comes free. But I am not a poacher, and this was a fly fishing–only river.

I found the water was just over my waist and I could cross to the other canyon wall to espy where the fish had gone. Stepping through boulders, boot cleats rasping on granite, I was more careful than I used to be. Should I have fallen, and my leg been wedged between rocks, it would have snapped my femur easily. Days of stepping from crest to crest are a relic of my youth.

The west wall had a crease in the rock that afforded foot holds. Bum against the wall, I moved forward with my left and followed, but not crossed, with my right. Of course, the water was getting deeper, and the crease was narrowing. There were hardy grass shoots to hold, as I traversed the wall 10 feet above the river.

A willow grew from the wall, its red roots seeking hold in bare rock. I put my rod between my teeth and reached my left hand to grab the willow. The crease was an inch wide, and rotating my left foot to my toe was next to impossible. But then the toe held, and compromised, hanging, I launched my right foot, so my body swung out over the canyon, held only by my left hand and toe. My right toe touched rock, but I could neither go forward nor back. Face and rod smacking canyon rock, I was committed, and let go.

The river was chest-deep when my feet hit bottom. I left my rod balanced on a small rock. Until I had the fortitude to carry on down to the falls, my arms were spread against wet wall and my forehead touched dripping granite. I was in my mid-fifties and will never forget trusting that willow and swinging my body out and across open space.

Around the corner the steelhead had gone, 120-foot vertical walls opened into a small amphitheatre. Neck deep, I looked up into a spatter of water. Individual drops fell out of forest 10 stories above my face and dropped into the echoey room of rock. On the edge, from where larger music of falling water came, was a dipper. It dipped, and threw water over its head, happy, in its element. It dipped again, this small bird the size of my fist, then trilled down, over the falls.

I was struck by the cathedral around me that virtually no one had ever seen. The only ones of whom I was aware were the intrepid guys who swim rivers counting fish. They told me that in high water, steelhead are brought by the vertical eddy right up to the level of the falls, and snake upstream. I moved to the lip, slipped my hand along rock worn by water over the centuries. Fifteen feet down, river splashed into the next pool. I knew it from bushwhacking a mile below the bridge. The fisheries guys must have to jump right off this ledge to the pool below. What a job of amazements.

I was in no danger, looking down at cutthroat trout swum up the canyon 10 kilometres. They wavered in their lines and I watched them for a long time.

My way back was one hand reaching for a rock, the next reaching above it. My body flowed out horizontally, as I "swam" the shoreline back to my rod. Then I swam across the river to where my fly had fallen, left hand with my 696 fly rod sort of helping me move: fly rod, right arm, fly rod, etc. Back to the safe one-foot shore, where I hauled my body out and quietly let the river drain out of me. I thanked my good fortune for moving into the unknown, and back, safely, another wonder for me to think about for the rest of my life.

Of course, there was the 100-foot vertical cliff yet to be climbed, but I moved to the right, where it wasn't quite so steep, and rose. Put my rod above me and lifted my right leg. Put my right hand higher to a number 10 clump of fern and lifted my left leg. Repeat. When I reached the vertical scary part, I didn't look down. I didn't move more than one limb at a time—held on with three. The top was a scrubby, bushy, bunch of white alder, ones you never touch. Even when two inches across, white alder snaps off, and there, that meant certain death. Fern, the simple fern, is stronger than alder.

I resolved to buy a rope to leave on this slope for my safety in years to come. And a black rope got bought. So no one can see it, unless they know it is there, I tied it to a stump and payed out as I descended into the canyon another day. Ten years later, in my aged sixties, I find it is still there, hidden by browned leaves turned back to soil. Not willing to trust it, I become a spider once again, holding lightly. At the top I yank on it for all I am worth. It will hold, and I find some broken-down greenery, evidence someone else has found my rope. Hmm. Maybe I'll have to cut it most of the way through ... maybe I won't.

And then another cliff, on another day. I looked closely at topographical maps and it took several times to find the right logging spur into a clear-cut, with its jumble of crossed stumps, Jimsonweed, and fern.

I descended a hundred vertical feet to the bottom of the cut and then looked down the even steeper tree-covered slope. It bent down and out of sight. At the time, I did not know that when a slope disappears, it is a canyon wall and vertical. Having looked down into such first-growth cedar before, I brought a bright red, high-quality climbing rope, never thinking it might not be long enough.

I was so scared, I mapped out five separate legs from top to edge and told myself I would stop at the end of each one, to decide whether I felt safe enough to take the next leg. The second last had a log so large I could straddle and sit while leaning out over the edge. Another hundred vertical feet, and only from a tree I had to edge down to in the silence of a canyon and tied my rope. Of course, I had not left instructions of where I was going, just trusted my own good male instincts that I would get through. The usual.

Holding the line circled around my fist, rod in the other hand, I slid the wet, grey and white granite rock down to the river. The rope ended six feet above the gravel, and I let go. Orange-tailed coho fry scattered like melting nails. After a half hour going upstream, I came to a canyon wall some 100 vertical feet on both sides, leading to a frothy chute. I would have to swim into it, then around the corner, where I couldn't see, to where I might haul my body out. So, I said no.

I went back to my rope and jumped up and down to get enough of it in my hand. Rod cork crunched between my teeth, and hand over hand, I hauled my carcass back up to the tree. I hung to the bottom of the tree, its roots growing into rock like bent fingers, for a good 10 minutes, figuring out how I would get to the top side of the tree. Then I would have to slide the rope in a circle around the butt, so I could untie the knot and make for a log that looked far above me.

When I finally made my way up the wet, slippery rock slope and took hold of the log—it was 50 feet long and several tons—it moved with my hand. That's how slippery fir needles on wet rock can be. No soil whatsoever. It took another 10 minutes of fear to work up the log and cross over, all the while knowing it could give way and roll right over me. It was my great good fortune not to have died. Once back on the top, on the edge of the clear-cut, looking down the 300 vertical feet I had just come up, I told myself I would never do anything so stupid again.

But then, of course, I am a guy. More scary things will come my way. But let me end on one of beauty: a day in March when the river was too strong to be crossed, yet had to be crossed, four times—upstream—before I dropped my fly in a cut rock seam not 10 feet long.

It was a day of blue-green water in a granite canyon, all alone. Into late winter air came the beauty of the invisible made visible. My next fly in the same slit of water brought another summer to my fly. And then a third cast and third summer steelhead in the cool of winter—a fish that could have been in freshwater since the previous May.

Several miracles in a few minutes: I had sweated upstream, hauled my body up a rock bank, rod thrown high in the bush, and hands grasped a dozen ferns each so I would not fall back out of the forest into the river and be swept away. I will always have these memories. I am sure you have your own. Hold onto them.

Chapter 23

TECHNICAL FISHING TIPS AND INFORMATION

The following sections give you good usable fishing techniques and information to help you catch more fish. They, are, of course, useful in any river on Vancouver Island you choose to fish, as well as estuaries and saltwater beaches, two of the real joys of fly fishing in summer months.

1. Salmon—The Five Easy Bites

You may never learn to play the piano, but if you fish, you can bone up on salmon behaviour and catch one fish after the other. In saltwater, salmon bite most frequently to feed, from the plankton/krill sockeye and chum, through omnivore pink and fish-eating Chinook and coho. In freshwater, the transition to spawning turns off that eating behaviour and turns on what is needed to be successful in salmon life—impressing others with an arpeggio of attractants.

Salmon, of *both* sexes, bite for one of five reasons in freshwater: passive, aggression, hormonal, territorial and curiosity. And they present themselves in useful ways to capitalize your day on the water. First, form an image of your water's 3-D structure and increase your chances dramatically, as salmon location is strongly affected by the bottom, side, log structure, and the surface, which is also structure—salmon don't swim in the air, after all.

Once you picture your structure, remember that salmon typically bunch together in schools of much higher numbers of fish, in a much smaller volume of water than saltwater, and are, by and large, on the bottom. Salmon also help you out by invariably swimming into current, and that puts their eyes and mouths facing upstream, looking at your offering coming downstream, across current, or in retrieve upstream.

Remember the five-note octave of fish bites and catch as many as you possibly can:

Passive Bite

I have written on this bite in several chapters, but here is a more in-depth treatment, along with the other bites. The Nitinat has Chinook, coho and chum, but other than the very small run of spotted sockeye, no sockeye, or pink salmon, call the river home. The text that follows is for all five species, and thus has information for all Island rivers.

The passive bite is most frequently observed in Chinook, pink, and chum, in that order. What this means is that an object like a lure or fly that moves horizontally downstream, through the school, will be touched by salmon in their mouths and then let go. If you gut a Chinook, for instance, you will find things like twigs and flotsam, evidence of this behaviour.

You have to detect the passive bite, either on your fly-rod hand's finger that you pass line over in stripping, or by seeing your float disappear from the surface on a gear fishing setup. In gear fishing, with line mended from float top to rod tip, you are set for the most effective strike, because there is no excess line.

Both pink and Chinook stop the offering without moving toward or away, including sideways, from it, so you will not feel a strike by a fish, say a coho, that turns on the bite and swims off in another direction. The gear offering that best suits this bite is a dink float, with weight on the mainline below and a leader to the fly/lure.

The alternative of skipping the float, casting the lure across a wall of flesh and reeling in, is not fishing; it is snagging. You need to change to passing down the current-line of float fishing. When fly fishing, you fish with a sink tip or line, with a maximum of 6 feet of leader to a fly—to keep the fly at the level of the line—and repeat your cast, following downstream, until you pick up a fish in the mouth. If you wear a spandex "glove" on your rod's stripping finger, you will instantaneously pick up the passive bite, and turn your day from fighting foul-hooked fish, because your finger feels the line rasp over fins and flesh, and thus you don't strike, until the fly stops; then you'll be fighting fairly hooked fish.

In most systems, sockeye do not bite in freshwater. But they are still caught, some by flossing, which is legal where meat-fisheries are authorized, for example the Somas River's Paper Mill Dam. In rare systems, there are bity sockeye and they exhibit the passive bite; the Gold River, for instance, its Muchalet fish.

Another useful thing to separate out rubs from passive bites is using circle hooks. These have points bent back within the hook's "circle." So, the point slides over flesh, fins, etc., and only sticks when a mouth has clamped down on it. Circle hooks almost completely eliminate foul-hooking. On a big day of Chinook, for instance, not foul-hooking 25 fish means not fighting an extra 500 to 1,000 pounds of resisting fish. A huge amount of effort. Chum are worse, because of their huge schools. They can present flesh anywhere in your lure's passage. You can literally foul-hook a chum almost every cast, a total waste of time and energy. Circle hooks might as well be called chum hooks.

Aggression Bite

The aggression bite occurs because sex hormones make salmon bolder; they will whack anything that moves. In addition, there are small fish cruising around, and cutthroat/Dolly Varden, that are interested in salmon eggs. Salmon want to clear them out of their zone—even errant eggs washing downstream. Salmon are large, after all, and only a small bit of aggression has a large impact on lure or fly presented properly.

Typically, you will feel this bite as the fish has moved to the lure and is trying to whack it out of existence. In Chinook, this may mean a couple of inches of line are taken out, or more, if it is carrying it out of the way. As mentioned, my way of putting it is that, when fly fishing, you want "slippery fingers," so your hands don't strike on line rasping over flesh, but only when some small bit of line passes out from your reel.

Territorial Bite

Similar to the aggression bite, this bite represents the pre-spawning behaviour that all salmon have of protecting a spawning space from anything and everything that comes within it. Sometimes, you will see small depressions in the gravel, along with their algae moved aside, often the result of Chinook pre-spawning behaviour that they may exhibit for a month before spawning proper.

Typically, you will catch male salmon in this phase of behaviour, they being interested in defending a female, good spawning territory, or impressing a female with their nifty bedroom setup. You want to make sure that you are not fishing over spawning salmon, of course, as that is unethical.

The point in this one is that you fish the bottom sector of the water column, or in shallow water. Riffles have higher oxygen in them, and more oxygen passing through the gravel pieces that have had their silt and sand washed right through. Females scent tailouts for the amount of oxygen they can smell coming through the gravel, particularly pink salmon that can spawn in very shallow water.

Hormonal Bite

The hormonal bite is the “I don’t know why I am doing this, but I’m going to whack that thing out of existence” bite. The purpose of steroids is to make the fish/person/animal want to have sex, remove inhibitions, and make behaviour erratic. A day when you see Chinook jumping and turning end over end is a day of hormonally affected fish. And, of course, let me add that “jumpers are not biters, they just tell you where the fish are.”

Fish that seem to have bitten for no good reason are often those affected most by hormones. Do note that hormonal stimulation can come and go, so on a day you receive bites that can’t be easily categorized as any of the other bites, they are likely hormonal.

If you are not getting bites, alter your approach. If, for example, you have been doing the passive-bite, dink-float setup thing, but find you get bites not in the drift, but in the retrieve, this suggests you will catch more by continuing to retrieve in a grid pattern from beginning of school until its end downstream, and a further foot from shore each cast, rather than the passive bite drift. Note that you should be using circle hooks to avoid foul-hooks.

A variation on this for chum: new chum, moving into or up a river, are the young Turks of the system, and you will see them, particularly males, looking here and there and advancing through the water together in schools of hundreds of fish. These fish get bold and become snappy, almost like coho in the curiosity bite. You feel an active bite, but not one that immediately takes off in another direction.

Curiosity Bite

The curiosity bite is almost completely the bailiwick of coho. More like steelhead than steelhead, coho are the most forward and curious of the five species. They are attracted to silver or metal surfaces; hence you will catch five times as many with a baitcaster and spinners and spoons—Mepps, Bolos and Gibbs' Coho, Ironhead and so on.

Do remember, Chinook have one behaviour no other salmon has (well, a rare chum will do it too). They will go down to the bottom and pick up shiny things and swim back up into the school. So, if your lure/fly sits on the bottom—let's hope it's not a sticky bottom—then gets up and moves, strike the rod for a great big spring.

On a fly, a bit of Krystal Flash or Flashabou will single out the coho in a school of 5,000 Chinook and you will catch virtually all coho in the day, even though you can't see a single one. But don't forget coho are primarily found on monsoon days in the *deepest part of the soft water*, for most of their season.

You will see coho follow a lure for an extraordinarily long way before biting; on days you can see them, and this means in shallow runs after fall's silt has gotten rid of the system's algae, cinnamon coho positively glow. No other species of salmon will do this in freshwater. When you feel a spinner's drag stop and start, this can be evidence of a coho following and touching the hook with its nose (hence why a black hook they can't see is added). They will follow 30 feet, then smack the lure and take off in another direction.

Moodier than pooled-up steelhead, coho do the "coho roll" thing on the end of your line, and if you don't have the drag a lot tighter than for soft-mouthed steelhead, you will not land the fish. On long, high pressure periods, you can be looking at thousands of coho, and not a one will move an inch to your offering, nor will the passive bite drift attract them. Get out in the rain when they are moving into side-streams and get that metallic sheen in their face. See **Baitcasters for Coho** below, for more information.

But for the best action, be the last angler on the river in November/ December and cast so your lure swings 18 inches in front of a coho face, watch it turn and follow, then begin twitching its nose for binocular vision, and when it locks on, bang, you receive the curiosity bite. Almost reminiscent of Jack Nicholson and his shining, veiny, half-crazed smile. Remember the five easy bites, and you'll catch more salmon than Jack.

2. Baitcasters for Coho in Rivers

October and November are the only months I carry a baitcaster and trigger-fingered rod rather than a fly rod for river fishing. The reason is that you will catch five times as many coho, and that's high on my list. Add the right gear, coho behaviour, lures, rain, and you have a winning combination. I will repeat some of what I have said, as it is worth hearing more than once.

Rod, Reel, and Line

Pick up a quality reel and rod. Reels include: Penn 965, Abu Garcia 6500 or 6600, Shimano 400, Okuma, or Diawa 300. You want quality metal that doesn't rust and that won't wear out, because you will have the reel for a very long time. I have two Penns and make a point of fishing one in top shape and promptly having the other serviced. Worm gears wear out, and levelwinds often stick on one or the other side. Best to have reels in top condition.

When casting, after the catch is released your thumb on the line in the drum provides pressure to allow mainline to run freely, but not so freely that it overruns. Good reels should have an adjustment to run tension, and you want an intermediate setting to prevent overruns.

When your educated thumb doesn't get the pressure right and you end up with an overrun on the reel, slowly pull the main line by hand until a "V" of line impedes the mainline. All overruns are "loops within loops," in other words, they are not knots. So, once you have found a "V," pluck it a few times lightly, then continue pulling out the mainline. If you do this alternately between mainline and "V" you can clear almost any overrun that typically forms while the lure is in the air, moving away from you, and you will be pulling the fouled line out as the lure is carried by the current downstream; hence, do it quickly, particularly if you are fishing a sticky bottom.

Load the reel with quality braided line of 20- to 25-pound test, a minimum of 100 yards. It is thinner diameter than mono, seldom gets nicked, so seldom breaks, and more can be put on a reel than mono, an advantage in a fast river or when you hook a Chinook of larger weight that can, simply by turning sideways, have the current steadily push it away from you and cannot be stopped, unless you run after it.

An example of braid is Sufix 832 or Sufix Performance Braid. The 832 helps the line sink quicker. The thin diameter means you can load more distance on your reel.

Braid's main advantage is that its lower drag results in longer casts, and in the swollen rivers of autumn this can be important to reaching fish that will be farther away from you. Do a figure-eight knot on the tag end of the braid and mono, then martingale the two together. Use 20 feet of quality 15- to 20-pound mono leader. Each time you snip the leader to replace a lure, this helps clear nicks that can break mono. When down to six feet, replace the leader.

As for rods, you are looking for a quality 9.5- to 10.5-foot trigger finger rod. Examples include Shimano, Fenwick and Rapala. Most coho are five- to 20-pounds, so you want a rod with butt strength, yet give in the tip. I have several rods and mix and match tips and butts, depending on what weight the target is for the day.

Coho Behaviour

Coho have characteristics that make them prime targets among salmon in rivers. They most resemble steelhead in that they are aggressive and whack the lure with abandon. As mentioned, the coho roll is unlike any other salmonid, and it's why you set your drag tighter or you won't get them in. As they have harder mouths than steelhead, you will land more coho at higher drag tension than steelhead.

Coho behaviour changes as their time in freshwater increases. Fresh minty fish are so aggressive they can be few among thousands of Chinook, and if you throw something with flash in it, they will beat the rest of the species to the fly/jig/lure. After a few weeks and migrating upriver, coho tend to get mighty choosy in sunlight and less inclined to bite. It is in this high-contrast period that you search for them in shade, particularly first thing in the morning, or late in the afternoon.

The Nitinat Hatchery clips off the adipose fin of all their coho, so they are marked and can be told apart from wild coho, an issue in distinguishing them, allowing a fishery for marked fish and assessing how many hatchery-raised, clipped coho get back to the river.

While annual fry numbers are often amended, at the time this book was published, the Hatchery released 4M Chinook into the river, 600,000 to the Sooke netpen project, 100,000 into Henderson Lake (some years) and 500,000 to the Sarita annually as fin-clipped fry, the purpose being to assess the wildness of this stock near Bamfield. They also produced 10,000,000 chum to the river, and this has been as large as 30,000,000.

Coho preferentially move up in shade and rest in shade. Good coho anglers look for shade and concentrate their days fishing. The longer the sunshine and high pressure last, the staler coho become. In runs where you can see the fish, you will note they won't move an inch to a lure.

As the season progresses into fall, the rains begin and coho move into pools. This is the golden time of high action. You will catch the most fish in "the deepest part of the soft water." Keep an eye out for coho just touching the surface. Once, fly fishing for pinks on a north Island river, after three hours, I noticed one coho touch the surface at the tail end of the pinks, though I had no idea they were there and had received zero bites from them. When I moved down and cast, with my baitcaster rod, directly to them, I caught one right away, and then several later in the afternoon.

Your river will have a number of pools with back eddies, where coho rest, and as the rain increases, you will have days where the bite is electric, so much so that you feel the fish in your body and can hardly tie lures on, your hands are so jittery. As side-stream spawners, and since seasonal creeks only flow in the highest amount of rain, coho get excited to move into the sex and death part of their lives.

Then, in November, once the major rains have settled in, leaves are gone, and rivers have fallen, those coho still remaining get, as I have said, "all lined up." You will see them in straight line, thigh-deep runs, as ones and twos simply waiting for the next spawn, which can be as late as February in Van Isle rivers. During this period, stay out of sight, or cast to fish that can't see you. Draw your lure across on a diagonal that passes within 18 inches of a coho's nose. If the fish locks on and its nose starts twitching side to side, get set for fun. They will always bite.

The final part of the season occurs when side-streams that can peter out hundreds of yards from the river in dry season, 12 feet above the river, get seeded by the full-on monsoons. In these circumstances, you will find "pools" or back eddies that don't exist in summer—in the river itself, downstream from the seasonal stream—and this is where you will catch your coho on the worst possible rain days of the year. You determine where these streams are in summer by investigating pools left in drying tributaries. As mentioned, if the fry have orange tails, you have found a coho side-stream.

Spinners and Spoons

Coho love metallic surfaces with action, and this is why they bite spinners and spoons. You will want a full collection of different colours of Bolos (the quarter-ounce size), Mepps (particularly the glow in size 4 and 5), Blue Fox (size 4 and 5) and Gibbs spoons (Kit-A-Mat, Illusion and Ironhead) as well as generic gold wobblers.

Then determine the colour progression in the rivers that you fish. The Nitinat starts with gold and red/orange, particularly Bolos, because they cast farther. Do try and retry the Mepps glow, as it can be a real sleeper some years and get the most fish, even though it looks unfishy. Then your full range of Blue Fox with silver spinners in silver/gold and bodies in orange, blue, pink, and finishing with chartreuse with a silver wing. Finally, in dirty water, try gold, as it transmits the best, and finally those large ugly spoons that you never use at any other time of the year. They are more easily seen. When you are faced with broad, deep pools, the Gibbs line comes into its own, as they are higher weight-to-volume spoons that cast farther and sink quicker.

Tea-stained rivers usually fish purple and white better. And where bait is allowed, put some on the hook. Once, casting an old, blue, knubbly wobbler from the '60s that had sat in someone's trunk for 40 years, I put on some salmon eggs, and, as mentioned, cast it across a steelhead in milky water. As the lure passed 10 feet in front of the steelhead it started to move forward, when from out of sight—at least 25 feet—a coho at missile speed left the steely in its vapour trail and whacked the lure. I would guess the smell is a pheromone to fish and thus gets a high response during mating season—so high it will move after it, even though it can't see the bait when it starts.

Tuning Spinners and Spoons

All these lures should be modified before use. Take off the silver hook, often a treble or Siwash, that comes from the package, add a black split ring, and then a black steelhead hook or black Kirbed Mustad hook, size 2 to 3/0. This makes the hook invisible to the fish and thus it bites in front of the hook, so the hook is down its throat before the fish makes contact. You will land dozens of fish over the years with this trick. If fish are very choosy, add a black barrel swivel as well as another split ring to put the hook even farther behind the pulsating lure. If you only have straight shaft hooks like Siwashes, take your pliers and hold the hook from shaft to point and bend to add a 15-degree Kirb.

Mustad has a full range of black hooks, its Ultrapoint for instance, which come with an open circle above the shaft; this allows you to insert it into the bottom side of a barrel swivel and close the circle with pliers. Gamakatsu also has a full range of black hooks, with closed circles, and thus need that second split ring. The farther back the black hook, the better.

Retrieve lures slowly, only fast enough that you can see spinner thump on your rod tip. And if the spinner slips a beat, meaning its drag has collapsed, you will know there are fish even though you can't see them. Return the cast to the same spot or change to a lure with a longer hook setup.

Also make up some Colorado blades. Copper does not work on Vancouver Island but does in the Lower Mainland. The other colours are silver, gold and brass. They are fished on a dink float set up with pencil lead and a leader of two feet to the lure. Cheap, simple, but sometimes the ticket.

As mentioned, I keep a simple red and white bobber in my raincoat. It clips onto the mainline, so I don't have to cut it off and insert a dink float. The bobber gets used when the coho are where I can't reach them by casting—for example, there are branches two feet from the water, or the coho are two hundred feet down from me, and I'm backed into the trees. Just float the float down to them, trip the drag when the bobber reaches them, and the spinner lifts up into their faces and stimulates a bite. Then take the bobber off when not needed, without wasting time having to re-rig a dink float setup.

Fishing Technique

In Chapter 1, you will remember that guide Bill Patterson told me long ago that coho only bite moving upstream. It is the most important thing to remember about coho, and I have emphasized this in several chapters. When you look at a pool and back eddy, start your casting at your feet into the current moving downstream from you and then successively cast farther out and then farther back, then into the seam, then the inside of the seam. When you are faced with the eddy moving '"up-current" back to you, move yourself downstream, and cast "upstream." In this way, you cover the entire pool—for example, the rock above the former boat launch.

Also, move around so your cast crosses the water from slightly different directions. Coho are unpredictable, and sometimes that is all it takes to stimulate a bite. So, make a cast or two, change your position and cast again. Also cast to water you have not covered for 10 minutes, and those fish might have calmed enough after watching a buddy or two being removed from their school.

The other important technique is to try different colours. If you start with orange and it doesn't work, move to red, blue, to pink, chartreuse, silver blade, gold blade and so on, until you find the one they want. That colour will usually work for the rest of the season but do change up until you hit that day's preferred colour. And remember the colour progression from sunny September into early winter.

3. Fly Fishing for Anadromous Species

On Vancouver Island, fly fishing in the ocean, on beaches and in rivers has as its targets anadromous fish, meaning fish that spend part of their lives in saltwater and part in freshwater, typically for spawning, rearing and/or feeding. Adult salmon do not feed in freshwater but bite flies, so they are not biting a food source but for the reasons described in the first section of these technical tips: **Salmon, the Five Easy Bites**. The trout in the anadromous crowd include Dolly Varden char, searun cutthroat trout, and the occasional brown.

The issue with anadromous species is flies. As these species spend part of their lives in fresh- and salt-water, they don't necessarily recognize food in the first couple of weeks after moving to the new type of water. This means that their feeding/biting choices are based on being attracted to a small object moving past them rather than the annual chironomid cycle prevalent in lakes. The latter does exist on Van Isle, but it is the former that prevails in rivers, including the Nitinat and those from below dams that fish cannot rise above.

That means the flies we use are attractor or stimulator patterns. They don't represent any particular natural food; they just attract a fish's attention. Add to this that winter and summer steelhead are so aggressive they will whack anything that moves. Hence our flies do just that: attract attention. Look at the patterns in this book and you will find that, for instance, the bunny patterns often use three contrasting colours, unlike anything in nature, but which aid in being seen as the fly zips past our quarry. Woolly Bugger variations also fall into this category.

Adding a guinea fowl feather or pheasant rump on top of the fly changes its silhouette. On days when no one is biting, you need these and other flies in your box because the change can make a difference. Do note that you need a straight feather over top, as a curved one can make the fly spiral, leading to leader tangles. It also changes presentation.

Having said this, you will also see stoneflies, nymph-style flies, and some dry flies among the patterns here. When fish are hitting a hatch, you give them a dry fly, necessitating carrying two reels in the spring to early fall period, one with a sink tip, and one a full floater to switch to. When you suspect the spot is more likely a trout spot, you fish nymphs with rubbery legs. Similarly, gaudy, flowery marabou patterns with bead chain eyes get attention. An example is red over orange over yellow marabou, a very simple, very effective pattern in the warmer months, particularly for steelhead. The bead chain eyes aid in fly penetration.

While I have seen hatches in January, there is no point putting on a dry fly, for many reasons: the river is too high for a trout to see a dry; there are very few trout in winter; the hatch is slight; the water is too cold for much activity; and turbidity can play a role.

On the other end, keep your eyes on the insect larval stages on small, algae-covered stones. Make sure that you are seeing nymphs. In the Nitinat, these species complete their in-water life stages by early September, and you will see no more. As mentioned, searun cutthroat trout stop biting on large stoneflies and other nymphs at this time, meaning that they do recognize the natural food and when it is not there. These fish precede Chinook into the river in August, and if you intercept a large school, you will have excellent fishing for your day. Once the Chinook are in the river, you may try egg patterns or switch over to fishing for Chinook. Note the Nitnook and Tutu flies for this purpose. Searuns tend to get marginalized once salmon come into the river.

When fishing for steelhead, you want the fly under connection with the tip at all times. For cutthroat, try a dead drift from time to time if you pass through good water without a bite. Searuns prefer slower water with woody debris. Steelhead prefer rock.

4. Being in the Zone

When fly fishing for salmon in estuaries or bottom pools in rivers, in the Nitinat's case, Poison, Gary's and Sturgeon pools, the term *being in the zone* has several meanings. The most obvious is that the person who is catching the most fish is *in the zone*. That is straightforward, but being *in the zone* is the result of many factors. And these make for a complex puzzle.

The first is that the fish have to be there, and also be bity. If the fish aren't there, they can't be in the zone, and thus no angler would be in the zone. Typically, on beaches or in estuaries, salmon arrive in schools, particularly pinks, sockeye and chum, to a lesser extent coho, and finally Chinook, which are individuals found in the same place at the same time, rather than densely schooling.

And fish aren't just anywhere or everywhere. Repeatedly, fish are in certain spots based on level of tide and 3-D structure of the beach under the water. Changes in tide level eliminate beach structure that influences fish position by rising over or falling below it, thus emphasizing other structure. *If you memorize 3-D structure, you know in advance where fish are going to be on any given tide.*

After all, an estuary may be a mile or more long, and fish move with the tide. They move up with the flood and fall with the ebb. However, they can move into a position, and stay there, regardless of the tide; this happens most frequently where a trench/crease has been gouged out by current and provides enough depth for them to feel safe while waiting to move forward. Salmon can spend almost a week going in and out for their gills to switch from breathing oxygen in saltwater to freshwater.

Popular estuarial fishing spots get many fly guys plying their trade at the same time. And usually, one person gets the most bites compared with other anglers—the etiquette of fly fishing is that you can't jump in on top of anyone else or enter a line of casters at any old place; if you are late, you normally get relegated to either end of the line. You need to first assess where the fish are and where they are going to be. There is no point starting to cast at the end of the line where the fish have moved through or fallen back from.

So, anticipate, based on who is getting bites and whether the tide is flooding or ebbing, where the fish are going to be, then move there. Having said this, "being in the zone" starts with the fish *being in the right spot at the right time, and the angler's fly presenting where they will bite it.* And, based on tide, the spot can be hot for an hour and then the tide changes, and thus fish position changes.

One more concept: estuarial water is moving because a river is flowing out over saltwater, and thus is moving downstream, even though the fish may be underneath in water moving in the opposite direction. The opposite: water that is not moving, like a lake, would carry a fly directly down to the bottom if you were not stripping; it will not swing to either side as there is no current. And, though gauging the sink right to get in the zone in moving water takes time and skill, a swung fly presents itself in front of many fish because it covers a greater horizontal distance combined with sink rather than simply straight down.

Now, receiving bites in an estuary of moving water is the result of a number of other factors, and this is where fly line, fly line tips, leader length and weight of fly come into the equation. All must combine to put the fly in front of the fish in a place they will bite at it, as in the fish zone.

If your line is too light, it will be swept off by the current and not penetrate the water column to the fish. The solution to this one is to toss 10 feet of line into the cast after it is on the water, and the slack will result in your line penetrating more before it comes under connection with your rod tip. Another caster who nixes his lips at this scruffy method is failing to realize the purpose is to allow the fly to penetrate before coming into connection. Alternatively, mend the fly line upstream just as the extended fly line has settled on the surface. Again, the result is more sink, and for purists, is the important point in the argument over the classical "greased line" fly fishing method.

On the other hand, if your line is too heavy, it will present below the fish zone, or worse, hang up on bottom, where, each time, you need to bring in the fly and check it for algae or other detritus. If you have 60 feet of line in your hands (and up to 30 feet out the rod tip in the water), placed sequentially over your fingers, in loops of shorter lengths, you have to drop them and deal with the fly before the line gets tangled with other loops, not to mention getting caught on your clothing, net, wading staff and so on. A casting basket is a better alternative.

In either case, too heavy or too light, this can also be solved by adding/changing tips between the fly line and the leader. Most people won't take the time, but that just ensures a skunk. Do consider this, as it takes only five minutes to change. You have to keep the leader in your mouth while changing the tip, using one that has a large enough loop to go over the fly, after it has been pushed through the loop at the other end of the leader.

Remember also that a longer leader of six to 10 feet makes the fly line and fly not present together in the zone. A heavier fly—one with bead chain or dumbbell eyes, or an epoxy fly—will present below the line. A lighter fly, any variety of streamer, or, for example, a California Neil that is fuzzy but not heavy, will float higher.

Remember also that shorter leader length, say four feet or less, in gentle estuarian currents (less than a river, for example) makes the fly line more visible to the fish, and the slower the swing, the more pronounced the visibility. You want to tie new leaders once off the water for the day, and thus not waste fishing time the next day. Once, in the *river*, however, don't increase leader length beyond four to six feet.

For example, while fishing above another angler one day, it was clear that he was getting more bites than I. He was in the right spot just as the fish began entering the estuary, but there were also fish in front of me. Added to this, we were both out on a flat where the fish could meander wherever they wanted, including behind us. Once the number of bites got truly galling, I politely asked if he had another of the lucky fly and would he kindly give me one.

He gave me the fly—a simple pink streamer with bead chain eyes on a number 4 hook—and while foaming at the choppers tying it on, once I cast it out, I immediately hooked bottom, meaning it was not in the zone.

The line on my switch rod was a Scandinavian one (a grain system line) with a full float 30-foot, white head. I had on a fast sink tip before it (they have a super fast as well, but the water was too shallow and slow for it). Meanwhile the other fellow just kept on getting bites. He was in the zone, while I was not.

So, I queried him on his line, which was a full, light sink line. This explained why he was shallower in the water, and in the zone, while I was a bit deeper and not in the zone. The next day I brought out a single-handed rod with a Kust line, which had a 32.8-foot 262-grain light sink line. It is described as having a floating running line, but in practice it looked like a light sink runner behind a light sink head. I was in the zone and released 10 fish.

5. The Case for a Switch Rod

There are three kinds of fly rods: single-handed, switch and Spey. Most people begin fly fishing with a single-handed rod. There is good point in this, as learning the basics of a forward cast sets the stage for all other fly casting. While it used to be the case that big water led to learning Spey casting and the extreme distances the rods can throw, these days there is another option.

Switch rods came on the scene after the move in Spey to the Skagit-style lines and matching 12- to 13-foot Spey rods—rather than the long 14- to 16-foot Speys. The heavy Skagit tip is seldom longer than 30 feet and matches very well with the shorter rods. The line systems became very popular with coastal fly guys who fish for summer steelhead and salmon. In the former, the issue is reaching a lie, with the latter, the issue is lofting a heavy sinking tip easily.

And learning Spey casts sets a fly fisher up for switch rods. While the roll cast is the basis of Spey, and one can make a roll cast with a single-handed rod, too, it is the versatility of Spey casts that is useful. In both the Single Spey and Double Spey, for which the key is taking your time and being deliberate in setting up the D-loop behind you, the tip touches the water, and then the forward part of the stroke is last. Other casts, such as the Snap-T or Circle-C, are really variations of the other casts; still, the key is deliberately letting the D form, before the forward cast.

The important thing to remember is: *Spey casts are change-of-direction casts.* That may not seem so important until you get the casts down, but it is the key to its versatility. Both the single and double Spey begin with retrieving the line at the end of the swing below you, and laying it down close to your body, and then on to the rest of the cast. The forward part of the cast changes the direction of the cast—in this case 90 degrees—from downstream to laying the line out perpendicular to your body.

Once you can cast proficiently, you will find endless times in your day where you want to cast 45 degrees or even 120 from where you stand. If you see someone with a single-handed rod who seems to be able to land his/her fly virtually anywhere in front of him/her, you are watching someone who has learned Spey, and then uses it with a single-handed rod. Versatile.

In the middle of your cast, if a fish rises, or wind changes direction, you can use Spey casting to make instant adjustments and place your fly where you want. One more thing I have mentioned earlier in this book bears repeating: spend your day trying to put your fly within a foot of where you want it. If, for instance, you can cast all the way across the river, and into the forest on the far side, then every cast, try to put your fly within a foot of the opposite bank.

You will lose a lot of flies at first, but then your judgment of cast distance improves. If the cast is going long, lift the rod tip and the fly will land short, something that is done all the time when casting dry flies but rarely in the subsurface fishing we normally do on the coast. Your sensitivity to circumstances, and practised, fluent casting, leads to landing in front of, or beside, just above a surface branch, in a gap and so on.

If you are never willing to go through a period when you lose more flies, you will never be able to count on your fly going where you want it to go. Reconcile yourself, during the learning period, to making multiple, simple nymphs or marabou creations that are quick, cheap and light enough to make casting easy.

Now, think of switch rods as short Spey rods. And the single Spey, the easiest of the Spey casts, becomes your good buddy. A few years before publication of this book, line systems moved on to the Skandi system of specific grains, or weights. The other use of switch rods, like Spey, is: not having to do a single-handed back cast, to set up the forward cast; this means you are less likely to catch your fly on bushes behind you.

As a D is rarely 10 feet behind you, you are far less likely to be chagrined by catching flies. This is particularly useful in winter, when rivers are higher and force you back into the forest, as in closer and closer to sticky branches. The other thing to remember is that in a D-loop the fly line hangs vertical behind you rather than horizontal. A vertical line hangs on bushes without getting a hook tangled, and thus, even when your D-lays on vegetation, it seldom gets caught. And the cast goes well.

Moving to a switch rod (though the change was really made by manufacturers to sell more rods), allows you to cast farther than you do with a single-handed rod. And even more importantly, it is far less effort to Spey cast all day than conventional back and forward, false casting on a single-handed rod.

Add to this that switch rods allow you to land a fish without breaking the rod tip off, as happens with longer Spey rods. When you try to "surf" that fish to you, at the end, judge when the fish is tired enough to allow you to get its head out of the water, and "surf" it to you—the closer it gets, the more likely your rod tip, up in the air, is bent over double, and if it snaps that could be the end of your day, not to mention *ka-ching*. Fly fishers seldom kill fish, so releasing them unharmed, without having to drop your rod in the drink, or having someone with a net, is a bonus offered by most switch rods.

Always, always, take two rods with you when you have a day on the water. If one breaks, you are still fishing. And that versatility thing can help you out in trying conditions. I fish a lot on Johnstone Strait beaches, where the wind is always blowing up to 25 knots over my left shoulder. I am left-handed and simply learned to make a single Spey off my wrong, meaning right, shoulder. So, I don't hit myself in the side of my face almost every cast, as I would if I cast off my left shoulder. I wised up from breaking my glasses and burying fish hooks in my face in the Nitinat years earlier, as you will recall from stories in this book.

Another option is: lay the line in the water in front of you with a short single Spey, then lift it off the water—surface tension loading the rod—above your head, directly behind, and use a haul on the forward cast to reach out your fly. *Back and out casting* is very simple and has the other advantage that there is no false casting. Each false cast can lead to a failed cast and having to start over again. Some people will use as many as 10 false casts, each of which could lead to a failed cast. With Spey casts, there is no false casting, and far fewer failed casts. Just be deliberate, making those D-loops, and you will be Spey casting in no time. Back and out casting also makes a lot of sense when you are fishing within a line of gear anglers—you can keep the line out of everyone's way by a quick back, quick out.

Finally, make a point of buying more fly lines. Being stingy only ensures you won't progress as quickly in your fishing as you could by having and being familiar with lots of different fly lines. When you find one you particularly like for a particular purpose, consider buying a couple before the manufacturer stops making them and moves on to make different line types. As mentioned, the 60-foot head Snowbee XS, white (then made in pale pink) floating line, makes for longer casts because the head is longer than average at 60 feet, and this makes longer casts easier. And its colour makes it easy to see on the water.

So, I use the 60-foot head line for summer fishing in rivers, particularly when there is a hatch, or fish are feeding within a foot of surface. I have it on a reel I reserve for this purpose, but many manufacturers have cassette systems that allow you to put different fly lines on different cassettes, and change fly lines quickly and easily. I have ones from Grays and Snowbee.

Also, consider that if you buy some backups you can often get a discount for buying more than one line. Alternatively, at season's end, when current line systems are being sold at cost, or less, to get rid of them, buy a number of lines to give them a try. An example, for me, is the Scientific Anglers full sink Sixth Sense fly line, for winter fly fishing; it was mounted on a cassette, and simply clicked into a reel body for immediate use. And cost me only 25 percent of its in-season price. When fly lines are this cheap, it makes sense to buy a number and thus always have a new line to try for a particular purpose. If they don't appeal, then turf them.

6. A Note on Knots

There are a slew of knots, but knowing a few good ones is enough. **The Little Red Book of Fishing Knots** is good and can be had from Amazon for $4.96: http://www.amazon.com/The-Little-Fishing-Knot-Book/dp/0969873409. Alternatively, Google: fishing knots in diagrams, or, fishing knot pdf, and you will be shown. Alternatively, look at page 76 in my ***Maximum Salmon***, also at Amazon.

Reel Knot—Tie a simple overhand knot in the tag end of the line, backing or other line that will be laid down on the reel first. Thread the line around the reel drum and tie another overhand knot and a second, this time around the line itself. Pull and, voila, a sound, simple knot that will not come apart.

Palomar—This simple, strong knot is best used for lures tied directly to the mainline for use in either salt- or fresh-water. Form a loop in the mainline and push it through the metal loop or swivel on the item. Now tie an overhand knot, then slip the loop around the lure and tighten. A good strong knot results with great breaking strength, because the knot itself is not a breaking point.

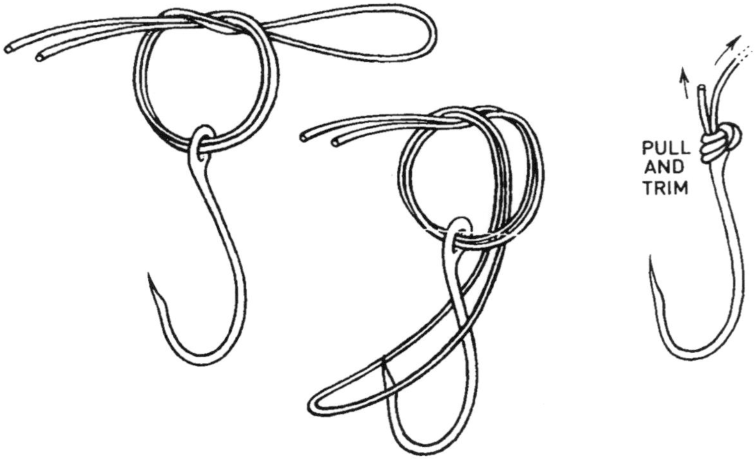

Figure Eight Knot—Perhaps the most useful knot in all of fishing. I stopped using Surgeon's Knots one day when, on five successive casts, I landed the fly in the bush on the other side of the Nitinat at Cutt Corner, on the first cast, and yanking simply broke the knot at the fly line; this was stepped down and thus three-different-test mono leader constructed on the spot with Surgeon's Knots. After half an hour and lots of expletives, I decided never to use a Surgeon Knot again. I had done the same earlier in my fishing with Blood Knots.

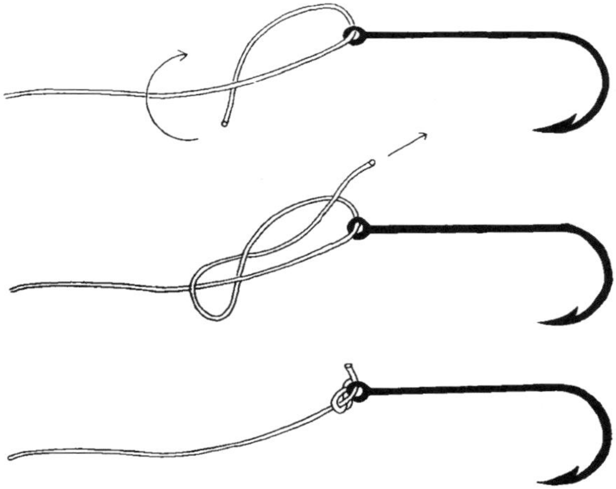

As a Figure Eight Knot results in a loop, you can use it any time you need one—stepping down leader; martingale; alternative to a Palomar. Make a loop in the tag end line, wrap it around your first two fingers, hold the line with your thumb of the same hand, take the line off your two fingers with the other hand, twist it in a circle and push the loop from your first hand through the second loop. As you tighten you will see the figure-eight form in the line and thus know it has been done correctly, before tightening all the way.

Another use for this knot is to make a loop large enough to pass around your fly reel, then, once the backing is wrapped around the reel, the loop passed through a fly line loop, the loop is passed around the reel and voila, you have a good tight knot on the fly line. This allows you to take off a fly line in the middle of your fishing day and put on another one.

Martingale—Often used in fly fishing or anywhere you may have to join two different types/weights of line or add leader. Form a Figure Eight Knot in each of the tag ends, then snip the tag end of each. The upper knot tag end, when in the end of the fly line, should be snipped right to the knot as you will catch line on the knot while casting, something that is a pain because you have to bring in the entire glumph—which if your fly/lure is rotating becomes a total mess—to lift the caught line off. This is because the knot faces "up" the line. The knot on the down side of the knot seldom catches line because it is not facing the line.

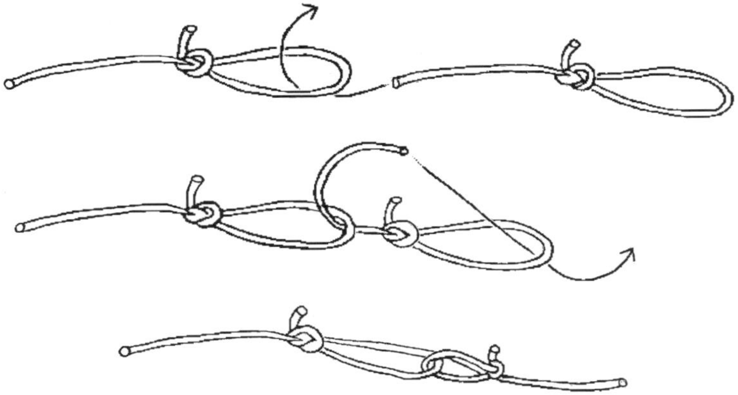

Take the upper loop, push it through the loop on the lower section of line, pass the tag end of the lower piece of line through the upper loop and pull that line all the way through; this loop on loop connection is a Martingale. It is important to always push the upper loop through the lower loop first, as if you don't you will find that sometimes after pulling the entire lower line through and tossing it into the water that you have just untied the second piece of line and lost it.

Clinch Knots—The most common fly-fishing knot for tying a fly on the tag end of the leader. The alternative is a loop knot. Slip the tag end through the eye on the fly, take the tag end around and, if there is room, slip the tag end of the line through the fly's eye once again, which makes it twice as strong. (Sometimes, when you have used too much head cement on the eye, it gets too clogged to push the leader through a second time).

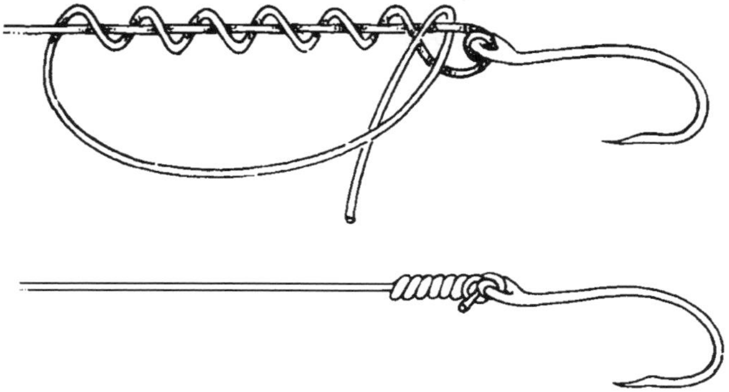

Wind the tag end around the standing line seven or eight times—alternatively, twist the fly around in seven to eight circles—then the tag end goes through the small opening of line near the eye. Tighten and you have a Clinch Knot. Even better, before tightening, bring the tag end back through the loop formed by putting the tag end through the small opening, and you have an Improved Clinch. Even better, as you tighten, stop and pull the tag end. This results in an Improved Clinch that has a loop between it and the fly eye. The purpose is to give the fly more action, as it can freely move because the knot is not tightened onto the eye but the line itself.

Nail Knot/Nailless Nail Knot—Commonly used to tie a loop in the end of a fly line. Form a loop in the fly line tag end and form a loop of leader along the fly line loop. Make the leader's tag end extend an inch beyond the fly line loop. Wrap the leader loop around the fly line loop six to eight times, secure the loop and pull the tag end. This lays down a nice compact knot around the fly line loop. Snip the knot on the upside as close to the knot as possible, to avoid line catching on it during casting. Finish with head cement, nail polish, or other adhesive that covers the upper tag end. Then use a Martingale to connect to your leader.

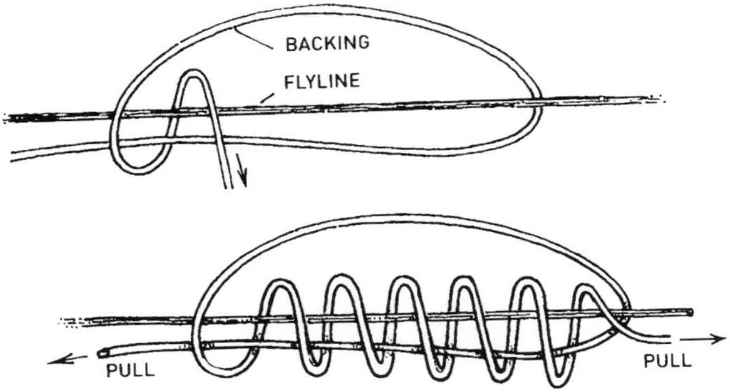

7. Cleaning Fly Lines

Fly lines need cleaning after use in saltwater, brackish water, and extended use in freshwater, particularly with lots of suspended solids or algae. You will find a dirty line ceases to cast as far, is more difficult to pick off the water and sticks to rod line guides on the cast. It can stick to your hands as well, and if you are managing several loops of stripped-in line in your line hand, the bottom of each loop is in the water, and it will stick to that water, too. Clean your fly line more often if used in brackish water, the worst combination of fresh- and salt-water, typically in estuaries.

All dirt problems lead to reduced casting distance; this can be as much as 20 feet, which for the average caster can be 33 to 50 percent of casting distance. Dirty lines also take more oomph to cast all day, to compensate for their unwillingness to slickly rocket out to land within a foot of where you aim the fly.

Always have a target in mind, and over the years, you will become amazingly accurate, even with other problems in your casting. Such accuracy is critical when aiming for rising fish and when you are laying a fly just off vegetation providing cover, typically on the far side of a river.

If your cast is a foot long, a tug of war ensues, with your fly getting broken off if it is stuck on vegetation. The most important thing to do in a long cast is to yank the line back asap, before the fly has gotten settled in green or wound around twigs. Accept that you will lose a few flies as the price of becoming more accurate and catching more fish.

Once a new line has worked through its best, new days—I don't clean a line until it is through this early period—put the reel with its line in a bowl of warm water after each day fishing. Use a small amount of dish soap, water just covering the reel. Don't use too much, as soap can degrade the surface of your expensive fly line. Leave overnight. Rinse the reel and dry with a cloth towel, rather than a paper towel. Then wipe the reel with the towel.

Check your line for cracking or patches where the coating has come away from the braided cord on the inside. If your line is cracked, chances are that it is sinking, even if it is a full float line, because it is full of water. Patches of missing coating are usually from fishing in weather below zero, and water forming ice on lines and guides. When the line gets stuck, a patch of *ka-ching* fly line breaks away, the beginning of the end for the fly line. Don't just keep using it, as the "hinging" of a patch of lower density line between two lengths of higher density line will ruin many casts, driving you bonkers. Any fly line surface cracked along its length should be replaced.

As above, I would say that not buying new fly lines soon enough is the number one problem fly anglers face with casting distance, regardless of level of casting skill. As fly lines cost $50 to $100 each, replacing them hurts. On the other hand, not casting properly, getting the distance and accuracy that comes with casting practice, is a complete waste of your time.

So, replace fly lines sooner rather than later. And keep the old one for a while. I have changed only to find that the new line caught fewer fish because the old waterlogged line was putting the fly in the fish zone, while the new line put the fly above the fish zone. This happens more frequently in beach and estuary fishing for incoming salmon, in salt or brackish water.

While you can buy fly line cleaner containers, I prefer to clean lines by hand. Most fly lines come with a small bottle of fly line cleaner, or slick. These are applied after your gentle cleaning step. Cut a two-inch square of cloth fabric from an old shirt that has been put in the cleaning-use pile in your house. Pick something that won't lose particles onto the line surface, the equivalent of putting dirt back on a cleaned line. Similarly, don't use paper towel, as these "bleed" paper particles back onto the line as you draw it through.

Keep a poster rolled up for cleaning purposes, then roll it out, face down on the floor, so that you aren't stripping line onto a dirty floor. Saturate your square of fabric with cleaner/slick, then with the drag on your reel almost fully off (don't fully eliminate it or, the first time through, dragging line off the reel, you will end up with line over-runs on your reel, and having to sort that out with hands covered with slick "grease"), fold the fabric around the fly line, and strip it smoothly through onto a clean surface below.

Prior to using a fly line or after completely cleaning the line, mark the end of the "head" on the line, where the thicker head ends in slimmer running line. Most manufacturers change colours between head and running line these days, so spotting the change is easier than in the olden days.

Take a black or other contrasting-colour marker and mark two inches of transition so you will know the end of the head, something that comes in very handy when casting. You simply put the marked line within the top rod guide and the line will not hinge, resulting in longer, more accurate casts. Also, strip another 20 feet and mark that spot with marker as well. That is for the lengthy casters who want to reach fish that are further away. It also indicates proximity to the end of the fly line where it contacts the backing line, something every fly fisher wants to know, as once that expensive line completely leaves the rod on a long run, we become worried about losing the fly line.

Returning to the cleaning stage, strip the line through the fabric—head and 20 feet to the running-line mark—to one side of the clean poster paper. Saturate the fabric square again, taking the fabric in your opposite hand, and strip the line back through the fabric, placing the pile on the other side of the poster paper. Change position of the fabric stripping point frequently, as you will find the gunk on the line gets stripped onto the fabric, and you want to present cleaner fabric to the fly line surface.

Finally, take the saturated fabric in your opposite hand, and bring the line through the line slick for a third time, making a pile on the side of this hand. Go wash your sticky hands, let the line dry overnight and put the fabric in the garbage. The reason for putting the pile on the stripping hand side is that with as much as 80 feet of line stripped onto the poster, you can tangle line very easily if the next strip results in one pile mixing with the other pile.

The next day, with a new two-inch square of fabric, fold it over the line and strip the pile through, three times, each time making a pile on the opposite side of the poster. Frequently change the fabric square position so that fly line is moving through clean fabric. Once done, you will find that the fly line has picked up a lot of particles of gunk, and the fabric will have dirty streaks where fly line was pulled through it. Finally, the next time you are out fishing, revel in how well your line strips, casts and lifts from water's grippy grip.

8. Winter Steelheading

January and February are the peak winter steelheading months on Vancouver Island, with the Nitinat high season including March. The season can extend from November to June, but late in the season, please don't fish over spawning fish. Most rivers have small wild winter steelhead runs on the Island's inside, with more wild summer steelhead occurring on the West Coast outside. Many rivers have both summer and winter, as small wild runs, all requiring fish release after catch. Please be kind to the fish.

With climate change now starting to affect our winters, too, you should always check the weather for as much as a week ahead of your planned date to fish. We now have more biblical deluges than we used to, and rivers get blown, with zero visibility more often than in the past.

If rivers are so high that they are over their banks and into the trees, you may not even be able to get to the river to fish, the trees being in the water between you and your quarry. And, the higher the river the lower the concentration of steelhead. Added to this, do remember that canyon rivers blow quicker but also come back quicker because they drain off rock, rather than through spongy soil. The Little Nitinat is an example, and a river that requires lots of muscle to get into and out of.

Get to know many rivers, and if the Nitinat is prohibitively high, have already planned your next, and canyon, river, as possibilities for your day, the Klanawa, Sarita, Caycuse, Gordon or Harris. This means a lot of driving in one day. The Cowichan can stay up for three weeks, but it can be clear and high.

Do note though that high water can give you advantages not normally available. In turbid water, steelhead tend to lie within a foot or two from shore, something that can change a fly-fishing day from no chance to some chance. Another area of higher success is where seasonal creeks flow into the main stem. Usually, some are clearer, and slower, than the main stem, and steelhead like to sit here.

Clear inlet streams have fewer suspended solids, have higher concentrations of oxygen and make breathing easier. Parker Creek would be an example, as it originates in Tuck Lake and thus is clearer than other entry streams.

Many canyon rivers, the Little Nitinat included, have falls that are generally unpassable, or only so at certain water levels. Another such river, that has no public access toward and including the beach of Robson Bight, is the Tsitika. Three kilometres up from tidal water is an obstacle that some species can get over at higher water. Other species can't. The regs are here: http://www.env.gov.bc.ca/fw/fish/regulations/docs/1719/fishing_synopsis_2017-19_region1.pdf,

If there is an impassable section, fish will be right below it, as in a falls pool. Falls pools generally have more fish of all species, as the fish migrate up to them and mill about before dropping back down for feeding, spawning or seasonal migration. In a steelhead river, the fish will shoot over small falls in rain to spawn above, and thus if you know they are below a falls in a certain month, and it rains, you will find them higher after rain. Another reason to get to understand a river's full length.

The drier our summers become, the more important falls pools become as barriers— the Stamp River, for instance, below the provincial park. You should take a look at the rivers that were snorkeled by Dr. John Volpe et al, on Vancouver Island, looking for Atlantic salmon and their progeny. See one of several posts on my fish farm blog, then go to his documents and read them: https://fishfarmnews.blogspot.ca/2017/12/atlantic-salmon-in-bc-rivers-bad-news.html. Their river-specific info is very interesting and one of the few places where you will find actual science on the species and their numbers in our rivers from July to November.

Typically, the best water for winter steelheading is rising or falling, somewhat coloured water. Low water, like high water, can spell doom—the fish become stale. The other water to consider is where a lake empties into a river. Because lakes are not moving, dirt and other solids settle to the bottom. By the time the lake is spilling into a river, it will be clearer than the river below or above it. That top section below the lake will hold the most fish.

Some examples include Great Central Lake, Sproat Lake, Cameron Lake, and Cowichan Lake. Lakes can save your bacon on days when the Nitinat is blown. Drive to the lake exit, instead, and fish. This gives you an idea of how much time you need to spend fishing, to understand the rivers you fish. It takes 10 years to understand one river in all its seasons and for all its species.

Now, a bit more on weather and water conditions. As mentioned, the murkier, or more blown, the river, the greater the importance of hitting a steelhead on the nose with the lure/fly, as the visibility for them can be less than a foot. This means covering good water several times before moving on. And it makes good sense, when the wading is difficult because of deeper water, to take a float- or drift-boat, to cover more water. And cover water that those on foot cannot reach. You will find untouched fish in these spots. In other words, you get "first water," where fish have not bitten or been disturbed, much more frequently, and longer in the day.

As for weather, the longer it has been between rain storms, the staler the fish. Water grows clearer the longer it drops, and the fish bite far less than on rising or dropping water; they become more wary, "pooled up," as steelheaders put it, particularly for summer steelhead as the summer wears on. The other part of pooled up is where steelhead come to rest in a deep pool and wait for rain to stimulate them. *Unbity*, to coin a term, they sit and wait months until spawning.

The other weather condition is: cold. When it is below freezing and ice forms in your line guides, steelhead sink to the bottom and will not move to your lure/fly. It really does have to bonk them on the nose. We tend to forget that rivers can be colder than the ocean, which, while cold for humans, is the natural temperature range for salmonids. Rivers can be colder because they have far less water to be cooled off by the cold air in winter than the ocean.

One cold, clear day in February, I stood on a tributary of the Gold at a spot that a guide, who was taking me fishing in return for my writing an article on the fishing, said was good. He said there was a fish there and that I would catch it. I just had to keep fishing, in this case gear. A pink worm at sinker level.

Well, I ran that worm down the run a dozen times, making little adjustments to the downriver "slice," six inches closer to me, or successively further away. I thought there was no chance of catching a fish. About my 40th cast, a nice male winter whacked the worm and the fight was on. Since then I have been a believer about giving the best water more casts before moving on in cold weather. Don't waste this time on low percentage water, though.

On the other hand, anyone who fishes steelhead knows you don't stand and cast. You cast, take a step, cast and take a step. Steelhead are plenty aggressive and there is no point wasting your time staying in one spot—they will move to your fly or lure. You have the day planned, in advance, of the spots you will try, hitting the highest percentage water first, and then head elsewhere. The point is to get first water, and the more difficult it is to reach a piece of water, the greater the likelihood it will not have been tried by anyone else.

In addition, do remember where you see footprints in the sand. These are places where others know the spot, too. It is important to pay your dues and find other good water spots, and ones where you find no footprints. Also, get to know whether the footprints are new or old. New prints have crisp edges, while old ones have softer ones—commonly wind will soften tracks over time. In addition, it is common for the surface to have a different water content than just below it. For example, if the sand/gravel is dry, but you can see a footprint that is in wet sand, that means you are looking at a very recent print, that has gone through the surface into the deeper substrate but has not yet dried. Similarly, if the sand/gravel is wet, but you find a track with dry material below the surface, then someone is just in front of you.

Other track features come to mind. If it is raining and the track you are following has no pool of water in it, it is recent. On the other end, if it is no longer raining and the track has water in it, it is likely from yesterday, if it also is a crisp-edged print.

As for trails, any time you are following a well-worn trail, that means you are moving to a high-percentage spot that a lot of anglers know. The trails on the Cowichan and Stamp come to mind. On the Stamp, for instance, downstream of Money's Pool, there is more than one track. You go down, as close to the water as possible. The river breaks into boulders, and rock is fishy steelhead water. On the other hand, boulder water is hard on the feet, and awkward wading.

A bit less than a mile down, at Black Rock, the river bears to the left. You fish down a ways, then find the second path back up. It cuts the corner off and runs through the trees up a side slope back to Money's. As mentioned, it takes years to find all the paths on rivers you intend to know well and fish often.

Another trail issue occurs on a path you use often but don't want others to know. An essential vest tool is a pair of pruning snippers that fit in a side pocket. Leave the first 50 feet of the trail unclipped, then start clipping growth, which grows back every year, hence the need for clippers. The unclipped portion conceals that there is a useful path beyond and makes it look like no one uses the spot, so it can't be good.

I have a few that are as long as three miles on the Nitinat. I am left-handed, so I carry clippers in this hand and cut the left-side branches on the way out. On the way back, clippers still in my left hand, I clip off growth on the other side of the trail; that may add up to as many as 300 in a day, and so it doesn't take using the path more than a few times and you have taken a thousand twigs out of your face.

Another useful thing to remember is: continue walking at all times. Don't stop to cut off a branch, just take them in stride. If you miss them one day, you will catch them another, and still have gotten to the water you intend to fish before anyone else gets there, and with time in the bank for reaching those second- and third-bet waters in the same day.

Yet another tip is that you should, over time, investigate all seasonal streams that you pass while walking on a trail. That means on the way back—don't waste time on the way out—you walk down the stream to where it enters the river you have been fishing. Thus, you know a shortcut to a certain stretch for when the water is too high to wade down the river and can get to high-percentage water that very few other anglers ever get to.

One final thing: pick up one of those hats that have LED lights in the front brim, make sure the batteries are charged, and wear it on days you will start or end in dark. This commonly happens in the fall, as the days get shorter. The lights keep you from tripping and falling.

One more final thing: get to know your river, as sometimes, it does not pay to fish a stretch early, particularly in summer. When water is dead calm or before the caddis and mayflies start hatching, which is based on temperature, fish bite less frequently than once a wind has set up to ruffle the water, or the higher temperature has brought fish out in search of surface food. Dry fly fishing using mayflies in the Nitinat seldom begins before 10 a.m. Use nymphs, and stone flies before you see the hatch. And once the Nitinat wind comes up, shallow runs come into their own.

Okay, yet another tip: you fly guys should get to know the cycle of insects in your river. On the Nitinat, mosquitos and no-see-ums are munching on your arms and face in March, the moment you get out of the car—so carry bug spray. In every river, caddis-, may-, damsel- and stone-flies may hatch at different times. I've seen mayflies in January, though that is uncommon. When you see flying insects, your chances with dry flies are higher. But throughout the season, take a look at the nymphs on the gravel and rocks. They tell you what to match.

And remember that those stonefly nymphs can be deadly, because they are the largest nymph you will carry, and in a current, the easier a nymph is to see in the split second it goes by a fish, the greater the likelihood it will get a bite. Note that typically by early September all the nymphs are gone from the Nitinat and thus there is no point fishing them. Time to switch to bright, generic flies like marabou Popsicles, or fish for salmon.

A truism about steelhead is that the fish are found where they are found. They move around a lot, and thus you may find one in a spot where you did not expect it, nor will catch one again. In other words, fish more water than just hotspots.

Having said this, winter steelhead are found most typically in: heads of pools, tails of pools and straight line runs of three to eight feet deep. And there is pass-through water and holding water, too. Steelhead move through pools to the head, where they tend to lie under the frothy water, out of sight, with lots of oxygen and being first to see food swept from the riffle above. Make sure to fish that top foot, rather than step into the water.

Tails of pools are spots where steelhead have come up a riffle or fast water with higher than usual downward gradient. They stop to rest for a while before continuing to the head of the pool. Sometimes they may be in direct view, depending on how high you can get above the tailout.

Usually, though, they melt into the rocks and are not seen. If they see you, however, then they will not bite.

There is nothing more aggravating than wading down a river and having a steelhead swim by you. Typically, you have disturbed the fish and they move up or down. Do remember these fish, as where you find one, you will find another in the future. Make sure your fly or lure plumbs that water before you disturb it by wading. The tail end of Rock No Rock Pool is an example of this situation.

Runs present a crease in bottom structure where the water is deeper than the rest of the cross-section of the river. Seldom do you see fish, as the water is too deep and flow patterns destroy the windows—calm surface patterns flowing down-current that allow momentary sight through to the bottom—but they are the highest-percentage spots in most rivers. In these circumstances, steelhead stop for a period of time, many days for example, before moving on.

Note also that you should fish a river—the Nitinat or any other—often enough to see its evolution over time. Bottom structure influences fish position, and if structure changes, so too does where fish come to rest. I have mentioned, for example, that I caught three "yearling" winter steelhead in a small depression caused by scouring gravel beside a shoreline log on Glass Run.

Over the next few years, the riffle below changed from right bank, where the fish were, to the left, leaving the water little more than calf-deep and without a route directly upstream into it. Not expecting much, but because I had caught fish in the spot several times, I plopped in the spinner I happened to be fishing one day (I typically fly fish for steelhead).

On my third and last cast before moving down, a steelhead took my lure, streaked to the left and downriver. This was the fish I chased 600 yards downriver. When it was finally subdued and hook removed, held up, it was longer than from the end of my arm to the middle of my chest—more than 34 inches, hence more than 20 pounds and the largest steelhead I have ever caught.

The only reason I caught it was I had put a lure into a spot I caught steelhead before, even though it had since become a very low-percentage spot. Had I done what other anglers would have done and passed by the water, I would not have ended up with my largest steelhead. I surmise the spot had a cool spring, so in warmer months, fish would lie there, in a second-rate shallow spot, rather than move up.

For gear fishing, many terminal tackle arrangements include variations on a theme: Gooey Bobs, Spin n Glos, Pink worms and so on, on a leader of 18- to 24-inches, or longer/lighter in ultra-clear water. Tackle is taken to the bottom by weights of varying description. Hollow core lead can be crimped lightly to the tag end of the mainline below the triple swivel tied on—so that in a bottom snag, it slips off, leaving you with the rest of the tackle. To the third eye of the swivel is tied a preassembled hook, lure, and leader of typically 10 or more pounds test, except for ultra-clear water.

Casting pattern depends on covering all the good water in front of you and mimics the pattern of passive-bite fishing for Chinook. The gear is cast upstream, and the rod tip is high in the air so line can be mended, so you are in contact at all times with the float. If the float goes down, strike. If the float continually points downstream, the tackle is dragging on the bottom and the distance between weight and float is shortened.

Once the gear passes you and carries on downstream, you are free spooling the reel, a circumstance that lets centre-pin reels shine. The point is to be in contact with the tackle and strike quickly when the float disappears. Steelhead are not passive fish; they whack and run.

You make successive casts run straight down-current, each one adding a foot to the cast. In other words, you fish the entire run from side to side and up- to down-stream. On cold days, add less distance in successive casts, or make multiple passes before moving on—remember the 40 casts I put over a male steelhead in a frigid Gold River tributary before it bit.

Comment needs be made on two types of water: pass-through and holding water. The first is typically slow water, perhaps the inside of a bend, and the incoming steelhead simply swims slowly through it up to the next head of a pool or run. You pass down the water fishing, and then, because new fish can always come through, you can actually go back to the top and fish pass-through water again.

Holding water, on the other hand, is where steelhead sit for some time. Typically, a lower speed spot in faster water, behind a rock—steelhead are found in connection with rock far more than they are with wood.

When fishing, you need to bear in mind that from holding water, once you are finished, you have to move on because you have disturbed the fish there, rather than in pass-through water, which can have new fish in it at any time. So, your day will depend on planning to hit several high-percentage spots, and you may fish pass-through water more than once. The Stamp has more of this water than the Nitinat, and also larger, hatchery runs.

Finally, steelheading reaches its highest percentage days when the river is rising or falling, and clarity is restricted to a few feet or less. Rain stimulates fish to move into a system, rise in the system or perk up wherever they may be. It makes sense to fish lower ends of rivers toward estuaries on days that rain starts in earnest, then move to other hotspots. If you are fly fishing, it makes sense to fish pass-through water, as it is moving slower than other sections of a river, and thus maximizes fly penetration.

9. Climate Change and Pacific Salmon

First let's talk about climate, and then move to effects on salmon. It is generally accepted that climate change, with its increasing temperatures, will have negative effects on BC salmon. DFO put out a paper in 2009 that studied more than 350 related papers, covering Korea, Japan, Russia, Alaska, BC, Washington, Oregon and California: http://www.npafc.org/publications/Special%20Publications/LRMP_Synthesis.pdf. Beamish and Riddell, well-known science names to sport anglers, took part. Do read it, as it is much more than I can summarize along with my own observations.

Factors include offshore weather patterns, decadal shifts in the Aleutians, winds, ground water discharge, iron concentration, El Nino/La Nina events, ocean currents, temperature, ice cover, ocean migration patterns, run-timing, interspecies competition, coastal upwelling, ocean acidity, zoo- and phyto-plankton effects and, also in freshwater, precipitation and forms of precipitation, snow pack and snow melt, increase in ice-free periods in lakes, temperature, size and timing of freshet, composition of stream- or river-type Chinook, coastal versus lengthy migration into interior rivers and so on.

Surprisingly, commercial catches have risen dramatically in Russia, and climate warming is seen as a good thing into the middle of the 21st century—because ice effects in fresh and saltwater depress salmon numbers—while competition between chum and pink fry results in size and productivity differences greater than other factors right now. Similar "local" variations occur, and sometimes opposite results can occur in different regions from the same stressor.

Sockeye are the first species to come back and can be as early as April in the Hobiton River on Van Isle, May to September in the Somass, May to June in Skeena and Nass rivers, and from early June to September in the complex, multi-component Fraser run. Sockeye are the most sensitive to temperature, and diversion from Johnstone Strait to Juan de Fuca Strait can result from a one-degree temperature change. Fraser River entry is also partly triggered by water temperature. In fresh water, sockeye tolerate 20 degrees C, and then begin dying. I once stood on a balcony overlooking the Somass River confluence, and the bottom of the river was littered with what looked like silver bars. It was sockeye dying—and little wonder. It was 42 C in the shade where we sat in Margaritaville, sweating like pigs, doing nothing.

The farther a run must go upstream, sockeye to the interior, for instance, the greater the pre-spawn mortality with respect to temperature; but greater marine fat levels brought back into the Fraser result in lower mortality, implying that several factors can affect the portion of escapement that successfully spawns. You may recall Dr. Kristi Miller's work on the Viral Signature—meaning disease—of Fraser sockeye can result in up to 90 percent pre-spawn mortality.

And if there is greater ice or rain precipitation, eggs can be wiped out. And sockeye typically spend a year or so in a lake before migrating. Higher temperatures are thought to result in higher fry mortality in saltwater, because they may be too small to survive the ocean. Longer periods of sunlight on saltwater are consistent with greater algal blooms in Georgia Strait, associated with higher mortality of smolts. And when the ocean is warmer, sockeye don't grow as well, and thus do poorer on entering rivers to migrate the distances.

The Fraser River accounts for 30- to 40-percent of all BC salmon production. Because numerous stocks of sockeye, pink and chum are near the southern limit of their range, the early impacts of climate change should be detectable in these stocks first. Warm water during spawning results in earlier hatching of fry and higher fry to smolt mortality.

Chinook, with their large bodies, have difficulty entering coastal rivers depleted by long, hot summers, with a lack of precipitation. They need almost a foot of water to torpedo up shallow sections. The same can be said for their fry and that of coho surviving a long, hot summer in rivers. Poor development in rivers leads to coho, sockeye, and Chinook doing poorer in saltwater. It is not yet clear whether the mechanism that causes ocean-weather regimes to shift will be exacerbated or muted by increasing levels of greenhouse gasses.

Coho come on the tail end of Chinook runs, but tend to hang on beyond all other species, waiting for the high rainfalls of late autumn and even winter before entering side-streams, where they preferentially spawn. Less rain means fewer coho, which are the second most temperature-sensitive of the five species, because the side-streams become isolated pools in summer, with coho fry frizzling in summer temperatures, waiting for fall flows to escape. Most of our rivers have had their trees logged in the past century, resulting in very open, gravel moonscapes that further elevate temperature. Go look at the San Juan, near Port Renfrew, for such a devastated river. On the other hand, walk the easy trail and pretty Big Qualicum, with its forest cover intact and cooler summer flow. Vastly different productivity.

Where it rains is important, too. A watershed can receive different amounts of rain and snow melt in different sections of the same river. So, some subcomponents of salmon runs do better if they return to tributary rivers, based on both water level and temperature. Ditto oxygen.

Chum are notoriously poor at spawning in good locations. As mentioned, they tend to spawn on the highest rains of fall, and when the river drops, up to 90% of eggs are wasted. So, less, rather than more, rain would conserve them, forcing them to spawn within the river's usual banks.

It has also been shown that BC populations north of 50- to 55-degrees latitude oscillate in ocean numbers differently from those of more southerly rivers. Warmer weather allows cold water predators like hake and mackerel to move north and eat more salmon. Predation is a big problem, even in Alaska, where 75 percent of Prince William Sound pink fry are lost to predation during their first 45- to 60-days in the ocean.

Temperature differences in the northeast Pacific play a role in sorting out different salmon species to different areas. Along with higher temperatures above the water, currents flowing north to south split the near-shore and offshore regions and also distribute salmon for foraging. Higher temperatures will influence marine distribution.

Salmon also stray from their own rivers by as much as 10 percent. Pink and sockeye are now reported in the Beaufort Sea. Chinook are the least temperature-related strayers. I have witnessed pinks and sockeye in rivers where there are no historical runs, for example, the Nitinat. As mentioned, I have noticed sockeye—because they are so easily identified as red fish before coho turn—spawning in the same patch of gravel below Tree Island in succeeding years, even though the river has no identified sockeye run.

There has been a decline in hatchery coho in Georgia Strait since the mid '80s, while wild coho have remained stable but at low levels. Growth, survival, and abundance occur earlier in the year for wild coho than hatchery coho. Growth between July and September is inversely related to marine survival, indicating that faster and earlier growth may improve lipid storage, increasing the chances of survival over the winter. This study suggests that fish farms have caused a 50 percent decline in salmon numbers: http://fishfarmnews.blogspot.ca/2013/01/fish-farms-kill-more-than-50-of-wild.html. This effect would be lower on a river like the Nitinat that has no fish farms within the salmon's normal access or egress pathways; this assumes that fish do not enter Barkley and Clayoquot Sound on their migrations to and from the open oceans.

10. More Climate Change Effects on Salmon

Let's look a little closer. Here is a summary document that, at four pages, is short and worthwhile reading: https://cmsdata.iucn.org/downloads/fact_sheet_red_list_salmon.pdf.

There is more to higher temperatures than simply immediate death. Higher temperature has been accompanied by lower precipitation in summer, monsoon rains in the fall, and either lower or higher snowpack in winter, setting up early floods, then lower flow, and lower oxygen all summer long.

Lower oxygen is the result of fewer riffles that mix air and water together. And as Chinook are mainstem residers for more than a year, they suffer the oxygen effects the most.

Pink and chum hatch in March/April and migrate to sea almost immediately, a period of high flow. The downside for them is that greater precipitation in winter smothers or washes out egg bearing redds—of all species, really.

But low flow in late summer can eliminate most water for pink spawning. They mate in very shallow water, particularly riffles hardly six inches deep. If those prime spots are only a couple of inches deep, in addition to lower oxygen, they don't give pinks enough depth to spawn, and thus they move to other water with small pebbles.

There are other effects. If spawning channels have no water to enter, those fish may not be able to spawn or may move to areas of lower success, or higher use by other species. If river flow is very low, it affects Chinook the greatest, as they need almost a foot for a 20- to 30-pounder to screw through.

It may be that the sudden rise in merganser numbers about a decade ago represents another climate change effect. If prey is easier to see—water is slower and shallower—fry are easier to catch and eat, so add predation to climate change effects.

As mentioned, sockeye are the most heat-sensitive of the five species, and over 20 degrees C is lethal to them. Pre-spawn mortality rises, as shown in Dr. Miller's work, on Fraser subcomponents to as high as 90 percent (also a disease effect, PRV, for example, meaning Piscine orthoreovirus), they get an easier pass by residing in lakes, like Great Central Lake and Sproat Lake near Port Alberni. The downside is that, like Ontario's Lake Erie, which has algal effects some years, lakes can acidify and become more lethal, in some cases changing the plankton (a bigger problem in the open ocean), the base of the food chain.

One effect that is less obvious is that lower, smaller rivers have less spawning space than when at normal levels. That means there is less main-stem place to spawn, and thus, the respawning phenomenon I have mentioned, and by more than one species. And the last to spawn would be the fry of greater numbers, usually chum. However, as Chinook are the largest and can move the largest gravel, the chum effect would be greatest on pink salmon and secondarily Chinook, and sockeye. Note though that chum spawning, as the most indiscriminate, can result in high egg wastage.

As mentioned, coho are a special case. In my winter fishing, I check on several side creeks to monitor the spawn. As coho fry can spend an entire summer in seasonal streams, they are most susceptible to low precipitation—even though coho hold on in freshwater the longest, in some rivers into February, waiting for highest water.

These days, several Nitinat side-streams don't get filled up enough to offer a good spawning chance. Some don't fill at all anymore, and some where I watched coho spawn for a decade have not had water for the past five years, meaning none of those coho survived (unless they spawned in other water, crowding other coho, too).

And seasonal creeks shrink in low water, so potholes around root balls provide the only habitat for coho through one summer and back into the next high-water event. Over the years, I have watched those small pans of water disappear completely, particularly in the upper Nitinat. It is hard to watch water that will support coho disappear with fry in them. As pink and chum migrate out immediately, Chinook are mainstem spawners, and sockeye are associated with lakes, chances are, fry cut off from river flow are likely coho. And when those small pools cut off from flow disappear, it kills all fry, a year's entire brood.

11. Epigenetics

It has long been known that hatchery enhancement of wild salmon can lead to unexpected results. In the States, for many years, hatchery spring Chinook were planted in many rivers in several states and came to be known as Springers. This led to obliterating natural genetics through inter-breeding between wild and hatchery fish. Diversity of natural genetics is key to the survival of salmon, as they are adapted to the waters in which they were raised. Wipe out diversity, and ability to adapt is also wiped out. Ditto for survival.

In Canada, we did not follow the same route. The intent was to use a raised stock in close-by waters that have similar genetics, rather than a generic fish for all rivers. For example, in the Nitinat hatchery, its Chinook are used in the close-by Sarita, Sooke and Sooke Basin net pen.

There are other approaches. Alaska, for example, does "ocean ranching," which means pumping out billions of fry, most commonly pink salmon, and reaping the abnormally high numbers of returning salmon to make the most money. Again, this wipes out genetic variation in wild stocks, but Alaska has chosen to make a commercial catch, in some basins, and ignore the genetic destruction. Catch results can be impressive. Alaska's catch of all species was 243 million in 2017.

In BC, right next door, the 2017 commercial catch was pretty much nonexistent; a staggering comparison of side by side abundance and dearth. There are many reasons. The big four are lack of adequate amounts of freshwater habitat restoration, DFO itself, fish farms, and climate change. And factors like "the Blob" offshore in rearing areas have led to problems. As well, the Pacific Salmon Foundation's project for the Salish Sea is showing other effects, such as seal predation of juvenile Chinook to 40 percent and coho to 47 percent, and phytoplankton differences in spring, among other things. See the Salish Sea Marine Survival Project, 2016 Canadian Progress Report: https://marinesurvivalproject.com/wp-content/uploads/Canadian-SSMSP-Status-and-Findings-to-Date-2016.pdf.

In the 2010 decade, though, the genetic considerations in enhanced fish received more study. While genetics may be the same in a wild fish from the same river where a hatchery fish is produced, the expression of those genes may be different and account for different outcomes, especially as the gene expression can begin and end in different periods of a salmon's life cycle. Measuring those effects out in the ocean is difficult, because it is difficult to find the fish. But the effects can be studied during raising of fry, and in mature fish when they return.

This field is known as epigenetics. See this article for a non-technical take on the issue: https://www.hakaimagazine.com/news/hatchery-fish-often-fail-in-the-wild-now-we-might-know-why/. Approaches to raising those fish are key. Here is a short quote: "Epigenetics is the physical and molecular processes that control how the instructions contained within DNA get expressed or turned into the proteins that affect day-to-day life. Often, epigenetics causes a gene to be expressed more or less frequently than it otherwise would. Everything from stress to chemicals to natural processes like puberty can cause epigenetic changes. Some of the changes are temporary or reversible, while others last forever."

Louis Bernatchez, working at Laval University, found that feeding and crowding in hatcheries accounted for much of the differences in gene expression. Perhaps surprisingly, this effect was consistent for fish of different stocks raised at different hatcheries. But if you were brought up to gorge on brown pellets that nice people or machines tossed at you, rather than be pretty hungry all the time, have to hunt to find something to eat, and stay out of the way of predators, the expression of some genes could dramatically differ.

You will recall that evolution functions through "natural selection," a concept that is the basis of all Darwinian thought. Do hatcheries "select" gorgers, or is the food, temperature, and inactive life modifying gene expression? Regardless of the explanation, hatchery fish don't always respond as well as wild fish.

It is common, at least for Chinook, for the fish to lose some or all of their ability to spawn in the wild, particularly males. This may be good for wild genetics, but it suggests an important reason to rely more on habitat restoration than enhancement, something made all the more difficult in this time of climate warming.

I think the time is coming where we will see convoys of trucks and helicopter buckets moving salmon above impassable river sections and depositing them in large, cool pools to rest until the later rains of fall do the deed. This would serve the interests of Chinook, coho and chum due to their October or later spawning pattern, when rain is more likely to be expected. I am not so sure about sockeye and pink, that can, due to their smaller size, navigate shallower water, and do spawn earlier, though sockeye have that problem with temperature above 20 degrees C.

Spot fishing closures, as annoying as they are, to let wild fish through can make a lot of sense, as can producing hatchery fish that do not return migrate at the same time as their wild compatriots. But what about "fake" food, couch potatoes and endlessly clicking iPhones?

The Nitinat Hatchery did interesting experiments to try to find some answers. Researchers Kristi Miller and Sean Rogers worked with them. As above, Miller was well known from her Cohen Commission presentation on her "Viral Signature" work, showing sockeye dying at advanced rates of pre-spawn mortality. In addition, in 2017, she showed that PRV causes HSMI (Heart and Skeletal Muscle Inflammation), a serious problem for wild fish as up to 95 percent of farmed fish have PRV.

Hatchery Manager, Rob Brouwer, pointing to the epigenetic Chinook set up. Feed is set up for delivery that does not make the fish connect food with humans. Objects have been inserted in the race way for them hide in and eat the natural fawna found in river settings. And a hose inserts a more natural current.

You may have had a serious laugh at the Jimmies, as one-year returnee hatchery male Chinook salmon have been dubbed in the Sarita and Nitinat. Take a six-weight rod and plop a generic Tom Thumb dry fly where they are snapping away, and you can pretty much ding everyone in the pool. They look like small pink salmon, but have sharp black teeth, and that unmistakeable smell of a Chinook. Presumably these, along with Jacks, sexually mature two-year-old males that no one really wants—except in very low water—are the result of epigenetic changes in hatchery Chinook.

The Nitinat Hatchery, with both coho and Chinook, found out interesting things by varying food, lifestyle, size of smolt at release and so on. They do both small and large Chinook smolts and yearlings. They also compare standard raceway fry with others that have an "enriched" lifestyle, including putting objects, bushes, and flotsam in their water to explore, hide in and feed on those mayflies, stoneflies and caddis flies that show up on high algae objects, rather than solely pellets.

There is also the alternative of putting fry into local lakes to bring themselves up, particularly coho. The aim is to produce fish with more wild behaviour, fish that have a greater chance of wild spawning, and a reduced percentage of young, sexually mature males. The more the epigenetics are right, the better the fish; and the more that enhancement becomes a better option for increasing salmon spawner numbers of wilder fish; in other words, a true companion to the overarching need for freshwater habitat restoration, the crux of the other half of the story.

Some experiments involving smaller, fitter fish led to larger adults, and for Chinook, the larger fish are typically female, the sex we want to return, not to mention that more five-year fish are returning as, yes, larger fish. Current experiments suggest that environment enrichment doubles smolt to adult survival, an important consideration when wild return is about 1 percent to maintain a run. So, we may be heading to lower density, lower growth rates and enriching environment more consistently across the Salmon Enhancement Program.

Acknowledgements:

Chapter 3: "Dennis's Pool" has been previously published in ***The Summer Book*** anthology, Mother Tongue Press, as well as specially selected for appearance on the Tyee.ca website, and onfishingdcreid.blogspot.com. "I could simply give in," and "Where children leave no footprints" appear in ***These Elegies*** – DC Reid. "The Dipper" appears in ***The Spirit of the Thing and the Thing Itself*** – DC Reid. "I shall fear no evil in the valley of the Nitinat," appears in ***The Hunger*** – DC Reid.

Text, Images, knots from Maximum Salmon, courtesy of DC Reid.

Sky Horse Press is thanked for the Roderick Haig-Brown quote from his book: A River Never Sleeps.

For the Figure Eight, Martingale and Circle Knot, Andrew Kolasinski is thanked for his artwork.

Thanks to Izaak Walton, for the quote from his The Compleat Angler, published in 1653.

Thanks to Trey Combs for permission to use a quote from his superb book, Steelhead Fly Fishing, Lyons Books, 1991.

other fishing titles from Hancock House

Fishing the Canadian Rockies
Second Edition 2022
Joey Ambrosi
978-0-88839-425-5
8.5 x 11, 248pp
100 maps, 650 photos
$39.95

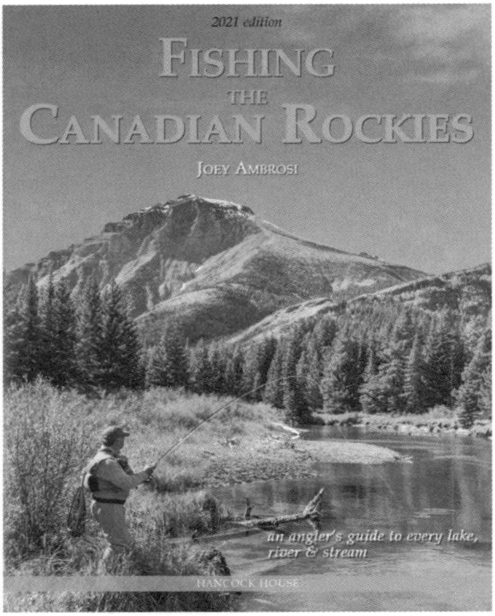

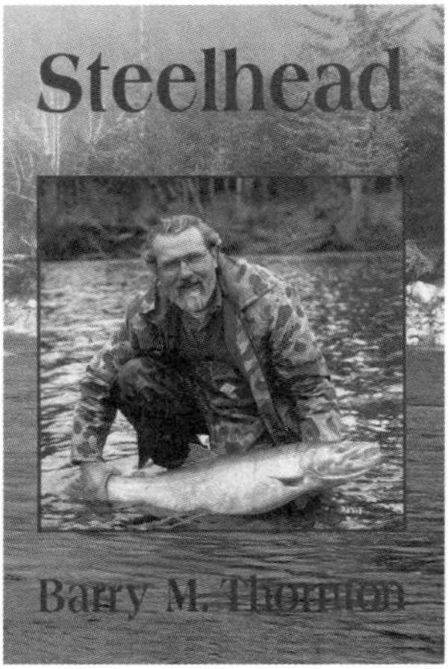

12 Basic Skills of Fly Fishing
Ted Peck & Ed Rychkun, *2000*
978-0-88839-459-0
5.5 x 8.5, 96 color pages
$12.95

Steelhead
Barry Thornton, *1995*
978-0-88839-370-8
5.5 x 8.5, 192 pages
$17.95

hancock house

Hancock House Publishers
19313 0 Ave, Surrey, BC, Canada V3Z 9R9
#104 4550 Birch Bay-Lynden Rd, Blaine, WA, USA 98230
www.hancockhouse.com info@hancockhouse.com
1-800-938-1114

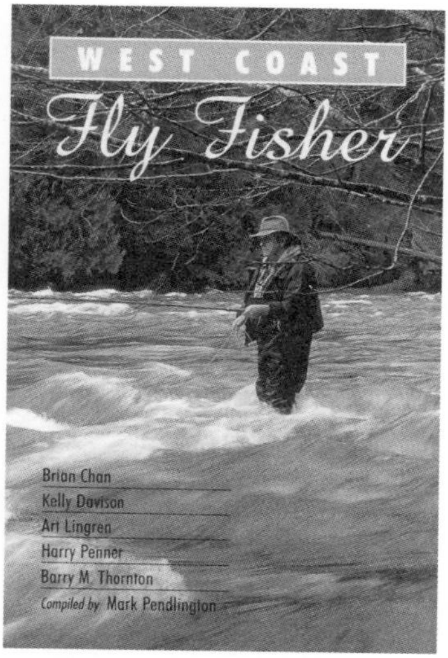

West Coast Fly Fisher
Brian Chan *et al*, 1998
978-0-8883-944-0
5.5 x 8.5, 152 color pages
$19.95

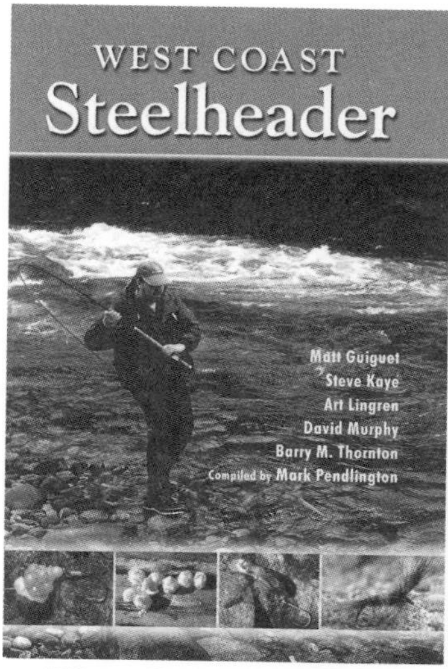

West Coast Steelheader
Mark Peddlington *et al, 2000*
978-0-88839-459-0
5.5 x 8.5, 96 color pages
$12.95

Trout Fishing
Ed Rychkun, 1994
978-0-88839-338-8
5.5 x 8.5, 120 pages
$16.95

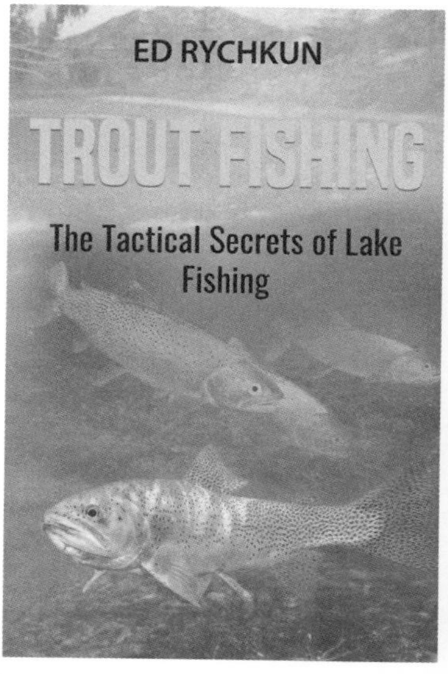